Paris in the Dark

Paris in the Dark

Going to the Movies in the City of Light, 1930–1950

Eric Smoodin

Duke University Press   *Durham and London*   2020

© 2020 Duke University Press
All rights reserved
Printed and bound by CPI Group (UK) Ltd, Croydon, CR04YY
Designed by Drew Sisk
Typeset in Garamond Premier Pro and Kabel
by Westchester Publishing Services

Library of Congress Cataloging-in-Publication Data

Names: Smoodin, Eric Loren, author.
Title: Paris in the dark : going to the movies in the City of Light,
    1930–1950 / Eric Smoodin.
Other titles: Movies in the City of Light, 1930–1950
Description: Durham ; London : Duke University Press, 2020. | Includes
    bibliographical references and index.
Identifiers: LCCN 2019032714 (print) | LCCN 2019032715 (ebook)
ISBN 9781478006114 (hardcover)
ISBN 9781478006923 (paperback)
ISBN 9781478007531 (ebook)
Subjects: LCSH: Motion pictures—France—Paris—History. | Motion picture
    theaters—France—Paris—History. | National characteristics in motion
    pictures. | Culture in motion pictures. | Paris (France)—History.
Classification: LCC PN1993.5.F7 S66 2020 (print) | LCC PN1993.5.F7 (ebook) |
    DDC 791.4309443/6—dc23
LC record available at https://lccn.loc.gov/2019032714
LC ebook record available at https://lccn.loc.gov/2019032715

Cover art: Details from a map of Paris showing the city's twenty arrondissements,
or neighborhoods, and also some of the major cinemas from the period 1930–1950.
Map by Michele Tobias. Inside covers: Neon signs at night, Avenue des Champs-
Elysées, Paris (VIIIth arrondissement), 1936. Photograph by Roger Schall
(1904–1995). © Roger Schall/Roger-Viollet.

This book is freely available in an open access edition thanks to TOME (Toward an
Open Monograph Ecosystem)—a collaboration of the Association of American
Universities, the Association of University Presses, and the Association of Research
Libraries—and the generous support of University of California, Davis. Learn more
at the TOME website, available at: openmonographs.org.

For Caren

T'as d'beaux yeux, tu sais . . .

CONTENTS

ACKNOWLEDGMENTS

I feel as if I've been working on this book for over forty years, now and then, in different places and at various jobs. When I think of the book like that, the results seem a little slim. But there you have it. This short book about Parisian film culture has had quite the *durée*.

With a project this long and this winding, a lot of people have been extremely important to me along the way. I started graduate school at UCLA in 1977, at a time when most of us did our scholarship on national cinemas because that's how film studies was organized then. I took required seminars in Italian neorealism and German expressionism, and I concentrated on American and French cinema in my own research. My dissertation dealt for the most part with American films, but I formulated the idea for it while I was spending one year as a student in Paris, and getting the chance to work with Raymond Bellour, Jacques Aumont, Marc Vernet, Jorge Dana, and others who were doing pioneering work in the field.

Well before that, I think I may have seen my first French movie, at least the first in a theatre rather than on television, with my sister, Roberta Smoodin. When I was fifteen or sixteen and she was an undergrad at UCLA, she let me tag along with her to an evening screening of Jean Cocteau's *Le Sang d'un poète* (1930). This was certainly the first avant-garde film I had ever seen, and I remember being completely mystified by it and sort of bored, but also feeling very grown-up. I remember Robbie's kindness in asking her younger brother to go with her, and she remains one of my favorite filmgoing companions.

Jon Lewis and I have been close friends since we joined the UCLA doctoral program together in 1979. Jon and I have also worked together on several projects, and I can't think of a better writing partner or pal. For a very long time, I've counted on his friendship and support, and also that of his wife, Martha Lewis.

I first met Ann Martin when I had the luck to work with her at the American Film Institute in Los Angeles, at my first job out of grad school. She has been a great friend since then, not only in LA but also in Washington, DC, Oakland, California, and elsewhere. Her support, and that of her partner, Bob

Reynolds, has been so meaningful to me for many years, not just in my writing but in so many things.

Inderpal Grewal and Al Jessel, and their daughters Kirin and Sonal, have practically become members of the family, and they've also welcomed me into theirs. Carolyn Dinshaw and Marget Long have been wonderfully supportive friends for a very long time, whether they've lived close by or across the country. They've also been terrific companions to hang out with in Paris. Minoo Moallem, Shahin Bayatmakou, Arash Bayatmakou, and Brita Bayatmakou have been valued friends for a very long time. Marisol de la Cadena and Steve Boucher are wonderful colleagues at UC Davis, but much more importantly, they're fabulous neighbors. Whether she's lived far away or nearby, Jennifer Terry has always been ready to talk with me about movies or research or work or the World Series.

David Lash visited me when I was a graduate student in Paris in 1981. By then we had already been great friends for about twenty years, and we continue to be almost forty years later. In fact, during my year abroad in grad school, I made a number of lasting friends. I would like to thank, especially, Richard Neupert, whose own work on French cinema has been so important to my own. Richard, his wife Cathy Jones, and their daughter Sophie have always been incredibly kind and generous. There are other students from that year in Paris whom I want to thank: Emily Calmer, Karen Wilde, Marie-Hélène Duprat, Karen Payne, BZ Petroff, Sylvie Palumbo-Liu, and Fabrice Ziolkowski, along with the faculty head of the program that year, Rick Altman. Just after I got back from Paris, Mark Zakarin became a wonderful neighbor and a close friend.

When I was completing a previous project about Frank Capra, I was invited to attend a Capra centennial conference in Sicily in 1997. The people I met there, and who organized the conference, have remained friends, and in particular I want to mention Franco Marineo, Federica Timeto, and Marcello Alajmo.

Over the years, I've had the chance to work with a number of amazing editors who have since become my friends: Leslie Mitchner, Rebecca Barden, and Bill Germano (who in a brainstorming session a few years ago helped me come up with the title for this book). When I worked at the University of California Press, I got to learn about books from some of the best in the business. Naomi Schneider, Monica McCormick, and Anna Weidman were mentors who became valued friends. There also were others at the press who taught me so much about what a book should be, and I've tried to apply those lessons to this project. I'd like to thank in particular Kate Toll, Mary Francis, Deborah

Kirshman, Reed Malcolm, Julie Christianson, Lynne Withey, Sheila Levine, Julie Brand, Linda Norton, Anna Bullard, Nola Burger, Nicole Heyward, Mari Coates, Howard Boyer, Leslie Larsen, Jim Clark, and Stan Holwitz.

When I began my job at UC Davis, I was lucky enough to join a group of scholars who soon would become my good friends. In particular, Carolyn Thomas, as well as her daughters Eva and Cat, have been encouraging and supportive, as well as great company and generous hosts. I would also like to thank my American Studies colleagues Julie Sze, Grace Wang, Ryan Cartwright, Javier Arbona, Anjali Nath, Charlotte Biltekoff, Michael Smith, Jay Mechling, Ari Kelman, Erica Kohl-Arenas, and Jemma DeCristo. My Film Studies colleague Jaimey Fisher has always been there with support, advice, and great friendship. I'd also like to thank Scott Simmon, Kris Fallon, Kriss Ravetto-Biagioli, Colin Milburn, Jesse Drew, Doug Kahn, Fiamma Montezemolo, Sergio de la Mora, and Michael Neff. Kay Allen, Karen Nofziger, Naomi Ambriz, Evelyn Farias, Omar Mojaddedi, Carlos Garcia, Tina Tansey, Fatima Garcia, and Aklil Bekele have made my job much easier, and saved me from terrible administrative and technological mistakes any number of times. Mapmaker extraordinaire Michele Tobias has not only improved the look of this book, but also its usefulness. My deans during this project, Jessie Ann Owens and Susan Kaiser, provided consistent support.

So many colleagues working on French cinema or related areas have been willing to read portions of this book or share their own work, and have welcomed me back into a field that I had moved away from for a number of years. I'd especially like to thank Judith Mayne, Kelley Conway, Chris Holmlund, Sabine Haenni, Brian Jacobson, Myriam Juan, and Annie Fee.

There have been so many other friends and colleagues who have been so helpful and kind, and often so much fun to spend time with, while I've been working on this book. I'm thinking here especially of Juana Maria Rodriguez and Mark Lynn Anderson. I also must thank Fred Davidson, Robert Ring, Lee Grieveson, Haidee Wasson, Victoria Vanderbilt, Cathy Jurca, Beth Becker, Nic Sammond, Cathy Davidson, Mary Ryan, Daniel Biltereyst, Peter Limbrick, Amy Bomse, Lisa Parks, Heather Hendershot, Marsha Gordon, Robyn Wiegman, Lisa Cartwright, Kathy Fuller-Seeley, Ella Shohat, Bob Stam, David Brent Spight, Jenny Horne, Caryl Flinn, Hong Guo-Juin, Melissa Riley, B. Ruby Rich, Greg Waller, Brenda Weber, Omnia El Shakry, Kathleen Frederickson, Parama Roy, John Marx, Laura Grindstaff, Gina Werfel, Hearne Pardee, Meredith Miller, Sigmund Roos, Ruthie Rohde, Sarah Juliet Lauro, Matthew Bernstein, Surina Khan, Molly McCarthy, Anna Everett, Jennifer Wild, Deb Gorlin, Nicole Baumgarth, Jun Okada, Regina Longo, Scott

MacDonald, Maureen Turim, Charles Maland, Sharon Marcus, Léopold Lambert, Florence, L'Huillier, Christina Cogdell, Andy Fell, David de la Peña, Sarah Gould-Waslohn, Rick Grossman, Lara Downes, Catherine Zimmer, Travis Milner, Leslie Blevins, Matthew Rosenberg, Natalya Eagan-Rosenberg, Valerie Venghiattis, Fernando Moreno, Gabriella Moreno, Paul Moylan, Jennifer Wadlin-Moylan, Arthur Janc, Kasia Koscielska, and Maja Janc.

When this project was just starting to come together, one of my mentors at UCLA, Nick Browne, invited me to come back for two quarters as a visitor. I had the opportunity to teach graduate seminars, and many of the students I met there have become friends as well as scholars from whom I've learned a great deal. I'd like to thank in particular Steven Charbonneau, Emily Carman, Deron Overpeck, and Ross Melnick. At UC Davis I've been able to work with so many terrific students in our Cultural Studies Graduate Group as well as other programs and departments: Michelle Yates, Marisol Cortez, Christina Owens, Cathy Hannabach, Magali Rabasa, Tallie Ben Daniel, Eric Taggart, Sara Bernstein, Elise Chatelain, Omar Abdullah, Kelley Gove, Julia Morales, Diana Pardo, Alexis Patino-Patroni, Ben D'Harlingue, Toby Smith, Jonathan Doucette, Abbie Boggs, Liz Montegary, Andrea Miller, David Laderman, Tristan Josephson, Terry Park, Nina Cole, Toby Beauchamp, Josef Nguyen, Alex Fine, Emma Waldron, Jinni Pradhan, Danielle McManus, Chris McCoy, Xiaolong Hou, Caroline McKusick, Jamianessa Davis, Jacob Hagelberg, Beshara Kehdi, Stephanie Maroney, Laurel Recker, Amanda Modell, Martha Stromberger, Heather Nolan, and many others.

Mentioning them makes me think of the students who were in graduate school with me, and who have been friends and mentors. Janet Bergstrom was the one who most encouraged me to attend the Paris program, and Michael Friend, who was in Paris the year before me, gave me his apartment in the fourth arrondissement. I'm still amazed that I was able to take classes and talk about movies with Lea Jacobs, Steve Ricci, Giuliana Muscio, Janet Walker, Frank Tomasulo, Dan Einstein, Michelle McGlade, Margaret Horwitz, Steve Seidman, Jonathan Kuntz, Eddie Richmond, Greg Lukow, and Richard de-Cordova, and that those classes were taught by people like Thomas Elsaesser and Dudley Andrew.

At Duke University Press, Ken Wissoker and Courtney Berger have been so steady in their support of my work and also in their friendship. This book marks my third project with Duke, and I want to thank Ken and Courtney for making me feel so at home there, and for their commitment to film history as a discipline. Everyone at Duke has been a dream to work with, and I'd particularly like to thank Jenny Tan, Sandra Korn, Christine Critelli, Susan Albury, and Emma Jacobs.

My family has been endlessly supportive. I would like to thank my brother- and sister-in-law, Mitchell Kaplan and Heidi Schulte-Kaplan. Henry Flax and David Norton have been incredibly generous in so many ways. My cousins Linda Benjamin-Pardee, Cathy Benjamin, Mindy Comitor, and Lynda Fisher have provided warmth and friendship. I want to give special thanks to Viviana Ramirez for helping make our family complete. My mother-in-law and father- in-law, Doris and Arthur Kaplan, both died during the last few years of this project. While I was finishing, I thought often about all of the help they gave me and the kindness they showed me for so many years and during various ups and downs in my career. I miss them both

Writing this book about Paris, having the chance to go there as often as I have, I'm very much aware that my parents, Mildred and Solly Smoodin, never had the same kind of opportunity. My mother, a member of her high school French club, never left the country. My father did only once, for three years in the Pacific during World War II. But I've thought of them all the time during this project, partially because of how important movies were to all of us, but mostly because they gave me the chance to have a very different kind of life, and to pursue what I most wanted to do. I wish they were here now.

I met Caren Kaplan in 1986. Since then, she and I have been to Paris to- gether a half dozen times, and I always have to stop and wonder at how lucky I've been to be able to spend my life with the perfect travel companion. She has been my primary source of emotional and intellectual support while I've been writing this book about a city we both love, and she has also been my role model as a scholar and as a writer. Over that first coffee in a café in Wash- ington, DC, thirty-five years ago, Caren and I realized that one of the things we had in common was that we had both been students in the Paris program, just a couple of years apart, and that as a result we knew several of the same people, and our paths had probably nearly crossed any number of times. When I think about it now, I can't help but feel at least a little like Vittorio De Sica in *Madame de . . .* (1953), when he tells Danielle Darrieux about meeting her, "C'est destin" ("It's fate"). For Caren and me, and thankfully without any of the tragic melodrama of *Madame de . . .* or some other Max Ophüls film, the long tracking shot of our life together began with that blind date.

Sofia Smoodin-Kaplan entered the scene about halfway through that shot. It's hard now to remember what life was like before her, and she has turned into a perfect pal for watching movies, or for traveling to Paris. Sofia has been there twice now, and each time she's been a terrific sport while I've dragged her off to find old cinemas that have been turned into Gap or Monoprix stores, or to look at the ones that still stand, like the spectacular Louxor in the tenth arrondissement. I can't imagine writing this book without her help, but that's the least of it. I'm ready for our next trip together.

Everyone here, in some way or another, has helped me with this book, even if that help came years before I began working on it. I know I've left people out, and I'll think of them later. But let me end with another Max Ophüls movie, one that's about the past and forgetting and trying to remember, *La Ronde* (1950). The film ends with a song, and I'll use the last lyric to conclude these acknowledgments, because the words seems so final when, really, they're anything but. *Je ne vous en dirai pas plus.* There's nothing else I have to tell.

A Walking Tour

1930–1981

When I was a graduate student in Paris in 1980 and 1981, I walked home from classes and always passed a cinema along the rue du Temple that never changed its bill. Fritz Lang's *Le Tigre du Bengale* (*Der Tiger von Eschnapur*; 1959) showed there for at least an entire year, and by the end of my stay I had come to count on the dependability of that one film at that same cinema week after week. When I saw *Le Tigre du Bengale*, there were probably only six or seven people in the audience, and I still remember the young woman who worked at the ticket booth, always smoking because she had nothing else to do. Practically no one was buying tickets to see the movie.

During that year in Paris, every Wednesday I bought the latest edition of *Pariscope*, which had complete listings of all of the films playing in the city and in the suburbs, a sort of weekly record of how new films and classics came and went and circulated through different neighborhoods. This was the kind of movement I had come to expect from growing up in Los Angeles, where subsequent-run cinemas changed their bills every Wednesday, except when a popular movie might be held over, and where new movies rarely played in first-run houses for more than a few weeks. I never really learned why, in Paris, most cinemas had a regular turnover, while a few never seemed to change. Someone told me that the cinema on rue du Temple and others like it were subsidized by the government, and so didn't have to change films, but that never seemed like a fully satisfying answer. Why did *Le Tigre du Bengale* never leave?

I'm fairly certain that's when I began thinking about this book, and about ways that movies came and went through the city, the relationships of cinemas to the movies they showed, to their neighborhoods, and to their audiences. I only really began working on it about fifteen years ago, after a trip back to

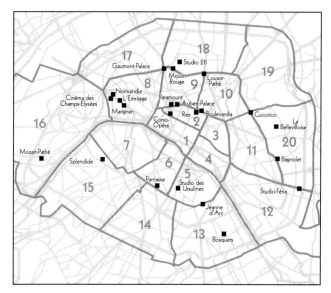

Map 1.1   A map of Paris showing the city's twenty arrondissements, or neighborhoods, and also some of the major cinemas from the period 1930–1950. Map by Michele Tobias.

Paris. While I was there I found an odd and now long-gone shop, Archives de la presse on the rue des Archives in the fourth arrondissement, stacked floor to ceiling with old French magazines. I went to the movie magazine section and looked through dozens of issues of *Pour Vous*, a popular film tabloid from 1928 until the surrender to Germany in 1940. On the last page of each issue there was a complete listing of the cinemas in the city, the movies they were showing, and the times they played.

These listings provided the now vanished cinematic geography of prewar Paris. One could chart how movies moved through neighborhoods, the development (and closure) of cinemas, and the relative importance of movies to different parts of town (typically around eighteen cinemas in the peripheral, working-class twentieth arrondissement and none in the first, which was spatially dominated by the Louvre). With these *Pour Vous* listings and with the more recent availability of other sources, particularly those put online by the Bibliothèque nationale on its Gallica website, I began work on a project examining Parisian film culture from the late 1920s until around 1950: the cinemas and the movies, the ciné-clubs and the preferred stars, the audiences, and also the role of film journalism.

Despite the abundance of possibilities for seeing movies during this period and the mythic status of Paris as a movie capital, we still know very little about

Figure 1.1   *Pour Vous* from October 13, 1933.

going to the movies there from the beginning of the sound era to the first films of the New Wave. Richard Abel has provided a full sense of the film distribution systems and exhibition experiences throughout France during the period just before World War I. Abel as well as Christophe Gauthier have unearthed and examined the history of the ciné-clubs and specialized cinemas that showed avant-garde, documentary, or animated films in Paris and elsewhere in France from the teens until about 1930, and Annie Fee has provided a history of gendered and politicized Parisian audiences in the post–World War I era.[1] From 1894 until the end of World War I, we have Jean-Jacques Meusy's encyclopedic rendering of all manner of exhibition sites in the city, including descriptions of the streets where they were located, in the aptly titled *Paris-Palaces*, as well as in his two-volume *Écrans français de l'entre-deux-guerres*.[2] But for that period from the late silent era until just after World War II, little attention has been paid to the average moviegoer and to the cinemas along the grand boulevards and in the neighborhoods that specialized in commercial, feature-length films, or to the ciné-clubs and other places for seeing movies.

A look at Parisian filmgoing and film exhibition from the period yields information that is both empirically and historiographically significant. While we have acknowledged the city's importance in film history, we still have not examined many of the basic aspects of the cinema in Paris, such as the number of cinemas and their locations. A close analysis of the ways films were exhibited and then moved through the city makes Paris itself, in the sense of a singular film culture, a problematic area of study. Examining films and filmgoing in Paris requires us to take our local study of the city to the micro level, to the neighborhoods within the city and the suburbs just outside it and the differences and similarities, in terms of film preference or audience, from one to the other. The city's film audience, from the working-class Ménilmontant, to the Jewish center of the Marais, to the bourgeois quarters in the middle and western half of the city, or to the leftwing political majority in the Clichy suburb, becomes a fragmented one, signifying not so much the "general Parisian" as the individual neighborhood itself.

Studying the varied audiences of Paris, the movies they watched, and their neighborhood cinemas also highlights significant changes in the practices of film studies. Increasingly over the last twenty-five years, the field has refined its understanding of the movie audience. I have written about this shift elsewhere, but for a number of reasons the field has moved away from an idea of a spectator mostly determined by the film itself, with one viewer much the same as any other. As Annette Kuhn has written, approaches to film viewing that developed in the 1960s and 1970s were "predominantly about a spectator addressed or constructed by the film text."[3] While these approaches still circulate, the prevailing belief is that issues of film viewing, and relationships between viewer and film, are far more complex and that empirical audiences are much more differentiated than can be accounted for by the notion of the textually produced viewer.

In a 1995 essay, "La Place du spectateur" ("The Place of the Spectator"), Christian-Marc Bosséno established some of the broad contours for studying the historical film viewer and for shifting the emphasis from that which took place on the screen to "the cinema itself" ("à la salle elle-même"). Bosséno posed a series of questions for conducting research on the audience: "Who went to the cinema, and why? How and under what technical and material conditions did they see films?" and later, "When can we date the death of the 'grand public' and the birth of specialized, micro audiences?"[4]

In asking about micro audiences, Bosséno had in mind those spectators who were interested primarily in particular kinds of films, in art films, or documentaries, or feature films. But one of the means for answering Bosséno's question, and for understanding these empirical audiences, has little to do with the kinds of movies they preferred. Instead, moving away from the "grand public," film scholars have engaged in regional and local analyses. As a result the city and the town have become central to contemporary film studies, much more so, in fact, than the nation. There might be nothing new about this emphasis on the local, as the 2001 translation and publication, in *Screen*, of Emilie Altenloh's 1914 dissertation regarding filmgoing in Mannheim, Germany, suggests. More recent scholars, such as Kathryn Fuller-Seeley, Lee Grieveson, Ben Singer, and Gregory Waller, have not only produced historiographies of local film habits, from the 1890s through World War II, but have also differentiated the varied audiences within a town or city.[5] In US-based film studies, scholars have analyzed the perceived tensions between city and town during the period in relation to taste in film and consumption practices, so that we might examine the full range of filmgoing habits and exhibition possibilities in such places as New York, Milwaukee, or Campbellsville, Kentucky, to name three test cases in a recent collection on movie audiences and film culture.[6]

In film studies, Paris has gone largely unexamined. We can, by inference, claim that Paris was both similar to and different from other major urban areas during the period. There were, of course, commercial agreements between nations, so that, as just one example, one of the major cinemas in London during the 1930s, the Finsbury Park, was part of the Gaumont British chain, which itself was a subsidiary of the French film company Gaumont, which owned so many cinemas in Paris and the rest of France. There also were the very determined systems of films opening in select, significant cinemas, typically in the "best" parts of town in London, Berlin, Los Angeles, or Paris, and then fanning out to cinemas in the neighborhoods.[7] Movie stars were understood as global commodities, as I'll examine in chapter 3, so that audiences in Paris as well as New York and London rushed out to see films with Greta Garbo or Marlene Dietrich. But these similarities only went so far. No other city during the period covered by this book, to my knowledge, had so extensive a system of ciné-clubs as Paris, and as I will point out in chapter 1, the people who wrote about such things understood significant differences in the architecture of cinemas between, for instance, New York and Paris. Those same experts, journalists typically, also felt that for every Maurice Chevalier, a star with an international following, there was also a Georges Milton, a performer of particularly Parisian appeal, whose films would leave American urban audiences as well as many European ones cold.

Purely in the French context, however, we probably have greater knowledge about modes of film exhibition and consumption in much smaller French locations than we do of the capital. Renaud Chaplain has examined the practices in Lyon, while Pierre and Jeanne Berneau have performed a similar study of Limoges from the beginning of cinema until the end of World War II, and Sylvie Rab has analyzed interwar film practices in Suresnes, the Parisian suburb.[8] But Paris remains a compelling case study because it functioned as a center of both national and international production, as one of the largest sites of film-going in Europe, as a hub of intellectual interest in cinema, and as the location of some of the most important film journalism on the continent.

By making sense of the information about movies in Paris we can also start to reconsider our ideas about national cinema. Since the 1930s and until fairly recently, film studies, at least as practiced in the United States and the United Kingdom, has made the term *national cinema* seem self-evident, with historians showing a clear sense of what French cinema might indicate, or German, or American for that matter. National cinema has meant, unproblematically, the films of a particular country. That is, national cinema has been defined textually as the narrative and visual mechanisms of large bodies of films. These come from filmmakers working in certain countries and languages or from movie companies with an important national presence and corporate headquarters (Gaumont, for instance, in the French context). They might also belong to significant movements primarily identified with a single country, for example French poetic realism in the 1930s or the French New Wave in the 1950s. But as I have argued before, we might also develop an understanding of national cinema based not only at the point of production, through analyses of the films made, but also at the point of reception—the ways in which audiences participated in film culture, the opportunities they had to see films, and the broad discourses about movies from such media as print journalism.[9]

This sort of examination helps us understand the national in both internationalist and fragmented terms. We can study the place of French cinema and French film culture in the rest of Europe as well as the United States and also their reach to France's colonies. But we can examine as well the similarities and differences between Parisian film culture and that of other areas in France—metropolitan, rural, and in between—to develop a more nuanced sense of French cinema.

In the case of Paris alone, by concentrating on the details of reception and exhibition, we acquire a way of reading that city in the manner of Michel de Certeau's "rhetoric of walking," from the ground, in terms of the spatial arrangement of film culture, the location of cinemas, and the movement of films through the city.[10] Studies of urban mobility by art historians and literary theorists typically have focused on representations of cities made by the artists and authors who walked through them: Walter Benjamin's focused inspection of the arcades of Paris, Édouard Manet's stroll on Georges-Eugène Haussmann's boulevard Malesherbes in the same city in the early 1860s, or Charles Dickens's evocations of London.[11] The important shift in film studies, however, has been to move beyond the study of representations of cities and the options of individuals to explore them, and to analyze the movements through space of the products of culture and of significant numbers of cultural consumers. This movement in the field has led to significant questions about a city and its films: How common was it for a single film to play in more than one cinema in the same neighborhood? What, if any, were the predictable distribution and exhibition patterns across the city? What were the connections between films and the cinemas and neighborhoods in which they played?

We also need to move away from just the local and get a sense of Paris's place within the film culture of the rest of France. In fact, how did movies make their way across the country? It is easy to assume that, at the very least, films opened in Paris and then went on to other cities and then to less urban areas. But what, really, were the patterns involved?

The evidence is hard to come by, particularly for the historian working in the United States. While it can be problematic enough to know much about Paris, it is extraordinarily difficult to find out many of the details of the film cultures of Havre or Marseille or Bordeaux, let alone any of the smaller cities and towns in France. If we take the 1930s, the period covered by so much of this book, as a brief case study, we have some national facts and figures. In 1937, in an example of just some of the numbers that the government acquired, a parliamentary inquest into the status of the French motion picture industry announced that there were four thousand cinemas in France, and that five hundred of them still had not been wired for sound (in fact, compared to Germany or Great Britain, the French film exhibition industry had been very slow to equip its cinemas with the technology required to show sound films).[12] It is very hard, though, to go much beyond that, and we have to get the evidence wherever we can find it.

The daily journalism from Paris in particular and from France more generally can help us here. A few notices from one of the most famous and available newspapers from the period, *Le Figaro*, serve as useful evidence. The paper always ran brief reviews of films and stories about them when they first appeared in the city. On October 25, 1931, for instance, filmgoers learned that the latest Janet Gaynor film from Hollywood, *Papa longues jambes* (*Daddy Long Legs*; 1931), had just opened at the Édouard VII cinema in the seventh arrondissement, and that Jean Renoir's "audacious" new film, *La Chienne* (1931), was bound to be "greatly discussed as well as at least occasionally condemned."[13]

Films less well known to us also opened that week—Viktor Tourjansky's *Le Chanteur inconnu* (1931), as well as Henri Chomette's *Le Petit Écart* (1931)—and the newspaper marked each of these films "P" for *parlant*, or "talking," to indicate that they took full advantage of the new technology.[14] Photos of the stars of the week often accompanied the brief reviews, in this case one of Gaynor from her film and also the French actress Madeleine Renaud from *Serments* (1931). Advertisements for movies hint at the range of important films in the city, and indeed in any single cinema. On October 31, 1931, readers saw an illustration of an airplane that had crashed nose first to the ground, and learned that Frank Capra's *Dirigible* (1931), dubbed into French, would begin its exclusive run at the Marigny cinema the following Tuesday, replacing Charlie Chaplin's far more intimate—and nontalking—*Les Lumières de la ville* (*City Lights*; 1930).[15] These ads and this information about movies appeared on an entertainment page, with a crossword puzzle, news about concerts, music hall performances, circuses, sporting events, and organization meetings ("Le Club féminin d'aviation" in the October 31, 1931, edition of *Figaro*, next to the advertisement for Capra's film). But *Figaro* provided cinema listings only sparsely, with schedules given for just a few venues for seeing films, because of the paper's mission of providing news and information for all of France.

The same is true for most of the other general-interest French newspapers that covered movies as just one amusement among many, and covered Paris significantly but not solely. As a result, some of the most detailed accounts of the cinema in the city and of the film culture there, at least from the early 1930s, come from *Pour Vous*, the movie tabloid that I came upon by a happenstance I discussed earlier, when I walked into Archives de la presse in Paris's fourth arrondissement. *Pour Vous* was just one of many movie magazines and journals that flourished in Paris and in the rest of France during the 1930s, with even a necessarily short and incomplete selection, yielding such titles as *Ciné Pour Tous, Ciné Magazine, Mon Ciné, Ciné Revue, Ciné Miroir, Ciné France*, and *Ciné Combat*. Paramount Pictures, the American movie studio, distributed its own journal, *Mon Film*, to advertise the movies that the company made in France—and in French—during the first years of the conversion to sound. As a sign of the importance of much of this film journalism, it was one of France's leading newspaper entrepreneurs, Léon Bailby, the director of the rightwing daily *L'Intransigeant*, who founded *Pour Vous*.[16]

Bailby's film tabloid focused most of its energy on Paris and on the films showing there. At least occasionally—or perhaps in a national issue meant for the rest of the country—*Pour Vous* ran the column "Aux quatre coins de la France ... ce qui se passe" ("What's Going On in the Four Corners of France"), announcing regional productions, the comings and goings of movie stars, and the films that had just opened. From the issue of January 22, 1931, readers found out that a comedy hardly known to us now, *Mon cœur incognito* (1930), had premiered in Marseille, at that time the second-largest city in France, and that René Clair's great, early sound film, *Sous les toits de Paris* (1930), had just started playing in Lille, around the tenth-largest city in the country.[17]

Mon cœur incognito was actually a German production. The film starred Mady Christians, who was Austrian, and Jean Angelo, a French actor who had had an extensive silent film career and appeared in sound films for just a few years. Two versions seem to have been made, one in French and one in German. At about the same time that the film opened in Marseille, it opened, as well in Paris, the week of January 16, 1931, at the Caméo-Aubert cinema on the boulevard des Italiens in the ninth arrondissement.[18]

This certainly doesn't count as definitive evidence, but it may well indicate that films opened more or less simultaneously in at least a few larger cities. Indeed, when *Pour Vous* announced *Mon cœur incognito* in Marseille, the tabloid also mentioned that G. W. Pabst's 1930 film *Quatre de l'infanterie* (*Westfront 1918*) continued its run there, which would closely match the film's December 1930 opening in Paris. By this time *Quatre de l'infanterie* had also already played in Havre, according to *Pour Vous*, and so it seems likely that Pabst's film had opened throughout France (Havre was only just getting *À l'Ouest rien de nouveau* [*All Quiet on the Western Front*; 1930], which for the last month had been a sensation in Paris).[19]

Other cities, even large ones, had to wait their turn. In western France, audiences in Nantes—typically the fifth- or sixth-largest city in the country—had been hearing about *Mon cœur incognito* for months after it first began showing in Paris. Throughout the late winter and early spring of 1931, there had been weekly radio broadcasts in Nantes of music from the movies, and songs from *Mon cœur incognito* always seemed to be featured, performed by the chanteuse and actress Florelle, who had a part in the film, Bernadette Delpart, and others. But *Mon cœur incognito* didn't come to Nantes until September 1931, when it premiered at the Majestic cinema there.[20]

Sous les toits de Paris presents a more difficult case than *Mon cœur incognito*. Clair's film also had links to the German film industry; Tobis Klangfilm, a German company created to produce sound films, opened a studio outside of Paris, in Epinay, to make French movies and recruited Clair for *Sous les toits de Paris*. The appearance of any Clair film at this time stood out as a major cultural event in Paris, and the press certainly treated the film as something very special when it opened, in April 1930, at the Moulin Rouge cinema on the boulevard de Clichy in the eighteenth arrondissement, and then as the film made its way to other countries in Europe and the United States. The details of its national release in France, however, are difficult to locate.

My best guess is that during the 1930s most French films opened in Paris and Marseille at about the same time. There may also have been different practices for films from different countries. Once again the evidence is difficult to find. As just one example, the Hollywood film *Les Quatre Plumes blanches* (*The Four Feathers*; 1929), with Richard Arlen and Fay Wray, opened in Paris in May 1930 but did not premiere in Marseille until July.[21] In an alternate instance, *Fox folies* (*Fox Movietone Follies of 1929*), which I will write about at greater length in chapter 4, opened in Marseille and Nice at least a few weeks before its contentious premiere in Paris in December 1929.[22]

There is no question that Paris was the most significant city in France for film exhibition. I have yet to find any evidence that a film might play anywhere else for months on end, in the manner of *À l'Ouest rien de nouveau* in the capital. The most typical case might be a film like *J'étais une espionne* (*I Was a Spy*; 1933), a British film with Madeleine Carroll, Herbert Marshall, and Conrad Veidt. *J'étais une espionne* was popular in Paris when it opened at the Élysée-Gaumont cinema in the eighth arrondissement in November 1933, playing there until the end of the year. Then the film moved to the Caméo-Aubert in the ninth, and then, a month later, to the Pagode in the seventh. The film seems to have disappeared for a few weeks after that, and then returned exclusively at the Lutetia in the seventeenth arrondissement in April 1934.[23] The French movie press duly noted this extended run in Paris. *La Revue de l'écran*, which covered cinema in the South of France, ran an advertisement for the film in May 1934, announcing not only the more than four-month success in Paris, but also that the film was being held over in other cities, in Metz and Strasbourg and Brussels.[24] In those places, though, the film was only in its third or fourth week, an indication that viewers there had to wait several months for the film, long after the Paris premiere.

Even if Paris was, occasionally, much like other cities in France in terms of when films might show there, it was also, most of the time, very much the first among equals. Thus we should keep in mind the absolute centrality of Paris to the nation's film culture, but also just how important other urban locations were to the success or failure of any film, and just how much Marseille, let alone Lyon or Nice or Toulouse or Nantes, meant to the French film industry.

The Archive of Parisian Film Exhibition

Understanding film exhibition and reception in Paris means reading through a range of primary materials from France and elsewhere. My focus on the period from around 1930 to 1950 reflects my own interests and preferences as well as the availability of materials. But it also is historiographically motivated. In these twenty years, the cinema in France moved from the introduction of sound, to World War II and German control of motion picture production and exhibition, to the postwar rebuilding of a national film industry infrastructure. The first years and the last also saw the adjustment of the American film industry in France, initially to the problems that the new sound technology posed to the internationally dominant Hollywood cinema and then to the opportunities of the years just after the war, when American films reestablished their central position in French film culture.[25]

This is also the period that marks what Colin Crisp has called the "classic French cinema," which developed with the conversion to sound technology in the late 1920s and lasted for about thirty years, until the broad industrial and stylistic changes heralded by the New Wave most famously, but that were as much bureaucratic as aesthetic.[26] As just one example, during this period, the Centre national de la cinématographie, which guided the French film industry, moved from the Ministry of Industry and Commerce to that of Cultural Affairs, under the leadership of André Malraux.[27] While historians have usually applied Crisp's sense of this classicism to modes of film style, we can also presume that the development of rules governing representation or narrative indicates the possibility of the same precision in other systems connected to the cinema, for instance exhibition.

From the recent work of François Garçon, in fact, we know that, at least during the 1930s, French film exhibition ran on a system of block booking and blind bidding, just as the American cinema did. Garçon provides as an example Marcel Pagnol's *Marius* (1931). We may think of Pagnol now as something of an independent filmmaker, having moved away from Paris, the cinematic center of France, to make films in Marseille. In fact, for *Marius*, Pagnol signed a coproduction deal with Paramount, the Hollywood company. Pagnol-Paramount then featured *Marius* as the lead film in a block of twenty; to show *Marius*, a film that was bound to be a popular one, cinemas in France also had to agree to show the other nineteen movies.[28] Garçon acknowledges, however, the baroque complexities of block booking, at least as it was carried out in France. He explains the dense practices of zones and clearances, again as in the American model, that mandated the length of time a film must go in and out of circulation (the "clearances") and the number of cinemas, and their proximity to each other, where a movie might play at any particular time (the "zones").[29] In France, then, at least during much of the period covered by this book, we do find an intricate administrative "classicism," but marked, in the tradition of French cinema, by intermittent yet steady chaos.

While the film journalism from Paris and the rest of France helps us chart these practices, so too does the reporting from the French film industry. The industry typically had an interest in finding out what it could about its audiences and the success of its exhibition practices, and so sources from the movie companies themselves often prove helpful, and in particular the 1948 document *Étude du comportement des spectateurs du Gaumont* (*Study of the Behavior of Spectators at the Gaumont*).[30] That report had been initiated by the Société nouvelle des établissements Gaumont (or SNEG in the dense alphabet soup of French cinema), the fully integrated production and exhibition corporation, in an attempt to find out why viewers went to, or stayed away from, the company's greatest showcase, the Gaumont-Palace, the largest cinema in Paris and one of the most important. Finally, of course, as erratic as the French film industry may have been during the period—and this instability is taken for granted in all of the histories—the cinema also was highly bureaucratized and linked to the national government, making governmental sources extremely valuable, and in particular two official reports almost twenty years apart: *Où va le cinéma français?* (*Where Is French Cinema Going?*) from 1937, and, from 1954, *L'Étude de marché du cinéma français* (*Study of the French Film Market*).[31] As this book moves chronologically, from about 1930 to the early 1950s, the concerns of these reports will come to seem remarkably similar.

A Few Notes on Method

This is also a book about a different kind of movement, about film enthusiasts making their way through the city, and movies going from one cinema to another, and about multiple uses of exhibition sites and the varying desires and activities of film audiences. How might this work in actual practice? Let me give a few examples—about cinemas, about a single cinema, and about a film—examples that inform much of the rest of this book.

Let's consider once again the 1930s. Had you gone to the movies in Paris with any regularity during that period, you would have had a difficult time avoiding the cinemas that belonged to the great exhibition chains. In the early years of the decade, of the two hundred or so cinemas throughout the city's twenty municipal districts, or arrondissements, around three dozen were affiliated with Pathé-Natan: the Marivaux-Pathé, Lutetia-Pathé, Sélect-Pathé, and the Excelsior-Pathé, to name just a few. About twenty-five were part of the Gaumont-Franco-Film-Aubert company: the Aubert-Palace, the Voltaire-Palace-Aubert, the Paradis-Palace-Aubert, and, of course, the Gaumont-Palace in the eighteenth arrondissement, the subject of that report mentioned above. These were among the best first-run sites in the city, the *cinémas d'exclusivité*, as well as smaller subsequent-run cinemas in the neighborhoods, the *cinémas des quartiers*.[32]

Chains might have connections with vertically integrated companies that produced and distributed films, with the Gaumont cinemas logically enough, often but not exclusively showing Gaumont films, while Pathé was connected to both Pathé-Natan and Paramount.

While these chains dominated the cinematic landscape of Paris (and, indeed, the rest of France), there were also some smaller affiliated groups of cinemas. At least during the very early 1930s there were two Family chain cinemas in Paris, the Family-Aubervilliers and the Family-Malakoff. A few cinemas were connected to newspapers, and typically specialized in documentaries and newsreels; the two Ciné *Paris-soir* locations, for instance, linked to the evening newspaper *Paris-soir*, or the four-cinema Cinéac chain, attached to yet another of the city's newspapers, *Le Journal*. And then there were a few cinemas with "Studio" in their names that may or may not have been part of a chain: the Studio de l'Étoile and the Studio-Haussmann in the eighth arrondissement, or the Studio-Féria in the twelfth, as well as the Studio-Parnasse (which at least for a time during this period specialized in Yiddish films) at 11 rue Jules Chaplain in the sixth. To attend these cinemas as well as those that were unaffiliated with a chain, movie patrons might pay anywhere from four or five francs up to twenty-five for admission (around $0.20 to $1.25), depending on the prestige of the cinema, the day, the time of the screening, and the quality of the seat.[33]

It is also worth taking a look at a single cinema that belonged to one of the major chains, moving back and forth through a few decades as we do so. Beginning in the 1930s, had you taken a walk on the boulevard de Rochechouart, not far from Montmartre, you would have had any number of opportunities to go to the movies. The boulevard borders the ninth and eighteenth arrondissements, and so you might have stopped in at the Palais-Rochechouart, or the Pathé-Rochechouart a few doors down, or the Roxy. If you wanted a smaller, neighborhood experience, you might have chosen the Clichy cinema just off the end of the boulevard, which seems to have been one of the numerous independent cinemas in the city. If you were interested in the overall spectacle of the cinema, and in spending a few hours in absolute opulence, you would have walked just a few more yards and gone straight to the Gaumont-Palace, situated just where Rochechouart ran into the place de Clichy and adjacent to the Clichy metro station.

The building's first incarnation was as the Hippodrome de Montmartre, dating from the 1900 World's Fair. Film entrepreneur Léon Gaumont bought the space in 1910 and shortly after that opened it as the Gaumont-Palace. Gaumont remodeled the beaux arts cinema in 1930 and reopened it a year later as an art deco showplace with six thousand seats. There was another renovation in the mid-1950s, and then a decade later the Palace converted to a site for Cinerama and then for 70 mm films.[34]

The reopening of the "new" Gaumont-Palace was a very big story in the French movie world in 1931. *Les Spectacles*, a movie trade tabloid for the north of France and particularly Lille, headlined "A Date in the History of Spectacle: The Reopening of the Gaumont-Palace," and called the new space "the largest and the most modern," and a "success for the entire French film industry."[35] The Palace was a showplace for Gaumont films, of course, but the company went in and out of film production throughout the 1930s because of financial difficulties, and so the cinema showed a range of first-run movies from a number of studios.

That was the Gaumont-Palace through most of the 1930s. With the beginning of World War II, however, things changed, really for all of the cinemas in Paris. As a German invasion and occupation of the capital seemed more and more inevitable, people left the city in droves, and many establishments shut down, including cinemas. By the time of the French surrender to the Germans in June 1940, all of the cinemas had closed. The best information available indicates that the Gaumont-Palace had been among the first to stop showing movies, perhaps because the operating costs for such a gigantic space were difficult to meet during a period of dwindling audiences and other scarcities.

The occupying Nazi force in Paris sought to give the illusion that the city had not skipped a beat since the surrender, and so reopened many of the cinemas there, including the Gaumont-Palace and the much smaller Clichy cinema nearby, perhaps a sign that the Germans hoped to emphasize both the importance of the great movie showplaces and also the more intimate, neighborhood locations. Possibly because it ran smoothly during the war, the Gaumont-Palace made an easy transition through the Liberation and the end of the conflict, showing the usual first-run French movies and also a backlog

Figure 1.2   The Gaumont-Palace cinema, as it looked in the early 1930s.

of American films that had been banned during the Occupation. For the new year in 1947, for instance, the Gaumont showed the MGM musical comedy *Bal des sirènes* (*Bathing Beauty*), from 1944, with Esther Williams and Red Skelton.[36]

I lose track of the Gaumont after this, with listings and other information difficult to come by. Although the Gaumont was torn down in 1972 (a Castorama shopping arcade and Mercure hotel now take up the space), at least by the late 1950s the site had lost none of its status as a Paris icon. In François Truffaut's *Les Quatre cents coups* (1959), it's a very big night when Antoine Doinel, his mother, and stepfather go to the Gaumont to see *Paris nous appartient*, although I'm not at all sure that the film ever played there. This was probably just an in-joke between Truffaut and his friend Jacques Rivette, whose film wouldn't even open until 1961. Antoine's stepfather is decidedly grouchy about going to the cinema at all, especially the Gaumont. He frowns when he hears what's playing there, and claims, anyway, that there are too many arsonists at cinemas, and at the Gaumont-Palace in particular.

What if we change our emphasis slightly, from cinemas to a single film as well as to the *cinéphiles* in the city? For a book about moving through Paris, there seems no better example here than Walter Benjamin, a movie enthusiast

Figure 1.3   The Castorama shopping arcade that now occupies the site
of the Gaumont-Palace. Photograph by author.

and also, of course, the theorist of the flâneur, of idly but purposefully strolling through an urban space. In fact, after Benjamin saw *L'Impossible Monsieur Bébé* (*Bringing Up Baby*; 1938) in Paris in the summer of 1938, he was moved to write to his good friend Gretel Adorno, Theodor's wife. "I recently saw Katharine Hepburn for the first time," Benjamin told her. "She's magnificent and reminds me so much of you. Has no one ever told you that?"[37] Benjamin had enjoyed the film and also Hepburn's performance immensely. But where, exactly, was he when he was struck by this resemblance between the star of Howard Hawks's great comedy and his very close friend? And how long had he waited to see the film?

Benjamin dated his letter July 20, about four months after the March opening of *Bébé* at the Miracles–Lord Byron cinema at 122 avenue des Champs-Élysées in the eighth arrondissement. The Lord Byron was not one of the very grand cinemas on the Champs-Élysées, but it was nevertheless a prestigious venue, and it was one of the cinémas d'exclusivité in the most fashionable parts of the city that specialized in foreign films shown in their original languages and subtitled in French. In the case of the Lord Byron, and in fact many of the other cinemas nearby, those films typically were from Hollywood. When *Bébé* opened at the Miracles, for instance, *Marie Walewska* (*Conquest*; 1937) with Greta Garbo showed at Le Paris in the eighth arrondissement just a few blocks away, while the Warner Bros. musical *Monsieur Dodd part pour Hollywood* (*Mr. Dodd Takes the Air*; 1937) was at the Helder in the ninth, and *La Rue sans issue* (*Dead End*; 1937) played at the Ciné-Opéra in the second.[38] There also were dubbed films showing in Paris. When audiences watched Cary Grant in *Bébé* during the film's opening in March, they could have seen the actor in another of his comedies from the period, *Le Couple invisible* (*Topper*; 1937), at the subsequent-run Mirage cinema on avenue de Clichy, although they would have heard a French actor speaking Grant's lines.[39]

Based on the available press coverage, it seems to have been a fairly big deal in Paris when *L'Impossible Monsieur Bébé* opened, and the movie had a healthy first run at the Lord Byron, showing for a little over two months until the end of May.[40] But that was hardly extraordinary. *Bébé* replaced another Cary Grant film at the Lord Byron, *Cette sacrée vérité* (*The Awful Truth*; 1937), which had played there for three months (before that, *Ange* [*Angel*; 1937], with Marlene Dietrich, had lasted only about one month, perhaps indicating that Dietrich's star was fading a bit in Paris at the time). Given the dates of *Bébé*'s run at the Lord Byron, it seems doubtful that Benjamin saw it there and then waited six weeks or more to write his letter to Adorno. The film disappeared for a short time after it left the Lord Byron, and then returned, once again with subtitles, to another cinema on the Champs-Élysées, the Ermitage. For a movie to go from one prominent cinema to another with not much time in between was common in Paris at the time, although the venues were not usually so close to one another.

Benjamin almost certainly saw *Bébé* at this second location, with the movie playing there from the end of June until July 20, the date on the letter. On July 21, *Bébé* left the Ermitage, to be replaced by Bob Hope and W. C. Fields in *The Big Broadcast of 1938* (1938). Hawks's film wasn't absent from Parisian screens for long, though, as it had reopened at the Courcelles cinema in the seventeenth arrondissement by the end of the month, and played there for a few weeks. This appearance at the Courcelles would mark the last chance for anyone in Paris, Benjamin included, to see and hear Hepburn and Grant in the film, because *Bébé* went straight from the Courcelles to the Mozart cinema in the sixteenth arrondissement at the end of August, but this time in a dubbed version.

It's difficult to tell whether other cinemas in Paris were showing *Bébé* as well by this time, because most of the available sources are somewhat sketchy. As I mentioned earlier, newspapers like *Le Figaro*, *Le Petit Parisien*, and *Le Matin* never listed all of the cinemas in the city, and even the Communist newspaper of record in Paris, *L'Humanité*, concentrated only on the "better" venues. If *Bébé* appeared in any other neighborhoods, however, it almost certainly would have been in the same French-language version showing at the Mozart, with this trajectory from exclusively in English at a single cinema to a dubbed format that played throughout the city establishing the pattern for the period. In addition, the film now played on double bills, first at the Courcelles, with the 1937 Barbara Stanwyck film *Déjeuner pour deux* (*Breakfast for Two*), and then at the Mozart with a film I have been unable to identify.

We can place these exhibition sites in Paris against those in the rest of France, to get a fuller sense of the importance of the capital and its relations to other locations. In the case of *Bébé*, during this period the film moved through the nation and also its colonies, as Hawks's film seems to have arrived in North Africa in the early summer of 1939. I haven't found any evidence of *Bébé* playing in Algiers, but it showed in a nearby suburb, Hussein Dey, in June of that year, on a double bill with *Révolte à Dublin* (*The Plough and the Stars*), the 1936 Barbara Stanwyck/John Ford film, at the Cinéma-Royal.[41] In fact the film reached the Algerian market even before it had played in many parts of France. *Bébé* didn't show in Nantes, for instance, in western France, until the week of June 13, 1940, at the Apollo cinema. *Gunga Din*, a Cary Grant film from 1939, was playing at the Palace that week, just a few days before the surrender to Germany, making these almost certainly among the last American films to play in Nantes until the end of the war.[42]

With some necessary detours along the way, examples like these make up the story of this book. Indeed, in the same manner that we might follow developments at the Gaumont-Palace or the place of *L'Impossible Monsieur Bébé* throughout Paris and the rest of France, this book will move through space and time, going from the late silent and early sound era, to the Popular Front and just after, then to World War II and the Occupation, and then to the postwar period, concentrating on Paris but extending to other parts of France, Europe, France's colonies, and occasionally the United States. Chapters will examine exhibition broadly as well as particular cinemas, individual movies, favored performers, and also and unavoidably the violence that was at least a small part of the city's film culture from the 1930s through World War II. Some of the great stars of French as well as international cinema—Maurice Chevalier, Marlene Dietrich, Jean Gabin, Michèle Morgan, and Danielle Darrieux—will come in and out of this narrative, as will those mostly unknown to us today, like the German actress Brigitte Horney who had a brief celebrity in Paris during the Occupation. German control of Parisian—and

French—cinema has a central role here, helping us make sense of some of the occurrences at Parisian cinemas in the decade before the war and those that took place just after, while also complicating our notion of what we mean by national cinema in the first place, as well as the cinema of a particular urban location. Of course, this project is mindful of alternative viewing sites, of the ciné-clubs of Paris and also of the ways that the activities in these specialized locations as well as at traditional ones interacted with other aspects of the Parisian cultural scene. On a small note about method, I have kept all film titles in French, except in those cases when sources use the original titles of foreign—typically American—movies.

So let's begin. Let's start our walk through Paris.

1

The Cinemas and the Films

1931–1933

In the ninth arrondissement in Paris, for the week of October 13, 1933, a film enthusiast might walk into the Paramount cinema on 2 boulevard des Capucines for a 9:30 a.m. show of *Un soir de réveillon* (1933), end the day down the block with a 3:00 a.m. screening of *Tire au flanc* (1933) at the Olympia at 28 boulevard des Capucines, and watch two or three movies in between at cinemas just a few steps away. In fact throughout the city that week, filmgoers could watch Fritz Lang's *Le Testament du Dr. Mabuse* (*Das Testament des Dr. Mabuse*; 1933), Max Ophüls's *Liebelei* (1933), Josef von Sternberg's *L'Ange bleu* (*Der blaue Engel*; 1930), and Frank Capra's *Forbidden* (1932), as well as *Je suis un évadé* (*I Am a Fugitive from a Chain Gang*; 1932), *King Kong* (1933), and Jacques Tourneur's *Toto* (1933). They might see Eddie Cantor in *Le Kid d'Espagne* (*The Kid from Spain*; 1932) and Boris Karloff in *Frankenstein* (1931), and also go to any number of films that have long been forgotten: *La Voie sans disque* (1933), for instance, or *Madame ne veut pas d'enfants* (1933), or *Rumba* (possibly *The Cuban Love Song*, from 1931).[1]

This brief but formidable list of viewing possibilities comes from "Voici les films qui passent à Paris"—the films showing in the two hundred or so cinemas in Paris—a section in that week's issue of the movie tabloid *Pour Vous*. The information here indicates that most of the large, first-run cinémas d'exclusivité were clustered in the more well-heeled neighborhoods, in the second arrondissement on the boulevard des Italiens (at 5, 6, 15, 27, and 29) and the boulevard Poissonière (at 1, 7, and 27), and in the eighth, on or near the avenue des Champs-Élysées, although there were others in neighboring areas such as the sixth and seventh.[2] The number of cinemas in the arrondissements varied, from only two in the fourth to eighteen in the ninth, which included

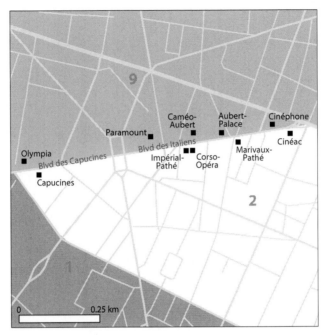

Map 1.1 The second and ninth arrondissements, showing the cinemas on the boulevard des Capucines and the boulevard des Italiens, 1933. Map by Michele Tobias.

the area around the rue Pigalle, and nineteen in the eighteenth arrondissement, around Montmartre, one of the more peripheral neighborhoods of the city. These numbers were tied to population density, but not strictly. The eighteenth arrondissement was, throughout the 1930s, the most highly populated area in Paris, while the first typically had the fewest residents. The ninth arrondissement, however, with its eighteen cinemas in 1933, as well as the second, sixth, and seventh, were on the low end of the Parisian population scale. The cinémas d'exclusivité in those areas almost certainly had more seats than the average cinema in the eighteenth, and so it becomes difficult to determine exactly the link between cinema space—in the broad sense of number of cinemas and number of seats—and the population of a particular arrondissement.[3]

Most of the cinemas ran their programs from noon or 2:00 p.m. until 8:30 or 9:00 p.m., typically every day, although in some cases only on two days a week, usually Thursday and Sunday. A few cinemas opened as early as 9:00 a.m., and some had their last screenings at midnight or even as late as three in the morning. Just as in the United States, more and more French cinemas showed double (and sometimes triple) bills throughout the 1930s, with many exhibitors responding to the Pathé cinema chain's aggressive July 1933 commitment to programs of multiple films.[4] In Paris during that week in October, the major first-run cinemas still only showed single films, but in the neighborhoods with mostly subsequent-run exhibition sites, the cinémas des quartiers, audiences could easily see two films for the price of one. In the third arrondissement, three of the five cinemas showed two films and usually maintained that practice from week to week. On the boulevard Saint-Martin in the third, the Kinérama paired two reissues of Hollywood films from 1932—Ernst Lubitsch's World War I melodrama *L'Homme j'ai tué* (*The Man I Killed*; 1932) with the Harold Lloyd comedy *Silence! On tourne* (*Movie Crazy*; 1932)—after having shown Marlene Dietrich in *Shanghai Express* (1932) the previous week, along with *Idylle au Caire*, the 1933 French version of a film from UFA, the German studio.[5] In the ninth arrondissement, five of nine cinemas showed double bills, while five of twelve cinemas reporting programs that week from the fourteenth, near the southern edge of Paris, presented two films each.

By 1933 almost all of the cinemas in the city showed, if not exclusively current films, then films that had been released before in Paris in 1931 or 1932. At least one cinema, however, still seemed to show silent films exclusively, and another specialized in them. In the tenth, the Boulevardia treated Greta Garbo fans to *Terre de volupté* (*Wild Orchids*; 1929) and then changed the program the following week to Douglas Fairbanks in *Le Voleur de Bagdad* (*The Thief of Bagdad*; 1924).[6] At the same time, the other Parisian cinema that typically treated fans to silent movies, the Corso-Opéra on the boulevard des Italiens in the second arrondissement, presented a reprise of one of the greatest hits of the last few years, *L'Ange bleu*, the film that made Marlene Dietrich an international star. The Corso, one of the oddest cinemas in a city full of them, hardly seemed like a cinema at all. The American trade paper *Variety* called it a "350-seat barn" with small stands at its entrance selling men's and women's clothing, and it was only the large film posters outside that indicated movies were shown there at all.[7] In keeping with the typical practice at the Corso, and as I will describe later, that print of *L'Ange bleu* may well have been the mostly silent version with French intertitles and all of Dietrich's songs in the original German that had played before in Paris, rather than the German-language subtitled copy of the film that also had been shown in the city.

The Conversion to Sound

In fact, at least until 1931 or 1932, silent cinema persisted in Paris, and certainly not because new silent movies were being produced. A few years after the 1929 Paris premiere of *Le Chanteur de jazz* (*The Jazz Singer*; 1927), audiences

Figure 1.1   The movie listings in *Pour Vous* from October 13, 1933.

could see silent films everywhere in Paris because of the exigencies of film exhibition—many cinemas in the city installed the necessary equipment for screening sound films only very slowly.[8] We know this because every week in its film listings by arrondissement, *Pour Vous* indicated exhibition technology, whether or not a cinema was equipped to show films "sonore et parlant," with recorded sound and also speech. In January 1931, *Pour Vous* showed almost seventy cinemas that had yet to be wired for talking films, with that number declining to sixty by April and to fewer than forty at the end of the year.[9] By 1933 *Pour Vous* had stopped the practice altogether of labeling cinemas as either silent or sound, which probably indicates that the conversion in exhibition technology had been completed.

Those exhibition sites controlled by the two major chains in Paris, Pathé and Gaumont, adapted to the new technology more quickly than others. The Pathé-Bagnolet was one of the very few in the first chain to be showing silent films in 1931; in early April, that cinema featured Greta Garbo in *La Belle Ténébreuse* (*The Mysterious Lady*; 1928), but this was a site on the Parisian periphery, in the working-class twentieth arrondissement, and so was probably not as important to Pathé's dominance of exhibition in the city as those cinemas more centrally located.[10] Neither location nor class counted for everything, however. In the wealthy and well-situated seventh arrondissement, two of the seven cinemas—the Pagode and the Récamier—had yet to be wired for sound by early April 1931, and in the sixteenth, on the western edge of the city and always one of the most exclusive neighborhoods in Paris, five of the nine still showed silent films exclusively.[11]

For many cinemas, especially those not belonging to an exhibition chain, the decision to delay conversion was almost certainly based on the expense of the new technology. The twentieth arrondissement seemed to have the slowest rate of change, with seven out of nineteen cinemas still not wired for sound in January 1931, and that number hadn't changed by the end of the year. Most of those seem to have been independent cinemas, and one of them served as a sort of all-purpose cultural center. The Bellevilloise, on the rue Boyer at the corner of the boulevard de Ménilmontant, was founded as a workers' cooperative in 1877, just a few years after the Paris Commune.[12] The building would be an educational site and also a cultural one, and showed films only erratically throughout the early 1930s. Because cinema was only one of the activities at the Bellevilloise, and far from the central one, it probably made little sense to install sound technology there, and this cooperative enterprise certainly would have had trouble coming up with the money to do so.

The last great silent film event in Paris during the early 1930s was the opening of Chaplin's *Les Lumières de la ville* in April 1931 at the prestigious Théâtre Marigny in the eighth arrondissement.[13] Anticipating that film, *Pour Vous* called it the first silent film made in the United States in eighteen months, since Garbo's *Le Baiser* (*The Kiss*; 1929).[14] This seemed to make silent film— or, at least, silent film production—fully a phenomenon of the past, to be brought back only by those artists, like Chaplin, working on their own. But if we shift our sense of history just a few degrees and concentrate on film exhibition, it becomes apparent that silent cinema had a significant place in Parisian film culture for far longer than we might have thought.

For this transitional period, however, we cannot just consider the binary opposition of silent and sound films, and the various means of exhibiting movies from the late 1920s until around 1933 tell us a great deal about the complexities of this era and the different opportunities for Parisians to hear sounds and voices at the movies. Film companies often made different versions of their films for different viewing—and hearing—constituencies. In the United States, when audiences watched *All Quiet on the Western Front*, they also heard the voices of the actors. German audiences seem to have seen and heard the German-language version (at least until the film was banned in Germany, shortly after its premiere), perhaps with German actors in some of the roles, or dubbing them, or a combination of both.[15] But Universal also made a nontalking film of Erich Maria Remarque's novel, with a musical score and sound effects. That film, now called *À l'Ouest rien de nouveau*, was the one French audiences apparently saw (the studio seems not to have made a French-language version); the advertisements in French magazines and newspapers announced that the film playing for month after month at the Ermitage cinema on the Champs-Élysées would be shown "sonore"—with sound effects—rather than "parlant."[16]

At about the same time, the French film *La Fin du monde* (1931), directed by Abel Gance, opened in Paris, naturally enough, "sonore et parlé," indicating music, effects, and synchronized speech. The same was true with *L'Énigmatique Mr. Parkes* (1930), an American film made in French, by Paramount, with French-speaking actors Claudette Colbert and Adolphe Menjou. An American film, *No, No, Nanette* (1930), was exhibited "sonore et chantant," which probably meant a silent version except when characters sang, in English, and the same seems to have been true with *Le Chant de bandit* (*The Rogue Song*; 1930), directed by Lionel Barrymore and featuring American baritone Lawrence Tibbett, with French audiences hearing the Metropolitan Opera star sing but not speak. The Panthéon cinema in the fifth arrondissement specialized in films "entièrement parlant anglais," and so showed the "version intégrale Américaine" of *The Love Parade* (1929), with Maurice Chevalier speaking and singing in English.[17] This version of Chevalier's film almost certainly had French subtitles, and the *sous-titré* movie in general held a privileged place in French cinema, at least in the early years of the conversion to sound.

Reading Subtitles

"The film is in German, but the subtitles by Colette make it easy to follow the action, which is already so involving."[18] That's how the French film weekly *Hebdo* ended its June 1932 review of *Jeunes filles en uniforme* (*Mädchen in Uniform*; 1931), with Leontine Sagan's classic already in the midst of a successful run in Paris at the exclusive Marigny cinema just off the Champs-Élysées, where *Les Lumières de la ville* had played. Certainly it was a mark of the prestige of the film that a writer as famous as Colette would compose the subtitles, and it made sense that the press would comment on her authorship. That same issue of *Hebdo*, however, also reviewed another German film playing just a few blocks away from *Jeunes filles* at the Cinéma des Champs-Élysées, *Quatre dans le tempête* (*Ein Mädel von der Reeperbahn*; 1930). The magazine mentioned yet again the author of the French subtitles, Jean Vincent-Bréchignac, a journalist and writer who was barely known at the time (and still remains little known).[19]

Figure 1.2   An advertisement for *À l'Ouest rien de nouveau* from the December 19, 1930, issue of *La Semaine à Paris*. Source: Bibliothèque nationale de France, Paris.

The subtitled film in France, it would seem, at least during the early sound period, might sometimes count as a significant literary event, with authorship duly noted and credited as much to the translator of the dialogue as to the original director or scenarist. But during this transition to recorded sound, as we have seen, there were other ways for audiences to view foreign films. In that same issue of *Hebdo*, the lead review was for *Frankenstein*, and the opening line alerted potential viewers that this was a "film spoken in French by 'dubbing.'"[20] That dubbed version was a big hit in Paris, playing for several months during the summer of 1932 at the Apollo cinema in the ninth arrondissement and then moving to another exclusive engagement in the same neighborhood, at the elegant Roxy.[21]

Sometimes any effort to translate a foreign film would meet with resistance. At the end of April 1932, *Shanghai Express*, another Dietrich film directed by

Josef von Sternberg, opened at the Cinéma des Champs-Élysées. Quite simply, in the wake of *L'Ange bleu*, any film by Sternberg and especially any film with Dietrich was a very big deal in Paris at the time (their previous film together, the 1931 *X-27* [*Dishonored*], was playing at nine cinemas that same week). Ribadeau Dumas wrote the review of *Shanghai Express* for *La Semaine à Paris*, a weekly listing and review of cultural events in Paris, and he extolled the artistry of the film, its technique, its editing, its cinematography. And then, as if any attempt by someone other than Sternberg to present the story to Parisian audiences was doomed to fail, the dependably snobbish Ribadeau Dumas emphasized the tedium of watching such a film translated with subtitles for the sake of those who could not understand English.[22]

The American Press, Alcohol, and Air-Conditioning

Complementing the statistical and qualitative information about exhibition in *Pour Vous* and other sources, about dates, times, and technologies, newspapers from the United States provide us with significant empirical data about Parisian cinemas and the movies they showed. The American press gives us, as well, ample anecdotes and impressions that also typically correspond to the conventions of American nonfiction from the period for reporting on Europe. Many of these entries on filmgoing in Paris repeat one of the clichés of much American travel literature, of a sort of unfathomable Frenchness and the complete difference of the French from the Americans.

Examples from the weekly magazine *Literary Digest* typify this balance of information and incredulity. The *Digest* compiled the best of middle- and high-brow journalism from a number of sources, and in 1929 ran an article titled "Why Paris Goes to the Movies," which acquainted readers with reporter Quinn Martin's recent "European Tour of Movie Houses."[23] One of the ongoing problems in film studies is that of determining precisely what people did at the movies. We know that they watched films and that they ate food, but we do not know much else; how intently they watched, how much they talked, what other activities took place at cinemas, and how that activity might be connected to first-run or subsequent-run cinemas, or to seats in the balcony or orchestra sections, or to time of day. From Martin, though, we get the amateur anthropologist's view of the bizarre practices of the natives, as he noted, first, that "the French go to the movies to rest." When Martin dropped into a cinema to see a reissue of the British film *The White Shadows* (1924), which was "preceded by a number of talking short subjects," the cinema was only one-quarter full, and the audience "sat there reading newspapers and eating sandwiches." Apparently the lights remained on during the movies there, at least brightly enough to let viewers read, but at another cinema on Martin's tour, the enormous Gaumont-Palace, the ambience may have been much darker, as "half the audience appeared to be drowsing," and the "other half was making love."[24]

Two years later, in April 1931, the *Digest* provided more information about when and how those Paris viewers used cinemas to make love and to rest, although here the source is perhaps no better than Martin, the amused tourist. In this case, the *Digest* cited a longstanding French satirical magazine, *Le Crapouillot*, and a special issue on "Pictures of Paris." The view from *Le Crapouillot*, then, was probably both distanced and ironized, as the magazine complained about the "continuous performance" in cinemas, "which open at nine in the morning and grind off reel after reel until two the next morning." *Le Crapouillot* then gave the sense of filmgoers less concerned about showtimes than with dipping into a cinema when it most convenienced them, as "Spectators are just as likely to enter the cinema at the middle or end of a picture as at the beginning." This casual viewer, though, had strong feelings about the movies being shown, and especially about film product from Hollywood. The critic in *Le Crapouillot* wrote that "I have . . . had the satisfaction of seeing honest folk leave a boulevard cinema at midnight, and stop to dissuade, in loud and unmistakable terms, those in the waiting line that they would lose both their time and money seeing and listening to an imbecility" from the United States.[25]

Thus in one essay we have the mythic binary of the French filmgoer, the flâneurs who go to the cinema when they feel like it, at the beginning, middle, or end of a program, and the dedicated cinéphiles who engage strangers in debate about movies. *Le Crapouillot* may not have been the most reliable source for information about film in Paris, given its emphasis on humor and satire, but there were other, perhaps more sober, sources that help us understand the film culture of Paris during this period, with the *New York Times* standing out for both data and opinion about cinema in the French capital.

As part of the paper's extensive international reporting, and particularly from urban centers around the world, the *Times* had a correspondent in Paris, Herbert L. Matthews, who wrote regularly on the films there, the audiences that watched movies, and the cinemas where they saw them. A quarter century later, Matthews's liberal cosmopolitanism would lead him to Cuba and to an infatuation with the revolution led by Fidel Castro, which he chronicled for an American audience.[26] In the 1930s, though, he was less the political leftist and much more the cultivated flâneur, reporting on the arts scene and taking the movies very seriously.

Matthews, as well as some of his colleagues at the *Times*, took a special interest in the city's cinemas. Reporting during the late summer of 1932, Matthews lamented that few new films were showing and audiences were dwindling, in part because "Parisian theatres do not employ the water-cooling system which entices so many sweltering New Yorkers off the streets and into the gigantic ice-boxes of Broadway." Of course, air-conditioning was one of the important advances of movie theatres in the United States in the 1920s, one that has not been given the attention of other technological innovations, such as the conversion to sound later in the decade, but that nevertheless marked a major difference between cinemas in the United States and those in France.[27] In spite of this American advantage, Matthews took pains to point out that "there are many cinemas here as modern, as large and as attractive as those along Broadway." He then mentioned the Paramount, in the ninth arrondissement, and approvingly wrote that it was "not nearly so pretentious as its namesake in New York" (both of which were owned by the American film company Paramount Pictures Corporation). Matthews also wrote about the Gaumont-Palace in the eighteenth, "which was recently done over in modernistic style," a reference to the renovation that I mentioned earlier. Moreover, "there are film houses along the Champs-Élysées of a smaller, more intimate sort which yield to none, anywhere, in attractiveness and comfort."[28]

So Matthews provides us with the range of cinemas in the more elegant neighborhoods, and approves of a more modest style than one might find in cinema architecture in New York. In next giving us some particular details of Parisian film culture, at least in the chic quarters, he more fully rounds out his comparison with the United States, and finds American movie houses wanting. Matthews reports that cinemas in Paris have a fifteen-minute intermission between feature films on a double bill, or between shorts and the main feature, or the stage show and the film. Parisians apparently put that intermission to good use, as did Matthews, the Prohibition-era journalist happily working in Europe. "There is one great convenience which Paris houses have, and the best of them in New York do not have," Matthews wrote, "and that is a bar—a real, old-fashioned bar where . . . the audience can go for refreshments that are indeed refreshments."[29] Thus, in weighing the comforts of cool air and those of a cool drink, Matthews preferred the latter, and therefore the French film exhibition model.

About six months later, in January 1933, Matthews began a report by writing about "an almost feverish activity in getting cinema theatres built," noting that "three were completed and opened within the last month, and several others are nearly ready for use." The buildings that marked this boom were "as fine as anything of the kind to be seen in New York," and then Matthews went on to tell his readers something of the style of the new Parisian spaces. For the most part, and quite unlike many of the downtown urban cinemas in the United States, the style in Paris was "toward small, exclusive, intimate edifices, with either no balconies or just a tiny one far in the back." Cinema architects in Paris emphasized "comfort and roominess, with splendid bars for the intermission," and their style was markedly "modernist . . . even to the extent of being slightly freakish about it."[30]

The Raspail 216, named for its address in the fourteenth arrondissement, was one of those new cinemas in Matthews's article, and it opened with Danish director Carl Theodor Dreyer's famous 1932 horror film, *Vampyr*. Dreyer's movie has come down to us as an art film, more suited to the university or the museum, but this German French coproduction originally was released commercially. Matthews provides us with an eyewitness account of the audience response to the film, a response that seems in keeping with the somewhat obscure narrative of *Vampyr*. Those viewers, sitting in the Raspail's "seats of white leather," were "either held . . . spellbound as in a long nightmare or else moved . . . to hysterical laughter."[31]

Other new cinemas played more conventional films. Shortly after the Rex opened in 1932 on the boulevard Poissonière in the second arrondissement, it had a great success with "that veteran comedian of the French state, Max Dearly." The film was *L'Amour et la veine* (1932), and it had been produced by the same man who built the Rex, the great film impresario Jacques Haïk. Matthews showed much more interest in the cinema than in the film, and he gave readers a sense of the Rex's appeal. "Outwardly it is a simple building in white stone," Matthews wrote, and then added that "it is the inside that is unique." The cinema seated close to three thousand "in an orchestra and two wide, sweeping balconies," and while this might compare to the largest, downtown cinemas in the United States, the Rex catered specifically to continental sensibilities. "What Europeans consider to be more suitable to their tastes," Matthews said, "the carpets, decorations, stairways, doors and the like, are not striking or rich or colorful, but simple and comfortable, and even elegant." The ceiling was especially so, as it was "made into a representation of the heavens at night—a summer's night on the Riviera." All of this fell under the authority of an American manager, Francis Mangan, apparently brought in from the United States to add some New York–style showmanship to Haïk's palace. The "36 Rex Mangan Stars" performed there as part of the stage show, as did sixteen rhythm dancers "doing their mechanically perfect cavorting."[32]

Figure 1.3   Jacques Haïk's movie palace, the Rex, around the time that it opened in 1932.

The Rex, just a few blocks away from the Corso on the boulevard Poissonière, stood as one of the grandest cinemas in Paris. The French press also took notice, with *La Semaine à Paris*, which usually only duly noted new locations for seeing movies, extolling the florid extravagance of this "cinéma atmosphérique," with its "starred ceiling . . . giving us the illusion of an oriental night" (although the reporter complained that too much exotic atmosphere made it a little hard to breathe in the place).[33] Despite its incredible ambience, the Rex, at least in the early 1930s, typically played new releases for only a week before they disappeared for just a little while and then fanned out to other cinemas in the city. This made the Rex a version of what, in the United States, would be a less important first-run house, a notch below the "run-of-the-picture" cinemas where a film might play for weeks on end. In the Rex's neighborhood, the second arrondissement, it would be the Marivaux-Pathé that would show some of the most important movies for weeks or months at a time, for instance in 1937 when the great Jean Gabin film *Pépé le Moko* opened there.[34]

From all of these sources, and especially from Matthews and other *Times* reporters from the early 1930s, we learn, then, about an expansion in cinema construction in Paris during the period that marked the conversion to sound. Paris entrepreneurs emphasized small cinemas, perhaps out of economic necessity or perhaps because of the city's spatial constraints, but the occasional new film palace still appeared on the grand boulevards. We can learn just how big these palaces were (not only the Rex but also the 2,500-seat Marignan, which opened on the Champs-Élysées in 1933).[35] According to the *Times*, this boom in building cinemas brought twenty-three new movie houses to Paris between 1930 and 1932, and seven to the suburbs just outside the city.[36]

Matthews also recorded responses to films, although here his remarks may be compromised by his continuing insistence on fully nationalist film preferences, with French—and primarily Parisian—audiences always looking for the "truly French" motion picture.[37] In spite of this, Matthews noted that Parisians particularly liked many early 1930s Hollywood films, all dubbed into French (with Matthews keeping their titles in English), such as *Frankenstein*, *Dr. Jekyll and Mr. Hyde* (1932), *The Crowd Roars* (1932) with James Cagney, as well as Lubitsch's *The Man I Killed*, Capra's aviation epic *Dirigible*, Greta Garbo in *Mata Hari* (1931), and three Marlene Dietrich films directed by Josef von Sternberg, *Shanghai Express*, *Dishonored*, and *Morocco* (1930). Among subtitled films, two gangster movies—*Scarface* (1932) and another Cagney film, *Public Enemy* (1931)—as well as the Eddie Cantor movie *Palmy Days* (1931), Harold Lloyd's *Movie Crazy*, and two literary adaptations, *Murders in the Rue Morgue* (1932) and John Ford's *Arrowsmith* (1931), were particularly successful.

Cross-cultural incomprehension, however, seemed to make a Hollywood adaptation of W. Somerset Maugham's *Rain* (1932), with the typically popular Joan Crawford, a failure among Parisian fans, who were also left cold by Mae West's films. These same moviegoers loved the latest film with French star Georges Milton, *Nu comme un ver* (1933), even though it would be safe to assume that "no American would enjoy" this French picture.[38]

City, Neighborhood, Nation

Milton's movie brings us back to our filmgoer in the ninth arrondissement, on the boulevard des Capucines. *Nu comme un ver* had opened at the Olympia cinema at 28 boulevard des Capucines in early May 1933.[39] By the end of May the film had moved to another exclusive run at the Gaumont-Palace in the eighteenth arrondissement, and then, within a week or two, disappeared from Paris cinemas.[40] By the beginning of September the film had returned for yet another exclusive showing at the Rex, the cinema that Matthews had so detailed, just a few blocks away from the Olympia.[41] By the week of October 6, *Nu comme un ver* had moved to cinemas across the city, in fashionable areas and also farther out toward the periphery, in the sixth, eleventh, fifteenth, and seventeenth arrondissements, and was also showing in four theatres in the twentieth. One week later, the run had contracted, and the film showed only in the fourteenth, seventeenth (in a different cinema from the week before), and eighteenth, and by October 20 the film once again had fallen out of circulation.[42]

Matthews's assertion of the "Frenchness" of Milton's film perhaps seems sensible, but also makes us ask about the relationship of a film like *Nu comme un ver* to the other movies in a city known for its international film culture. During the week in October that began this chapter, the films listed in *Pour Vous* numbered about 150. The movies were mostly feature length, but there were also shorts and documentaries, and six of the cinemas showed only newsreels.[43] I have been able to identify about 110 of the films playing that week, with forty-eight of them coming from French film companies. Hollywood accounted for thirty-four of the films, while at least nine were produced in French, and either in France or in Hollywood, by American film studios (Paramount mostly, but also Warner Bros. and Universal).

Assigning national origins at all to films from the period can be challenging, given the practice at the time of companies from Germany, Great Britain, and the United States to produce occasional multiple-language versions of movies or original films in French, and also the possibility of multinational productions. *La Vie privée de Henry VIII* (*The Private Life of Henry VIII*; 1933), a prominent British film, was playing in Paris then, but there were also three British films that had been produced in French and with French actors. Audiences had the chance to see at least one Italian French coproduction, a Spanish French film, and a French Belgian coproduction.[44] There were three German films in Paris that week, although there were a number of films that were either German films made in French for a French audience, or Franco-German coproductions. Showing that week in Paris, *L'Étoile de Valencia* (1933) typified this blending of national styles, workers, and economies. Directed by French filmmaker Serge de Poligny, *L'Étoile de Valencia* starred French leading man Jean Gabin and German actress Brigitte Helm (famous for her appearance as Maria in *Metropolis* [1927]), and was produced by UFA, the German studio.[45]

If we concentrate on just the week of October 13, we get no sense of the movement of films across Paris, and of the various patterns of film distribution and exhibition in the city. Examining the week before and the week after helps show those patterns, and the varying possibilities for audiences to attend movies at cinémas d'exclusivité and in the neighborhoods. In the grand cinemas in the second arrondissement, each new film played for at least a week. At the Rex on the boulevard Poissonnière, audiences could see the just-opened American film *Révolte au zoo* (*Zoo in Budapest*; 1933) the week of October 6, and then new French films, *Les Ailes brisées* (1933) the following week and *L'Abbé Constantin* (1933) the week after that. At the Cinéac, nearby on the boulevard des Italiens, Jean Benoît-Lévy and Marie Epstein's *La Maternelle* (1933) drew large crowds continually, and showed there for all three weeks and more.

The same pattern persisted in other major venues. In the eighth arrondissement, Capra's *Platinum Blonde* (1931), as well as another American film, *Jennie Gerhardt* (1933), showed at the same cinemas for the same three-week period. But also in the eighth, the Pépenière, which seems to have shown subsequent-run as well as first-run films, switched from *Conduisez-moi, Madame*, from 1932, to *Les Deux "Monsieur" de Madame*, a 1933 French film, to *Le Testament de Dr. Mabuse*. So far, then, the system in France seems fully as rational as that in the United States, which has been examined so extensively during the last quarter century.[46] The most important cinemas showed films, typically but not always in their first run, for one week. Those cinemas that, unlike the Rex, were contractually cleared for longer runs, held options for subsequent weeks if audience interest remained high.

As I mentioned earlier, the French cinema, like the American, followed a model of runs, zones, and clearances in order to produce efficient systems of where films might play, for how long, and the specific intervals during which they disappeared from exhibition altogether. A closer look shows that these systems, at least in Paris, were never quite so scientifically precise, or, at least, seem much more random than the practices in major American cities. *La Maternelle*, as well as showing in the second, also played for that three-week period in cinemas in the sixth and ninth arrondissements, in the latter case in two cinemas just a healthy but not uncomfortable walk away from each other, up the avenue de l'Opéra to the rue d'Athènes.[47] A Jean Epstein film in wide release, *L'Homme à l'Hispano* (1933), played at two cinemas each in the fifth and thirteenth arrondissements during the week of October 13, as well as at other cinemas throughout the city. In fact it was not uncommon for two cinemas in the same neighborhood to play the same film; in just one other example, on October 6 three cinemas in the eleventh arrondissement exhibited the American film *Je suis un évadé*, which seems to have been extremely popular in Paris. From week to week films might also move from one cinema to another within a neighborhood. In the thirteenth arrondissement, *Moi et l'impératrice*, a 1933 film produced in French by UFA and starring Charles Boyer, moved from the Bosquets cinema, where it played on October 13, to the Édens des Gobelins for the week of October 20, while during the same period *Rumba* shifted from the Casino de Grenelle to the Splendide cinema just a few blocks away in the fifteenth arrondissement.

King Kong in Paris

Two films with overlapping play dates in Paris demonstrate the extremes of film exhibition there. The Marivaux-Pathé in the second arrondissement hosted the Paris opening of *King Kong* in early September 1933. When the film first appeared, in a dubbed version, *Pour Vous* gave it only a lukewarm review, calling it more of a "photographic curiosity," because of its famous stop-motion animation, than a film that might inspire "fear" or any other emotion.[48] But the film was a popular one in Paris and stayed exclusively at the Marivaux for almost two months. This alone did not constitute an extraordinary first run at the cinema. *King Kong* had replaced *Théodore et Cie* (1933), a film much less well known to us now than *Kong* but that starred the great French comic actor Raimu and played exclusively at the cinema for about three months.[49] After leaving the Marivaux in early November, *King Kong* did not appear on any Parisian screen at least until the beginning of 1934 (by which time the film had also made its way to French colonial Algeria, where it was playing in Algiers and Oran). This kind of first run indicates that films might indeed have a significant clearance period in Paris before playing in the neighborhoods, with the comings and goings of *King Kong* almost certainly coordinated by RKO, the film's American production and distribution company.[50]

Another film, without the cachet of *King Kong* but significant nonetheless, presents a different model. *Toto* premiered in Paris at the same time as *King Kong*, at the Moulin Rouge cinema in the eighteenth arrondissement.[51] Jacques Tourneur had directed *Toto*, and although this was an early motion picture for him, and well before the distinguished films noirs and horror movies he made in Hollywood, Tourneur certainly would have been known at the time as the son of one of Europe's more distinguished filmmakers; Maurice Tourneur had been directing movies in France and the United States since before World War I. The star of *Toto*, Albert Préjean, began acting in films in the early 1920s, and was well known for his roles in such René Clair films as *Paris qui dort* (1925) and *Un chapeau de paille d'Italie* (1928). Pathé-Natan, one of France's leading film studios, had produced *Toto*, and so this was, indeed, an important film for French audiences, if not a release on the same level as *King Kong* or such other films as *L'Ange bleu* and *La Maternelle*.

Toto had an opening engagement of just a few weeks and left the Moulin Rouge by the end of September. Almost immediately, by the first week of October, the film had fanned out to three cinemas in the neighborhoods and away from the grand movie palaces; near the southwestern border of the city in the sixteenth arrondissement and in two cinemas on the northeastern edge of the seventeenth, both of which paired *Toto* with a short subject by Maurice Tourneur, *Lidoire* (1933), another Pathé movie, as if trying to capitalize on the familial connection between the filmmakers. The film lasted only one week in those cinemas, but on October 13 *Toto* opened in fourteen others. Ten of those venues were bunched very close together around the Montmartre and Pigalle sections of the city, more or less outlying areas in the hierarchy of Parisian cinemas despite the densely packed number of exhibition sites. *Toto* continued moving throughout the city the following week. The film still played at fourteen cinemas, but all of them different, and by this time *Toto* had made it to the interior of the city, in cinemas in the third and fifth arrondissements, although it remained, typically, on the geographical edges of Paris.

The system that brought *King Kong* to Parisian audiences looks familiar to anyone with a knowledge of the fully rationalized Hollywood model of distribution and exhibition from the period. The options for seeing *Toto*, however—almost three dozen different venues in a two-month period—look random and ill advised. In fact, seeing how *Toto* moved through the city, and noting the differences between that film and *King Kong*, the temptation is to assume that, regardless of any system that motion picture companies attempted to impose to regularize exhibition, Parisian practices simply exemplified the legendary chaos and economic instability of the French film industry of the 1930s.[52]

But there also may be some other possibilities. In just one practical example, and as Matthews noted in one of his *New York Times* dispatches cited above, Parisian cinemas seem generally to have been smaller than their American counterparts, and if this was the case, then it probably made sense to show a film in more than one cinema in the same or neighboring arrondissement in order to attract a wide audience. Other ways of understanding Parisian exhibition bring up significant historiographic issues, however, and make us reconsider our understanding of the relationships between film culture and the nation on the one hand, and the neighborhood on the other.

Cities and other locations produced multiple film cultures. In Paris, this meant not only the possibility of different audiences for commercial and avant-garde films, but also varied expectations, desires, and pleasures from neighborhood to neighborhood. Exhibition patterns in Paris, as in any city, indicate different ways of viewing films within the city itself, from the extravagant floorshows at some of the first-run cinemas to the more intimate pleasures of neighborhood venues. Rather than signifying the instability of the French film industry, the seemingly random exhibition of *Toto* in 1933, concentrated week after week in different cinemas around Montmartre and Pigalle, may indicate that film preferences can be isolated down to neighborhoods rather than broad metropolitan areas, and so might demonstrate the geometric precision of film distribution throughout the city, taking into consideration, as it did, microlevels of audience desire.

If this was the case, if we return to our filmgoer on the boulevard des Capucines, it becomes possible that this movie enthusiast would have stayed right there, in that neighborhood on the southern edge of the ninth arrondissement, rather than venturing to see a movie like *Toto* playing just due north in the eighteenth. Leaving the neighborhoods and moving to issues that are more regional and global, the example of Paris and the possibilities for seeing films there provide new options for considering national cinema. In the manner of Ruth Vasey, Andrew Higson, and others, we of course need to think of the nation in internationalist terms. As just one example, the French cinema of the period had significant impact in all of the country's colonies, while also reaching areas of less influence, such as the United States. Audiences may have experienced that cinema in particular ways depending upon location, and movie fans seem to have understood audiences even in nearby cities and towns as quite different from each other.

Pour Vous highlights these issues. The tabloid had a national circulation and perhaps even beyond, to other French-speaking countries and regions, and typically emphasized French films and film culture. But with its concentration on Paris, *Pour Vous* announced that French and Parisian film cultures were identical. In extending the reach of that culture to other parts of France, Europe, and the world, the periodical showed as well just how differently French cinema might be understood, and French film culture experienced, in different places.

That section in so many of the issues, "What's Going on in the Four Corners of France," asserted the reach of a French national film culture even to the colonies (and those colonies themselves constituting some of the "corners of France"). The column indicated the differences in available films, or cinema architecture, or the perceptions of varied audience desires and preferences from region to region.[53] Readers learned, for example, that viewers in Mostaganem, in Algeria, were particularly taken by the American film about Africa, *Trader Horn* (1931), because they so enjoyed movies about "mysterious voyages"; that audiences in Nîmes, in France, should not be "underestimated," presumably by Parisians, and that they would indeed fully appreciate the great German film *Jeunes filles en uniforme*; that film fans in Le Mans were staying away from cinemas, probably because exhibitors there depended too much on programs put together by the large movie firms. This section also provided information about international distribution practices, as readers learned that Renoir's *La Chienne* was only just appearing in Morocco in July 1932, after having opened in France the year before.[54]

Thus France's control of cinema in the colonies did not necessarily mean that colonials experienced French films and French film culture in the same manner as Parisians. Even in terms of France alone, we need to analyze much more fully the idea of local film cultures rather than national ones, with such an analysis providing a different understanding of the place of the city in film history. With some of the notable exceptions mentioned earlier—the work of Kathryn Fuller-Seeley, for instance, and Gregory Waller—film historiography, as practiced in the United States and Great Britain, and at least since the early 1990s, has concentrated on the links between cinema and cities and, in the words of Leo Charney and Vanessa Schwartz, has viewed late nineteenth- and early twentieth-century "metropolitan urban culture [as] leading to new forms of entertainment and leisure activity."[55] The cinema has emerged as the form par excellence of these activities, with Paris serving as one of the models of this new urban experience, which itself led to new forms of national culture. A study of cinema in Paris and other cities in France during the early 1930s shows the need to reconfigure this assessment. As we can see from some of the discussions in *Pour Vous* of Paris, Nîmes, and Le Mans, or Marseille and Lille and Cherbourg as well as other locations, there were marked differences, both real and imagined, between metropolitan areas that at first glance seem unproblematically French, and that make the idea of a cohesive French cinema from the period difficult to maintain.

We can only make these assessments of the international, the national, and the local if we shift our methodological focus. We need to move away from the films themselves and consider other materials. In the case of Paris, the French film journalism from the 1930s provides us with invaluable data about filmgoing there: the locations of cinemas, the times of shows, and the flow of movies across the city. The scope of film-related journalism in France at the time, so often centering on Paris, informs us of the ways in which Parisians' understanding of movies, movie stars, and gossip, for instance, came to be mediated by the periodicals that they read. *Pour Vous* along with other newspapers and magazines, specialty or otherwise, gave audiences the information they needed for seeing films and also many of the terms for understanding and enjoying them.

These materials make the exhibition site, and the progress of movies through the city, central to any consideration of the period's film history. Our film enthusiast in the ninth arrondissement might plan a day or week or month around the movies and their movement from cinema to cinema, choosing whether to stay in a familiar neighborhood or venture out, to see *King Kong* now or much later, to watch *L'Ange bleu* for the third or fourth time, or to enjoy or avoid the more fleeting and very local pleasures of *Toto*. The listings of the cinemas and their programs in *Pour Vous* and other sources give us the beginnings of both a geography and sociology of film viewing in Paris, allowing us to analyze the varied relations of spectators to the movies they saw, the conditions in which they saw them, and when and where they were able to watch films. "Voici les films qui passent," the title of the weekly listings, itself evokes movement and flow, from the verb *passer* (to pass), and the name of the tabloid made this movement of films specifically "for you," the film viewer. For the modern film scholar, *Pour Vous* and the rest of the archive of primary materials considered here lets us chart some of the relations of the city to the nation and to the world, and to determine the multiple film cultures that produced the Parisian cinema of the 1930s.

2

The Ciné-Clubs

1930–1944

During the 1930s, André de Fouquières wrote an occasional column as the resident bon vivant and man about town for *La Semaine à Paris*, the weekly listing and description of all of the cultural events going on in Paris from Friday to the following Thursday. He arranged possible activities—going to concerts, museums, lectures—day by day, and as much as possible he staggered events by time, indicating that those so inclined might go from one to the other. He rarely included anything about the movies playing at regular cinemas, but he paid careful attention to the ciné-clubs in the city. In the edition of April 12, 1935, de Fouquières wrote that on Friday, one might take in the opening of the Goya Exposition at the Bibliothèque nationale and then, at 3:00 p.m., move to the Musée d'Ethnographie du Trocadéro for a display of photographs of Indo-China and Siam. Following this afternoon of visual pleasures, one might then go to the Club George Sand to hear travel writer Marion Sénones explain "how she became a nomad," and then move on to the Théâtre des Ambassadeurs for a 5:00 conference on "that distressing problem: 'Will there be war?'" That evening, after the conference, there were a number of choices. The pianist Artur Schnabel would be playing at 9:00, but at about the same time there also would be a meeting of the Ciné-Club de la femme at the Marignan cinema on the Champs-Élysées. De Fouquières did not note the program at the club that night. For him, the gathering of the members of the club was significant enough.[1]

De Fouquières had been born in 1874, virtually the beginning of France's decidedly precinematic Belle Epoque, and he had grown up wealthy enough to be the consummate dilettante, writing some plays as well as many essays. Perhaps because of his upbringing and his artistic inclinations, the cinema itself—in its regular, daily, popular form—would not appear in his *La Semaine* column. So, we can get the sense of a difference, at least for de Fouquières and those like him, between the cinema and the ciné-club, with the latter fully on the level of Goya or Schnabel and just as important as a conference about the prospects for world peace. As much as it belonged to what we might call the broad film culture of Paris and the rest of France, the ciné-club was also marginal to it, given the dominance of the commercial cinema. Nevertheless the clubs had affiliations with a highbrow Parisian culture of the museum and the concert hall that the commercial cinema typically did not.

In both French- and English-language film histories, scholars have paid little attention to the ciné-clubs from around 1930 to 1945. Richard Abel has chronicled the club scene before then, and there has been some work on the postwar movement, particularly around André Bazin and those acolytes who would become so central to French filmmaking in the 1950s.[2] But perhaps because the evidence of the clubs in the 1930s and during World War II is so ephemeral—mostly in newspapers and magazines—we have little sense of where they were, how they worked, or what they showed. As a result, the history of the ciné-club from the period tends to follow a simplified, heroic narrative. With the coming of sound the clubs devoted themselves to preserving the art of silent cinema, or, as in the cases of the Ciné-Club de France or the Amis de Spartacus, to showing those films censored by French authorities, with the formation of the Cinémathèque française in 1936 standing as the only logical evolutionary step in the clubs' developmental history. After the catastrophe of World War II, according to this narrative, the clubs reestablished themselves as the place for the nurturing of the brilliant young men who would lead the French New Wave in the next decade.[3]

Even in Paul Léglise's encyclopedic *Histoire de la politique du cinéma français*, about all manner of industrial organization, the clubs get just a brief mention. Léglise brings up the children's clubs, such as Cendrillon (Cinderella), and also the club most frequently referenced in all the histories, Henri Langlois and Georges Franju's Cercle du cinéma, from which was formed the Cinémathèque française.[4] Despite the prominence of the Cercle du cinéma, however, even that club often disappears from standard texts, and so the Cinémathèque often seems simply to appear in 1936, fully grown and without a more modest precursor.[5]

The recent availability of so many online materials—newspapers, film tabloids, and magazines—housed in the Bibliothèque nationale in Paris helps uncover more of this history, so much of it obscure for so many years.[6] There remains a great deal we can probably never know, such as the prevalence of

LA SEMAINE A PARIS
ANNONCÉE ET COMMENTÉE PAR
ANDRÉ DE FOUQUIÈRES

VENDREDI. — Préludant à la Semaine Sainte, ces quelques jours vont se dérouler dans une atmosphère de calme et de repos. Peu de manifestations à notre bloc-notes. A la Bibliothèque Nationale, ouverture de l'Exposition Goya, le grand maître espagnol du début du XIXᵉ siècle. Nous y verrons quelques chefs-d'œuvre prêtés par le musée du Prado. Ce même jour, vernissage de l'Exposition Georges Lattès à la galerie « Le Petit Musée », 44, rue de Vaugirard.

De 15 h. à 18 h., au Musée d'Ethnographie du Trocadéro, inauguration de deux expositions : visions d'Indonésie et le Siam, avec de belles photographies de M. Raymond Plion, l'auteur d'un livre intéressant récemment paru sur le Siam pittoresque et religieux, « Fêtes et Cérémonies siamoises ».

Au Théâtre des Ambassadeurs, à 17 h., conférence contradictoire Marcel Déat-Henry de Kérillis sur cet angoissant problème : « Est-ce la guerre? » Au Club George-Sand, au Royal Condé, 10, rue de Condé, Mme Marion Senones nous dira comment elle est devenue nomade. A Rive Gauche, 28 bis, rue Saint-Dominique, conférence de M. de Monzie sur Rome, à 17 h. 30.

Au Palais des Sports, boulevard de Grenelle, ouverture de l'exposition-vente d'animaux (chiens, chats, poissons, serpents, etc.), de 9 h. à 23 h. 30 ; entrée 5 fr. Ce jour, entre 16 h. et 19 h., les vedettes du théâtre et du cinéma seront vendeuses bénévoles.

Ne manquons pas la belle exposition des azalées qui vient d'ouvrir, 3, avenue de la Porte-d'Auteuil. Quelle vision enchanteresse!

Figure 2.1   André de Fouquières's column in *La Semaine à Paris*, April 12, 1935.
Source: Bibliothèque nationale de France, Paris.

smaller clubs that met perhaps in private homes or small commercial spaces that newspapers never noticed. Information about the clubs during the Occupation of Paris is still frustratingly difficult to find. We can, however, now begin to move away from the simplified narrative about the clubs and learn more about the regular activities of so many of these groups, which themselves, throughout the 1930s and the various economic disasters that the French film industry faced, throughout the German control of French cinema during World War II, and then as France rebuilt in the aftermath of war, remained a constant part of the Parisian filmgoing landscape.

First, some definitions are in order, because it certainly was not unusual in Paris during the period for a number of nontraditional locations to show movies at least occasionally. One might see documentaries at the Théâtre national populaire at the Palais de Chaillot, a site usually reserved for live performances. Or, at the Agence Économique de l'Indochine, audiences could watch films about France's Far Eastern colonies. Other, more traditional cinemas often showed movies at special times for special audiences.

As just one example among many, the fashionable Lord Byron cinema in the eighth arrondissement sometimes showed matinees of cartoons and other films suited to children's tastes. None of these spaces, properly speaking, was a ciné-club, but rather a venue where one might see movies now and then, or a conventional cinema that might every so often cater to very precise groups of viewers.[7]

There was also an extensive club culture in Paris during the 1930s where films might often be part of an evening's discussion even for an organization usually unconcerned with cinema. In an event that I will return to in an upcoming chapter, on November 8, 1930, for instance, the socialist Club du Faubourg, which specialized in a wide range of political rather than cultural or aesthetic discussions, engaged in a "débat cinématographique," taking sides "for and against" the two antiwar films about to open in Paris, the first from the United States and the second from Germany, *À l'Ouest rien de nouveau* and *Quatre de l'infanterie*.

Despite the romance of the movement—its links to the French avant-garde of the 1920s and to the doomed-to-die-too-young Jean Vigo and André Bazin—the ciné-club came to be defined, and differentiated from other exhibition practices, by an extraordinarily specific level of bureaucracy and nationwide affiliation. In France during the early 1930s, the *Annuaire général des lettres* kept obsessive track of such things, and among its more than six hundred pages of lists of authors' deaths, awards to artists, university officials, taxes on artistic activities, and legislation affecting newspapers, there was also a section devoted to "Clubs Cinématographique." The 1933–34 edition listed three, and all apparently in Paris. The Fédération française des Ciné-Clubs was the parent organization for the national movement and also seems to have sponsored screenings at other clubs. This was by far the most important group and the one with the highest profile, with Germaine Dulac as president and Marcel L'Herbier, René Clair, and Abel Gance as members. There was also the Cinéregardo club, and a third called But. There were, after this, some sixteen "groupements adhérents," satellite groups, mostly in Paris but also in Reims and Strasbourg and Nice, where Vigo served as president.[8]

We tend to imagine the French film industry of the period as one marked mostly by instability. Think of the forced receiverships or bankruptcies of so many film studios during the Depression—Gaumont, Pathé, Haïk, Osso, Braunberger—which had such a devastating impact not only on production but also on exhibition.[9] The ciné-club, however, appears to have been one of the most orderly and longstanding aspects of the industry. As early as 1929 the leaders of all of the clubs in France assembled at the Congrès des ciné-clubs, with Dulac running the meeting. Club leaders discussed their mission of fore-grounding those films that initially had failed to find a public or had been for-gotten, or were now only seen in incomplete and compromised prints. They informed each other about efforts to develop clubs and audiences throughout the country, in Agen, Montpelier, Angers, Troyes, Avignon, and elsewhere, and of the need for rigid administrative practices. Club leaders understood that film distribution must be absolutely systematic, or else the club system would fall victim to the same random uncertainties that marked so much of the French film industry, and that the government would tax the clubs much more highly as individual entities than as members of a large federation.[10] This system developed by the clubs, and the nationwide clubs cinématographiques, seems to have lasted, more or less successfully, at least until the German invasion of France in 1940.

Much more than mere bureaucratic affiliation marked and defined the ciné-club. In Paris at the time, one could find, quite easily, clubs that appar-ently had no direct connection to the larger movement. Cendrillon, for in-stance, had no link to the nationwide organization of clubs, but still identi-fied itself as the "Club cinématographique d'enfants," and showed cartoons and kids' documentaries throughout the year. Cendrillon met at the upscale Gaumont-Marignan cinema on the Champs-Élysées, as did other clubs during the 1930s, and shared with practically all of the clubs in Paris and the rest of France their most distinguishing characteristic: public debate and discussion following screenings. Even the children who went to Cendrillon to be amused by Mickey Mouse or Flip the Frog participated in postfilm discussions and received guidance in the art of cinema, just as did those cinéphiles who be-longed to more adult clubs.

One of those, the Amis de Spartacus, aligned itself with the French Communist Party rather than, apparently, the national ciné-club organization, and typi-cally showed films that had been banned in France, such as Sergei Eisenstein's *Le Cuirassé Potemkine* (*Battleship Potemkin*; 1925). There were clubs, as well, with connections to other media, and particularly journalism. Many of the leaders of the clubs were themselves film journalists, and the clubs were often the offspring of newspapers. One of the longest-lasting and best known of the clubs was *La Tribune Libre* du Cinéma, established as an offshoot of the newspaper *La Tribune Libre*, and by 1939 the club had its own radio program, with debates and discussions led by the well-known French polymath Maurice Bessy.[11] Possibly because of the multimedia success of *La Tribune Libre* du Cinéma, the film tabloid *Pour Vous* established its own club, Des Amis de *Pour Vous*, around 1940 and lasting until the beginning of the Occupation, showing

Friday-night premieres of major French films as well as reprises of popular movies at a fashionable spot on the Champs-Élysées, but one that seems not to have been a conventional space for movies.[12]

The Screenings and the Viewers

Holding meetings in that kind of location was not unusual. The Ciné-Club de Phare Tournant showed movies in the ninth arrondissement at the building that housed the agricultural society of France, while *La Tribune Libre* du Cinéma screened films in the seventh arrondissement at the Salle Adyar, a theatre rather than a cinema. Wherever the films showed, most of the clubs— or at least those that we can find even sketchy records of today—met in some of the very best parts of Paris. Many of them—Cendrillon, the Ciné-Club de la Femme, the Cercle du cinéma, and others—had their weekly screenings at 33 avenue des Champs-Élysées at the Marignan, one of the most important cinemas in Paris.

The frequently posh setting, the people who attended, and the discussions that took place made the ciné-club, far more than the ordinary cinema, a special location in the cultural geography of Paris. So what, precisely, happened at the clubs that made going to one the equal of attending a concert or a museum? Of course the films were important, and the tabloids and newspapers from the period can give us an idea of the screening strategies of the clubs, and of the differences and similarities between them and also between the clubs and the commercial cinemas located throughout Paris. There were, as well, other elements of the experience of going to a club, elements that developed from the clubs themselves, but that also derived from the never less than baroque legislation that governed the cinema in France.

Naturally enough, cinéphiles went to the clubs to see movies. Looked at most broadly, throughout the 1930s the screenings tended toward several major and often overlapping categories: the director retrospective, the silent film, the thematic series, the avant-garde, and the sensational or censored film. None of these categories, however, was specific to the clubs, and in fact one might find the same films playing in the regular cinemas in Paris. At least in terms of these film choices, the clubs stand out not in binary opposition to the more available film culture of Paris (and, indeed, the rest of France), but as overlapping with it, differing in terms of presentation context, or in the frequency that they might highlight a specific performer or director or kind of film.

We can see the preferences of the clubs through a random look at the period from around 1930 to 1940. Just a few days before the surrender to Germany

Figure 2.2   The Marignan cinema, the site of so many ciné-club screenings in the 1930s, as it looks today. Photograph by author.

in June 1940, the Cercle du cinéma, meeting at the Musée de l'homme at the Palais de Chaillot in the sixteenth arrondissement, ran an evening's retrospective of the work of Bette Davis, showing fragments of *La Forêt pétrifiée* (*The Petrified Forest*; 1936), *Ville frontière* (*Bordertown*; 1935), and *Femmes marquées* (*Marked Woman*; 1937), as well as screening *Une certaine femme* (*That Certain Woman*; 1937).[13] Ten years earlier, in December 1930, *La Tribune Libre* du cinéma ran an evening's retrospective of the work of director Jean Grémillon, showing entire feature films as well as some clips.[14] Grémillon, of course, had a distinguished career, making films practically until his death in 1959. At the time of the *Tribune* retrospective, however, he had been a director for only a few years, and so we can see the interest of the clubs in fostering the work of young, promising filmmakers. More typically, however, the clubs showcased the major directors: a screening of Marcel L'Herbier's films at Ciné-Club de la Femme in 1936, or a Jean Vigo festival at the Cercle du cinéma in 1938, or a Jacques Feyder retrospective presented by the same club in 1940.[15] No director during this period, though, seemed more important to the clubs' sense of film history and French film culture than René Clair.

In October 1935, the Ciné-Club de la Femme presented an evening of Clair's *Un chapeau de paille d'Italie* and *Entr'acte* (1924), as well as clips from *La Proie du vent* (1927) and *Les Deux timides* (1928). In January 1937, the Ciné-Club Mercredi dedicated a session to Clair, showing a silent film and one with sound, *Les Deux timides* and *Fantôme à vendre* (*The Ghost Goes West*, Clair's first film in English, from 1935). Just two months later, the same club showed two more Clair movies, *Le Million* (1931) and *14 Juillet* (1933).[16] The list of Clair screenings at clubs might go on and on. Clair's films also showed constantly at French commercial cinemas throughout the period, not fully as retrospectives but often in reissue, while the opening of a new Clair film would be cause for celebration in all of the French film tabloids that catered to average fans rather than those frequenting clubs.[17] Thus the auteurist approach of the clubs served to reinforce the central position of individual filmmakers in French film culture generally, and, as the case of Clair indicates, also supported the period's standard notions of the patrimony of French cinema.

Clair's work shows the eclecticism of the clubs, ranging as it does from an avant-gardist tradition (*Entr'acte*) to a more precise narrative classicism (*Fantôme à vendre*). These wide interests were a constant of the clubs in the 1930s, with experimental cinema always holding a significant place. In May 1936, for example, the Cercle du cinéma mounted what surely must have been one of the most comprehensive screenings of French avant-garde cinema, with an evening of films by a who's who of experimental filmmakers: Clair,

Louis Delluc, Germaine Dulac, and Jean Epstein, for instance. The Cercle also included clips from Abel Gance's *La Roue* (1923), demonstrating the links between the avant-garde and commercial cinema, and the club did all of this at that standard and very fashionable location, the Marignan cinema.[18]

The chic address indicates that the clubs were very much in the center of Parisian culture rather than the margins, and also shows the fully respectable status of avant-garde cinema. Nevertheless, the clubs always stressed the significance of commercial cinema generally, and Hollywood cinema in particular. The same week as the avant-garde retrospective, and at the same address, the Ciné-Club de la Femme screened James Whale's *L'Homme invisible* (*The Invisible Man*; 1935), while just a short metro ride away at the Salle Poissonière on the border of the ninth and tenth arrondissements, the Ciné-Club de Paris showed the Gregory La Cava screwball comedy *Mon mari, le patron* (*She Married Her Boss*; 1935).[19]

The Paris ciné-clubs all emphasized the importance of silent cinema, and all of them concentrated on the necessity of preserving those motion pictures from before the transition to recorded sound. The popular press, at least, understood the mission of the clubs in just such archival terms, and viewed the clubs as the most formidable defenders of silent cinema. A 1940 article about ciné-clubs in the newspaper *Le Temps* argued that the clubs themselves formed the last outpost for a kind of cinema "ignored by the audiences in our grand movie palaces," a cinema that counted for much more than the current vogue for mere "recorded theatre." The article then went on to praise in particular the Cercle du cinéma, which posed as its statement of principles research and conservation of "the classics of the screen," and to show new prints of the films of Griffith, Stroheim, Wiene, Dreyer, and Chaplin, among others. The newspaper did not mince words about this project, praising the Cercle for "courageously attacking" this problem of a silent cinema overwhelmed by the technology of sound.[20]

The Cercle took its mission seriously, and showed a range of silent films, often French but also those from other countries. In less than a month, between the end of December 1938 and the middle of January 1939, the club screened an evening of early silent films by Georges Méliès and Ferdinand Zecca, Wegener's *Le Golem* (*Der Golem, wie er in die Welt kam*; 1920), Lang's *Metropolis*, and Sjöström's *La Charrette fantôme* (*Körkarlen*; 1921).[21] But silent films played throughout the period at most of the clubs, with movies by Chaplin, Murnau, and Feyder in addition to Clair always well represented. Here again, the clubs' screenings of silent films differed not so much absolutely from the more typical cinemas in Paris, but more in terms of volume and frequency. Reissues of silent films played in the city at least through the mid-1930s, and one cinema in Paris, as I mentioned earlier—the Boulevardia in the tenth arrondissement—showed silent films exclusively during that same period, while the idiosyncratic Corso-Opéra in the second arrondissement showed them more frequently than sound films.[22]

The clubs interpreted film history in other ways, and not just as the lineage of great directors or as the necessity for preserving a lost and now mostly ignored art form. Whether that history might be understood as ranging from the beginning of cinema to the present, or as a specific set of current concerns, the clubs often organized screenings around themes or genres or technologies, or alternatives to mainstream cinema as we have seen with the frequent avant-garde festivals. In stressing an educational imperative, in bringing to light linkages between films or eras, the clubs did indeed separate themselves from the other cinemas in Paris.

After the war had begun but before the Occupation, in February 1940, the Cercle du cinéma ran a retrospective of current movies that specifically addressed the crisis, showing a series of English propaganda films by Humphrey Jennings and others, mostly produced by the General Post Office. Just a few weeks later, the club staged an evening of two anti-Nazi films, *Kuhle Wampe* (1932), from Germany, and *Karl Brunner* (1936), a Russian film. Indeed, between 1938 and 1940, the Cercle du cinéma routinely scheduled such thematic events, but usually with more relaxed rather than pressing concerns, and taking a longer view of history: a festival of animation "from Émile Cohl to Walt Disney," two festivals of "films fantastiques," a retrospective on the "evolution of French cinema from 1888 to 1940" from Marey to Renoir, and, as well, a session on "Eroticism and the Cinema," with screenings and analyses of films by Pabst, Murnau, Stiller, Eisenstein, Lang, Chaplin, Renoir, Sternberg, DeMille, and others.[23]

As one might imagine, this last festival seems to have been a major event in Paris at the time, and fully showed the connection between the clubs and other cultural and educational organizations. French philosopher Jean Carteret presided at the screenings, as did members of the "groupe psychologique de la Sorbonne." The exact schedule of events remains unclear, but the screenings either were interspersed with, or followed by, broad discussions on the aesthetics, philosophy, and psychology of the erotic in cinema.

An event like this one constituted the fulfillment of de Fouquière's belief in a Parisian cultural landscape where ciné-clubs might engage with, and even be the equal of, a range of intellectual and artistic activities. This sort of engagement came to mark so many of the clubs, and to differentiate them from neighborhood cinemas and those on the grand boulevards. At that 1936 screening of *L'Homme invisible* at the Ciné-Club de la Femme, Germaine Dulac addressed the audience on the topic of "The Cinema in the Service of History."[24] The link between the film and the presentation is uncertain, but this has the sound of an important speech given by a prominent member of France's artistic scene, and highlights the pedagogical instinct and the outreach to the Parisian intellectual community of so many of the ciné-clubs' activities.

The clubs took part in broad aesthetic debates, and then might provoke an even wider discussion of them. In 1927, for example, *La Tribune Libre* du Cinéma staged an evening of films made from the various color processes available at the time. The event seemed significant enough that France's leading Communist newspaper, *L'Humanité*, gave it prominent coverage. According to the newspaper, debates followed the screenings, with partisans for and against color film each arguing for their cause. *L'Humanité* understood the scene at the screening as part of a simmering argument, one that the newspaper had examined before ("The question of the color film, on which we have already given our opinion, is more and more the order of the day"). The newspaper then weighed in on *La Tribune*'s screening ("In general, horrible pictures"), and then linked the entire event to a recent issue of the film journal *Photo-Ciné*, in which Jean Epstein had explored, at length, the issue of the color film.[25]

L'Humanité typically covered the movies, and with an understandable interest in the politics of cinema. The article about *La Tribune Libre* and color film was surrounded by an extended appreciation of Russian director Youri Taritch's proletarian drama *Les Ailes du serf* (1926) and by an ongoing call for protests against the Hollywood war film *La Grande Parade* (*The Big Parade*; 1925), that exemplar of the "odious mercantilism of an international bourgeois cinema."[26] Clearly the newspaper understood the fluidity between aesthetic issues, such as color cinema, and political ones, and saw itself as broadly supporting the efforts of *La Tribune*, which was hardly a club for Communists (that would be the Amis du Spartacus). The newspaper further understood the events at the club as contributing to a much broader and ongoing discussion that connected *La Tribune Libre* du Cinéma to a Communist newspaper and also to a film journal like *Photo-Ciné*, and that included a wide range of adherents, among them one of Europe's most important film theorists and filmmakers, Jean Epstein.

So many of the presentations at the club screenings seem too good to be true to the contemporary film scholar. There was the ubiquitous Dulac, who spoke at so many club meetings. In 1935 Jacques Feyder presided over a screening of his 1934 French Foreign Legion melodrama, *Le Grand Jeu*, at Le Club 32.[27] When the Cercle du cinéma presented a Jean Vigo retrospective in 1938, the late director's films were introduced by Jean Painlevé, who himself would continue to make movies until the 1980s and had already made his documentary series about sea urchins, crabs, and seahorses, as well as any number of other short films.[28] Here, then, we can see one of the important differences between the ciné-club and the more typical cinema. Fans understood the latter as a place for seeing movies. Those who attended the clubs, however, knew the former as a site for movies and also for active debate, discussion, and education, and as the place where they might encounter some of France's leading artists and intellectuals.

The ciné-club also came to be marked as a location for controversial films. In 1936, at the elegant Marignan cinema, the Club cinégraphique showed "le grand film de Gustav Machaty," *Extase* (1933), famous internationally for its frank sexuality and for Hedy Lamarr's nude swimming scene.[29] But *Extase* had also had a standard run in Paris when it came out, at the fully respectable Théâtre Pigalle in the ninth arrondissement.[30] Controversy itself, then, did not signify a film fit only for the clubs, but films banned in France might only be shown at the clubs. Film historian Yann Darré has claimed that the originating impulse behind the formation of so many of the ciné-clubs was precisely the showing of banned films, films that might now be presented because the clubs were private and not subject to the same laws as typical cinemas.[31]

From an eighty-year remove it becomes difficult to know, exactly, which of the films shown at the clubs may have been banned from other, more typical cinemas. Many of the showings, however interesting, remain fairly conventional, and Darré himself may have been succumbing to the romance of the clubs as spaces for alternative cinemas. By the end of the 1930s, however, the ciné-club as a safe space for banned films became a legislative reality. Jean Zay, the Minister of National Education and Fine Arts (who himself would be assassinated in 1944 by a pro-Vichy French militia) instituted a regulation that put into place the absolute distinction between the clubs and typical cinemas. Now understood as fully private rather than public spaces, the clubs would not be allowed to charge an admission price from anyone who might turn up to watch a movie. Rather, only club members who had paid their dues for the entire year might attend a screening. "Any infringement of these rules," as Paul Léglise has explained it, resulted in a club being declared a routine, public cinema, and therefore unable to show motion pictures that the state had banned.[32] The club might have screenings in a regular cinema, but the law of 1939 decreed the fluidity of that screening space from public to private, and determined when and to whom films deemed dangerous, and not fit for general consumption, could be shown.

The Gender of Ciné-Clubs

Even as France legislated this distinguishing characteristic of the ciné-club, there were, as well, nonregulated aspects of the clubs that also helped separate them from other locations for seeing movies. These aspects were perhaps not as immediately apparent as the constant debates and discussions that followed screenings, or the possibility for seeing banned films. From the available information, the club bureaucracies seem to have been much more welcoming of participation by women than the commercial film industry.

Of course, there was the indefatigable clubwoman Germaine Dulac. We know her today primarily for her work as a director, from World War I until the early 1930s, of commercial films that nonetheless incorporated an avant-garde aesthetic (*La Souriante Madame Beudet* from 1923) and for later and more inscrutable work (*La Coquille et le clergyman* from 1928). Also during this period, however, she performed tireless work in the formation of the ciné-club movement.[33] Her films often screened at the clubs, and Dulac herself was also a presence there, and not just in Paris but in clubs throughout France.

At that 1929 meeting of the Congrès des ciné-clubs, Dulac announced that she planned a series of presentations at clubs in Grenoble and Agen on the evolution of cinema, using some of her own films as examples as well as those by Dimitri Kirsanoff (*Ménilmontant*; 1926), Séverin-Mars (*Le Coeur magnifique*; 1921), Henri Chomette (*Cinq minutes de cinéma pur*; 1925), and others.[34] By 1932, Dulac had become president of the Section cinématographique du Conseil national des femmes françaises. The Conseil itself, which still exists today, dated from 1901, supporting universal suffrage and organizing around health, education, work, peace, and other topics and activities, including cinema. Under Dulac's leadership, the Section cinématographique seems to have been linked to the clubs, screening films at least occasionally as well as facilitating the national distribution of scientific and educational films that were a staple of the clubs.[35]

In the still mostly masculine administration of the ciné-clubs, Dulac stood out as extraordinary. At about the same time as her leadership of the Section cinématographique she also served as the president of the Fédération française des Ciné-Clubs. The significance of both of these positions, at least to those associated with a spectrum of leftwing political movements in France, motivated *Le Populaire*, the newspaper of the country's Socialist Party, to run a front-page story about Dulac, referring to her as both "a film master" ("Un maître de l'écran") and as exemplifying "the modern woman" ("la femme moderne").[36]

The case of Dulac seems somewhat overdetermined. Her fame was so exceptional, at least among the Parisian avant-garde and political left, that her standing in the clubs may not tell us much about the possibilities for other women interested in working in the cinema. Instead, another much more obscure career that intersected with the clubs, as well as with the broader cultural scene in France, indicates some of the gendered dimensions of the ciné-club movement. Lucie Derain made films, earned money as a journalist and novelist, and socialized with movie stars and other filmmakers from the late 1920s until the late 1950s, and she worked tirelessly for ciné-clubs at least throughout the 1930s. Her lengthy career on France's cultural periphery shows how the clubs might intersect with film production and with journalism, and the ways in which women no less than men could remain active in and important to a range of aesthetic practices.

Derain seems to have been involved in directing at least two short films, and the second, *Désordre* (1930), screened in October 1930 at the Ursulines cinema in the fifth arrondissement in Paris, along with a Mack Sennett comedy and a William Wyler western.[37] At the same time, and probably to support her filmmaking, Derain had begun writing about cinema for serious film journals: a 1929 appreciation of King Vidor's *La Foule* (*The Crowd*; 1928) in *Cinémonde*, and, a year later, a defense of the director Robert Florey in *Cinéa*.[38] She became well enough known as a critic that, when the film studio Sofar organized a 1927 luncheon at the very upscale Ledoyen restaurant in Paris, the journalists covering the event mentioned her presence there, along with that of Jean Renoir, Renoir's actress wife Catherine Hessling, and others prominent in the French film scene.[39] By 1933, the exhaustive *Annuaire général des lettres* listed her as one of France's two hundred or so film critics, a compilation that included only about a dozen other women.[40] Derain's notoriety may have been enhanced when she was injured in the 1931 car crash that killed the most famous passenger, the actress Janie Marèse, who had just starred in Renoir's *La Chienne*.[41]

Throughout the 1930s, Derain acted as a constant advocate for, and participant in, various Parisian ciné-clubs. With Dulac, we see a club career at the highest levels. She oversaw a nationwide organization of clubs, and she visited them in Paris and elsewhere to deliver lessons on film history and aesthetics. With Derain, we get to experience the clubs more from ground level, from the point of view of someone much more involved in the day-to-day activities of

Figure 2.3   A column in *Cinémonde*, from April 6, 1933, by journalist, filmmaker, and ciné-club activist Lucie Derain. Source: Bibliothèque nationale de France, Paris.

organizing screenings and debates, and whose movements from one club to another showed the connections between them. In particular during the mid- to late 1930s, Derain curated showings at the Ciné-Club Mercredi. These in- cluded Ben Hecht and Charles MacArthur's *Le Goujat* (*The Scoundrel*; 1935) followed by a debate on the merits of the film; Julien Duvivier's *La Bandera* (1935) once again followed by debates; a film of "the new school," Marcel Carné's *Jenny* (1936) with a discussion afterward with the star, Françoise Rosay; and *Winterset* (1936), along with a *Marche du temps* (*March of Time*) newsreel about the fighting in Abyssinia.[42]

By 1936, at about the same time as this flurry of activity for the Ciné-Club Mercredi, Derain had become the director of the Ciné-Club de la Femme, which dated from at least the early 1930s. During Derain's directorship, the club elicited the alarm of a cinema columnist in the newspaper *Le Temps*, who believed that the name itself might exclude, "a priori," any men from at- tending the screenings.[43] The fear seemed unfounded because, at the time, the Ciné-Club de la Femme had announced a retrospective of the work of Marcel L'Herbier, hardly a filmmaker of simply feminine, or feminist, appeal. Nevertheless, while Derain's screenings for the Ciné-Club Mercredi seemed in keeping with those of other clubs, with its broad array of national cinemas and types of film, the Ciné-Club de la Femme did at least have some commitment to a more feminist cultural sensibility. Along with the usual Clair retrospectives or showings of a film that seemed to make the rounds of all the clubs, Murnau's *L'Aurore* (*Sunrise*; 1927), the Ciné-Club de la Femme served as a location for screenings of films that might be thought to appeal to women, often presented by leading female intellectuals and artists, perhaps not at Dulac's level but sig- nificant nonetheless.[44]

In 1935, for instance, the club showed George Cukor's *Little Women* (1933), with a presentation by the prominent feminist attorney Yvonne Netter, and then a public discussion about a topic motivated by this film about the nine- teenth century, "the young girl of the past."[45] The club also screened Leontine Sagan's *Jeunes filles en uniform*, presented by the well-known feminist nov- elist and, in historian Mary Lynn Stewart's phrase, "fashion chronicler," Magdeleine Chaumont, followed by a discussion about adolescence.[46] Of course, there is no record of the viewers at either screening, but both seem to be programs designed with female audiences in mind, with films about young girls and families, introduced by the intellectual Netter on the one hand and the writer Chaumont on the other, and leading to discussions of presumed feminine interest, adolescents in general and young girls in particular.

If we return for a moment to Dulac, in her club work, and despite her bona fides as a feminist filmmaker, she appears to have been devoted to an idea of pure cinema aesthetics, and to presenting all manner of film while never forgetting the importance of the avant-garde. This was precisely the commitment, and exactly the same practice, of most of the clubs. From the late 1920s to the beginning of World War II, the clubs sought to explain, preserve, and expand an aesthetic of cinema that could contain both Hollywood commercial movies and obscure experimental ones, and the clubs' primary political commitment, endorsed by the state, was to an absolute openness in the kinds of films they might show. Derain, with the Ciné-Club de la Femme, both endorsed this general club policy and also made a commitment to a more specific feminist agenda. From examining club programs from eighty years ago, and without knowing the content of the debates and discussions at the clubs, we can have no way of knowing whether other groups, besides the Amis de Spartacus and just a few others, had any interest in ongoing political or cultural issues. Some of the clubs met in less well-heeled neighborhoods, which might tell us something about the clientele and their political inclinations, but so many of them, including the Ciné-Club de la Femme, gathered in the same fashionable screening space, at the Marignan cinema on the Champs-Élysées, that location might not tell us much at all. But the case of Derain and the Ciné-Club de la Femme indicates not only the overlap between the clubs in terms of interests and practices, but also the possibility for difference.

War

Evidence about the clubs from the end of the decade and the beginning of World War II remains scant, so it becomes difficult to determine whether screenings became more politicized around current events. Film periodicals often acknowledged the emergency of the war, with *Pour Vous*, for example, running a weekly "journal de guerre" and publishing frequent articles about the role of cinema during the fighting. But the tabloid's film club, Des Amis de *Pour Vous*, from the details that still exist, held fairly innocuous screenings rather than anything associated with the national crisis: premieres of major French films (*L'Enfer des anges*; 1941) and reprises of popular movies (Jacques Feyder's *Le Grand Jeu* and the Evelyn Brent vehicle *The Pagan Lady* [1931]).[47] Then, just after the French surrender in June 1940, the traditional ciné-clubs disappeared altogether, at least in the highly bureaucratized, government-approved system that had become such a significant aspect of French film culture. In their place, the Nazi occupying authority established two Parisian ciné-clubs, each one linked to a German film tabloid published in France for French film fans, *Vedettes* and *Ciné-Mondial*.

We have at least some evidence about the latter. *Ciné-Mondial* often ran notices about its club, which started toward the end of 1943 and met in a Parisian concert hall, the Salle Pleyel in the eighth arrondissement, and also nearby in the Salle des Agriculteurs in the ninth, both areas central to the concentration of Nazi power in the most prosperous parts of the city, those with the fewest Jews and immigrants.[48] The club itself served different purposes from those before the war, and movies might not always be shown. Instead, the club was a place for film stars and other celebrities to gather and entertain an audience. At a meeting in early January 1944, the movie stars Bernard Blier and Charles Moulin were present, and so too were Jean d'Yd and Piéral, two of the supporting actors from the Jean Delannoy/Jean Cocteau film *L'Éternal Retour* (1943), which had been produced during the Occupation and released in Paris just a few months before.[49] At club sessions a couple of months later, Blier returned, accompanied by Louis Jourdan and the performers Monique Rolland, Monique Helbling, and François Perier, the latter telling stories about the early years of his acting career.[50] The following week, Sessue Hayakawa appeared along with other actors and musicians.[51] To the extent that evidence exists, the stars appearing at the club always seem to have been French rather than German, or, as in the case of Hayakawa, foreign performers who had had extraordinary success in France.

Thus the club relentlessly stressed entertainment, with stars telling funny stories about their careers or musicians performing familiar numbers, or using such films as *L'Éternel Retour* to celebrate the possibilities of cinema-as-usual during the Occupation. There would be some very occasional debate and discussion, as when the journalist Jeander lectured at the club in March 1944 on the future of French cinema.[52] The week after Jeander's talk, however, all of the club's functions went back to normal, as guests would be amused by the movie stars Georges Marchal, Yvette Lebon, Alexandre Rignault, and Armand Mestral.[53] The Germans believed that this *Ciné-Mondial* club, at least, played such an important role in the Nazi cultural project in Paris that it remained open even as the city was on the verge of being liberated, and as power shortages closed down almost everything there. At the end of May 1944, *Ciné-Mondial* ran an advertisement stressing that its club would continue to meet, "despite the crisis in electricity."[54] While the ciné-clubs of the 1930s usually were regulated by the state, during the Occupation the Nazi-sponsored clubs served the state directly, by asserting the benign nature of German control and the continuity of French popular culture. The Occupation-era club preserved just the traces of the prewar ciné-club, merely the idea of a place for a different sort of interaction with the cinema.

Well before the Occupation and prior to the beginning of the war, a late 1930s article in *Le Temps* referred to habitués of the clubs as the "last amateurs of pure cinema."[55] *Le Temps* said this both admiringly and somewhat dismissively. The term might apply to de Fouquières, our flâneur at the beginning of this section, but hardly to Dulac, Vigo, or others who made clubs into such a vital part of their professional lives. Here *Le Temps* proposes the marginality of the ciné-clubs, demonstrated perhaps by the significant participation of women like Derain as well as Dulac, given the generally masculinist culture of French cinephilia at the time. Nevertheless, the ciné-clubs seem also to have been central to the broad cultural contours of Paris during the period. This was certainly true during the Occupation, when the Nazis used their carefully regulated clubs as one of the signs of the return of "normal" Parisian cultural activity. But it also was the case in the 1930s when, just as we saw with de Fouquières, the clubs would be among the desirable destinations of any well-brought-up Parisian's stroll through the city.

3

Chevalier and Dietrich

1929–1935

In February 1931 the French film magazine *Cinéa* announced its current topic of interest on the cover page and on the back: "In this issue: the French talking film."[1] Just under that, the names of two performers, with a photo portrait of each on the front and on the back: Maurice Chevalier and Marlene Dietrich. The rest of the issue served to confirm the linkage between the topic and the stars. Chevalier and Dietrich, whose photos bookended the issue, emerged on the pages in between as the first and greatest of a new generation of stars made possible by sound film, stars of international importance but who also could be claimed by the nation—by France—as two of its own.

The new sound technology that helped produce stars like Chevalier and Dietrich had a significant impact on the ways that films played in Parisian cinemas. The sound of the voice might help create a sensational, extended run of a single film in the city, or the cinematic geography of Paris might come to be understood in terms of the route a particular sound film might take as it made its rounds of different neighborhoods. During this transitional period, the screening of a sound film at a particular cinema followed a week or two later by a silent film threw into relief for neighborhood audiences the overlapping and also different pleasures of the two technologies. With the film journalism of the period, we can read not just where films played and for how long, but also what the responses might be to going to the cinema to hear a special voice, or to watch once again a particular face. Film exhibition, film sound, the film image, and the film press, all in a particular place, can show us something of what it meant, for the typical fan who picked up a magazine like *Cinéa* or the cinéphile who wrote for it, to experience a shift to a new technology and a change to a different kind of star.

Including *Cinéa* there were dozens of film tabloids and journals in France during this period; the *Annuaire général des lettres* for 1933–34, which kept meticulous track of such things, lists around thirty-five, most of them concentrating their attention on Paris, although there were others with interests beyond the capital.[2] *La Revue de l'écran*, for example, a trade journal for cinema managers, focused on Marseille and the area around it, while *Les Spectacles* reviewed entertainments in Lille, and *Les Spectacles d'Alger* examined film, theatre, and music halls in and around Algiers. Jean Tedesco, who managed the fashionable Vieux-Colombier cinema in Paris's sixth arrondissement, published *Cinéa*, and because of Tedesco's well-known interest in film history and the film archive (the Vieux-Colombier specialized in screenings of experimental films, documentaries, and early silent movies), his magazine's ongoing concern with developments in the medium made perfect sense.[3] Almost all of the film magazines devoted coverage to the history of cinema, and they signaled to their readers that the transition to sound film, even as it was happening, constituted an important period in the growth of motion pictures. These publications interpreted the transition, at least in part, through its effects on film stardom. Information detailing the sound of the language spoken by the star became a means of distilling news about the shift to talkies, much more so than discussions of the changes in equipment or industrial practice, or any of the other important but more mundane aspects of *le cinéma parlant*.

Among the most compelling of the stars of this new cinema were Chevalier and Dietrich, and reading about them in the film magazines of the period provides a sense of the experience of this transitional era in French cinema. Looking through the various narratives of the shift to sound films, in *Cinéa*, *Pour Vous*, *Les Spectacles d'Alger*, and other sources from the period, we can begin to understand how movie enthusiasts learned about film as a local, regional, and international phenomenon. These sources also help to explain audience preferences for stars and movies, as well as many of the nuts and bolts of the transition to sound; how films were shown and in what languages, for instance, or the stars whose appeal seemed limited to France or extended well beyond it, and also the impact on stardom of rapid technological innovation and implementation.

Studying stardom, film exhibition, and film reception through the primary materials of French film journalism provides the possibility of differential histories of sound film, and also helps complicate our understanding of national cinema. In the cases of Chevalier and Dietrich during the transition to sound, we can see how, for some audiences, stars themselves might signify the nation, often regardless of the country where their films were produced, and how, in

Figures 3.1 and 3.2   Maurice Chevalier and Marlene Dietrich on the cover and back of *Cinéa*, February 1931. Source: Bibliothèque nationale de France, Paris.

the case of Chevalier, a star's "Frenchness" might vary between France and France's colonies, or how Dietrich, the actress from Berlin, came to indicate a broadly understood cosmopolitan European identity that might be imagined to be as much French as German.[4]

Placing Paris as well as France and French culture at the center of this inquiry shows us how the transition to sound generated specific kinds of stardom. This combined history of film sound and movie stardom charts the impact of new technologies on an international commodity (the cinema) and on a specific industrial practice (the production of celebrity). In particular, this chapter's study of film reception and exhibition examines how fans in Paris and elsewhere in France as well as in North Africa came to understand and appreciate Marlene Dietrich and Maurice Chevalier in particular, but also other stars who emerged during this period, and to update and adapt their devotion to stars more fully associated with silent cinema. That cinema certainly had produced an extraordinary number of international movie stars; Asta Nielsen from the German film industry, Charlie Chaplin from Hollywood, and Max Linder from France come to mind immediately. For the new movie celebrities of the transitional period, however, the sound of the performer's voice became the marker of stardom, while for many of the great silent actors, even as they made their transitions to sound, the image remained transcendent.

Maurice Chevalier and the Era of the New International Star

A fan poll organized by the tabloid *Mon Film* named Maurice Chevalier "King of French Film" for 1930, just one year after he began starring in movies.[5] Chevalier displaced the previous year's winner, Jean Dehelly, who had started out as a leading man in silent movies in the early 1920s and would be out of films entirely by 1932. Thus Chevalier, the great international celebrity of sound film, supplanted a silent film star whose fame never really extended much beyond France.

The sound cinema created other major stars. Indeed, rather than eliminating the international performer from cinema (as in the well-chronicled demise of Emil Jannings, whose thick German accent made it impossible for him to appear in Hollywood talking films), sound movies produced new forms of global celebrity. In France alone, Hollywood stars such as Joan Crawford and Jeanette MacDonald enjoyed great vogue during the early 1930s, as did Dorothea Wieck, the German star of *Jeunes filles en uniform*, as well as many other performers from Europe and the United States. Many French stars made films intended only for French-speaking audiences but that were produced in other countries, or in France by foreign film companies: Charles Boyer, for instance, who starred in French movies made in Hollywood and Germany, and Francoise Rosay, who appeared with Chevalier in German director Ludwig Berger's *Le Petit Café* (1931) and also starred in other French films made by the American studio Paramount at its Joinville facility outside Paris. These performers, from Crawford to Rosay, were international stars in terms of where their films were exhibited, or where they worked and for whom.

Still other stars were more purely national, such as Gaby Morlay, who worked consistently for Pathé-Natan, or Pierre Larquey, who made films for Alex Nalpas, Les Films diamants, and other of France's myriad movie companies from the period. Their films were shown almost exclusively to French-speaking audiences, but even these viewers ranged beyond France, as they might be watching movies in Belgium or Switzerland or North Africa or Southeast Asia. As just one example among many that demonstrates the point, and the differences between these French stars and those with a more fully international appeal, during the last week of 1931 and the first of 1932, the Majestic cinema in Algiers showed Georges Milton's latest film, *Pas sur la bouche* (1931), while the Splendid cinema there exhibited Chevalier in *Le Petit Café*. This screening of *Pas sur la bouche* showed the full extent of Milton's fame, at its height in France (like Chevalier, Milton was a star of the Parisian music hall), but reaching only as far as North Africa. For a Chevalier film, an exhibition in Algiers counted as just one more stop on a global distribution plan.[6]

Jean Dehelly giving way to Chevalier, the silent star to the sound icon, shows the cinema's movement from old to fully contemporary technology. Even before the movie magazine fan poll that anointed this new king of French film, though, Chevalier had been hailed as an entirely modern hero in France, one who represented both the rise of a new cinema and the decline of an old one. In April 1930, *Cinéa* put Chevalier on its cover in a special issue on the star, on the occasion of the French premiere of Ernst Lubitsch's *Parade d'amour*. *Cinéa* ran dozens of photos of Chevalier, from childhood to his successes in the music hall to his trip to the United States and his film work at Paramount, as well as appreciations and histories ("M.C.," "Son Secret," "Le Succès de Chevalier"), in a section covering half of the forty-plus-page magazine.[7] But most of the rest of the issue, that part not devoted to Chevalier, considered the passing of the silent cinema and the kind of film that would be lost forever.

In the first sentence of his opening editorial, the publisher, Jean Tedesco, lamented that "the silent cinema is in its death throes." Another article considered that "misunderstood film," the avant-garde silent classic *Un chien andalou* (1929), perhaps the most talked-about film of the decade. Still another

Figure 3.3   Maurice Chevalier, the newly crowned "Roi du Cinéma,"
on the cover of *Mon Film*, July 11, 1930.

reproduced Pierre Mac Orlan's preface to *La Petite Marchande d'allumettes*, the novelization of Jean Renoir's 1928 silent film. At the end of the issue, after all the celebrations of Chevalier, Henri Baranger considered the state of cinema. He wrote that one of his film idols was King Vidor, whom he cited as the Dante and the Balzac of motion pictures, and whose silent film *La Foule* suggested the possibility of a "human cinema." As part of an issue so suffused with photographs of Chevalier, Baranger wrote that he himself still thought constantly of the great faces of silent cinema, for instance William S. Hart and Sessue Hayakawa.[8] This special issue on Chevalier not only celebrated the triumph of the Hollywood sound film in France and the rise of a new kind of film personality, but also contemplated the loss of an older and different kind of cinema, and a different kind of star.

The Sound of the Star

In the French film tabloids, and in the manner of Chevalier and Dehelly, Dietrich, too, found herself in competition, as it were, with another performer. But rather than displacing her, as Chevalier did with the now forgotten Dehelly during the transition to sound, Dietrich coexisted with the greatest international star of silent cinema, Greta Garbo. Dietrich had only become a leading woman in 1929, in a few silent films of varying quality. Her appearance as Lola Lola in Josef von Sternberg's *L'Ange bleu*, from 1930, stands out as one of the great star turns in cinema history, and made Dietrich the equal not only of Garbo and Charlie Chaplin among stars from the silent era, but also of Chevalier, who had already achieved much of his celebrity, in the United States and Europe, from his music hall performances.

Movie fans and film critics in Paris and the rest of France had anticipated *L'Ange bleu* for months, as it had opened to acclaim earlier in Germany and elsewhere in Europe. When the film premiered in Paris at the fashionable Ursulines cinema in the fifth arrondissement, it caused an immediate sensation. The Ursulines only had around three hundred seats, and it specialized in artistic rather than simply commercial films.[9] To give just a brief sense of the typical viewing experience at the Ursulines, *L'Ange bleu* replaced a program of short films made before the war and also some avant-garde movies that played with G. W. Pabst's *Le Journal d'une fille perdue* (*Tagebuch einer Verlorenen*; 1929).[10] More broadly, the screening of Sternberg's film at the Ursulines shows the cinematic fluidity of 1930s Parisian film culture. When *L'Ange bleu* played at other cinemas in Paris, the venues were often grander than the Ursulines, but in particular they were sites that concerned themselves with cinema-as-usual rather than cinema-as-art, with *L'Ange bleu*, as well as those other films that went from the Ursulines to other locations, clearly counting as both.

The film wouldn't go to any of those cinemas for a very long time. *L'Ange bleu* played at the Ursulines for almost a year, until early November 1931. That kind of a first run wasn't unheard of in Paris at the time, but it was nonetheless very impressive. Far more common for an extraordinarily popular film would be Eddie Cantor's *Whoopee* (1930), which opened a few months after *L'Ange bleu* in early March 1931, at another fashionable cinema in the fifth arrondissement, the Panthéon. Cantor's film played with a Thelma Todd short and a Krazy Kat cartoon until the end of May, and then was replaced by the Marx Brothers in *Cocoanuts* (1929) for just a few weeks and then Douglas Fairbanks in *Reaching for the Moon* (1930), which played for at least two months, all while *L'Ange bleu* kept on showing four times a day at the Ursulines, week after week.[11]

When Sternberg's film left the Ursulines, to be replaced by another German film, Pabst's *L'Opéra de quat'sous* (*Die 3 Groschen-Oper*; 1931), it was major news.[12] The newspaper *Paris-soir* took note, and in a way that stressed the cinematic geography of the city. *Paris-soir* wrote that after around a thousand screenings, "*L'Ange bleu* will cross the Seine and continue its magnificent career on the right bank," at the Aubert-Palace in the ninth arrondissement.[13]

In fact, for a few years, it seems as if *L'Ange bleu* played continuously in Paris, and as late as 1933 the film had an extended reprise in the very well-heeled second arrondissement at the Corso-Opéra cinema.[14]

During its opening week, *L'Ange bleu* was only one of a number of important films in Paris. The newest of all major French cinemas, the Miracles in the second arrondissement, opened with King Vidor's melodrama with an African American cast, *Hallelujah* (1929), in the same week that *L'Ange bleu* began its run at the Ursulines. Critics hailed *Hallelujah* as an important aesthetic and social document, as a film of undoubted "high class."[15] Vidor's pastoral film took its place as the folk equivalent of the great movie event in France, and probably the rest of Europe (before *L'Ange bleu*), Universal Studio's *À l'Ouest rien de nouveau*, which was still in a months-long first run in Paris. That film proved the capacity of the cinema to produce a vivid social document, to reach intellectuals and also average fans, and to align the motion picture with a global antiwar movement. That same week, the film that critics hoped would signal the future of French cinema, René Clair's *Sous les toits de Paris*, continued an extended run in the city, at the Jeanne d'Arc in the thirteenth arrondissement.[16]

When *L'Ange bleu* opened in Paris, the exhibition strategy was fitted only to that film, and emphasized the special nature of Dietrich's voice and the importance of hearing it. The film showed four times a day at the Ursulines, twice each in the afternoon and evening. For the first afternoon and evening screenings, audiences saw the French version of *L'Ange bleu*, a film sonore— music and effects over a silent film with French intertitles, but with Dietrich performing her songs in German. For the second showings, fans could see and hear *la version intégrale*, the German version, a fully talking film, with all speech and songs in that language.

La Semaine à Paris ran an article by Charles de Saint-Cyr, "Twenty Things about *L'Ange bleu*," that covered the opening of the film and that listed this dual-version exhibition "innovation" as the most compelling detail of Dietrich's movie.[17] For Saint-Cyr, the French, largely silent version emphasized the film's international appeal, while with the German version, even poorly understood by many audiences, "the words added to the voyage" on which *L'Ange bleu* took its viewers. Anecdotal evidence indicates that both versions were equally popular.[18] Of course, while the film also featured Emil Jannings, a star of great international importance at the time, the astonishing enthusiasm for *L'Ange bleu* always rested on the impact of hearing Dietrich, either in the French version or the German one. In just one example among many, when the film opened in Algiers in June 1931, *Les Spectacles d'Alger*, in its review, praised Dietrich's performance and then marveled at her "husky" and "captivating" voice.[19]

Figure 3.4   An advertisement for *L'Ange bleu* in *La Semaine à Paris*, March 13, 1931, emphasizing the two versions of the film playing at the Ursulines cinema. Source: Bibliothèque nationale de France, Paris.

The literature and mythology about Dietrich and *L'Ange bleu* are full of references to the importance of seeing the star. Heinrich Mann, for example, the author of the novel on which the film was based, reportedly told Jannings that the success of the film depended not so much on the great actor's performance, but on "the naked thighs of Miss Dietrich."[20] There is also ample evidence that the success of *L'Ange bleu*, and of its new star, depended just as much on Miss Dietrich's "husky" voice, and hearing it in the German sound film, or as practically the only instance of speech in the French version.

The Sound of Chevalier

Chevalier's voice, like Dietrich's, came to signify his stardom, and even, in some contexts, his historic importance to cinema. Chevalier's 1929 American sound film debut, *La Chanson de Paris* (*Innocents of Paris*; 1929), came to Algiers in

January 1930. For the opening, *Les Spectacles d'Alger* announced, "we have seen and heard, in our city, several artists onscreen with synchronized sound," and then dismissed those efforts as "interesting," but not really cinema.[21] Now, the Splendid cinema presented *La Chanson de Paris*, a complete sound film and the first shown in the city, with the star singing in both French and English.

Audiences in Algiers apparently had seen any number of sound shorts, the kind that the major movie companies and even some of the small ones produced in order to highlight the new technology. In fact, only the week before in Algiers, viewers at the Régent cinema had witnessed just such a program of sound movies.[22] If we believe *Les Spectacles d'Alger*, however, there was no true sound film in Algiers before Chevalier's, and no voice worth hearing there before his. The success of the film was such that it was held over a second week at the Splendid, and *Les Spectacles d'Alger* ran an update on the popularity of the movie and its star. Without Chevalier, *La Chanson* would have been a "bad film," but the actor's charm dominated everything else about the story. In the film, "he swims, he dances, he appears miserably dressed and then elegantly, in his smoking jacket and trademark straw hat, he plays the comedy simply and he sings." The report continued, as if to emphasize the star's voice, "he sings and one listens, thanks to the clarity of his diction and the perfection of the sound apparatus."[23] Chevalier's singing voice was the marvel of the film, which commanded the audience's attention, and was equaled only by the technology that brought that voice to the people in the cinema.

The impact of Chevalier's film and the sound of his voice in Algiers indicate something about global distribution practices during this period. *La Chanson de Paris* was ready for cinemas in the United States in May 1929 and opened in Paris in October of that year. The three months it took for the film to go from Paris to Algiers was not at all unusual and provides a sense of the relative peripheral cinematic status of North Africa to France and particularly to Paris. Chevalier's film played in Algiers even before Al Jolson in *Le Chanteur de jazz*. That film, of course, which had opened in Paris in January 1929, is the one that typically receives credit as the first significant sound film and for establishing the credibility of sound technology.

Jolson became a major star in France as a result of *Le Chanteur de jazz*. He was popular, as well, in North Africa, and when *Le Chanteur de jazz* opened in Algiers at the end of February 1930, *Les Spectacles d'Alger* acknowledging the film's success in Paris, called it a "marvel of cinematographic art," and duly noted the sociological importance of the representation of the "religious mores of North American Israelites of Polish origin."[24] But in that city and perhaps the rest of the region, it was Chevalier who began the sound era, and his film that signaled a new moment in cinema. For the French colonies, *La Chanson de Paris* served the same historical function that *Le Chanteur de jazz* did for most of the rest of the world.

Dietrich and Garbo

After her appearance in *L'Ange bleu*, Dietrich also seemed to mark the arrival of a new era. *Cinéa* put a photograph of Dietrich in *Coeurs brûlés* (*Morocco*; 1930), her next film, on the cover of its issue for April 1931. In an article about "Current Trends in Cinema" in the same issue, *Cinéa* claimed that the international successes of *Les Lumières de la ville*, *Sous les toits de Paris*, and *L'Ange bleu* suggested the possibility that films that added sound only sparingly to compelling images might be best suited, during this transitional period, for reaching wide global audiences.[25] At least to the film journals, however, and perhaps movie fans, Dietrich's greatest significance was the challenge she posed to the most important current star in cinema, and one whose sound debut seemed so long delayed, Greta Garbo.

A month after the Paris premiere of *L'Ange bleu*, *Pour Vous* posed the question directly to readers and to experts: "Whom Do You Prefer? Greta Garbo or Marlene Dietrich?" The writer Pierre Mac Orlan, still unconvinced of Dietrich's charm, chose Garbo. Ever the gentleman, the great French tennis player Jean Borotra refused to choose. The sentiment among several others echoed Mac Orlan, and tended toward a preference for Garbo.[26] Two weeks later, readers weighed in and also seemed to prefer Garbo, at least in part because Dietrich was so new to the screen. One fan pinpointed the difference between the two as precisely the difference between the kinds of cinema with which they were associated. With Dietrich, he wrote, it is her "sex appeal that speaks," while with Garbo, it is "the look."[27] For this viewer, Garbo represented the sensual pleasures of the old technology, so dependent on the image, and Dietrich, whose attraction "spoke" to the audience, those of the new.

Garbo's cinematic presence in France and the French colonies was a constant of the period. In Hanoi, for instance, the 1934 opening of *Grand Hôtel*, Garbo's film from 1932, was understood to be a significant cultural event, while in Paris there always seemed to be a Garbo film playing somewhere during this period.[28] Often, her films and Dietrich's showed at the same time. When Dietrich in *Blonde Vénus* (1932) ran in fourteen cinemas throughout Paris in March 1933, Garbo's *La Courtisane* (*Susan Lenox: Her Fall and Rise*; 1931) played in the ninth and eighteenth arrondissements.[29] In Marseille in April 1934, *Grand Hôtel* returned to cinemas, with this reprise indicating the earlier success of the film there, probably the year before, and just two weeks after a similar "seconde vision" for Dietrich's 1933 movie, *Cantique d'amour* (*Song of Songs*; 1933).[30]

Two Garbo films, however, point out the perceived differences between the stars, differences connected to silent and sound film technologies. In Algiers in 1931, Garbo's *La Belle Ténébreuse* played at the Splendid cinema just one week after *L'Ange bleu* had shown there. The review of this silent film, in *Les Spectacles d'Alger*, emphasized the experience of looking at the movie and particularly at Garbo's face, just as the same newspaper previously had lauded the huskiness of Dietrich's voice. "Greta Garbo," the review explained, "is that accomplished type of femme fatale whose magic face reflects a powerful interior emotion."[31]

That same year, Garbo's first talking film, *Anna Christie* (1930), which had been so carefully crafted by its Hollywood studio, MGM, and its director, Clarence Brown, opened in Paris. Of course this opening constituted a major cinematic event in the city, and most periodicals devoted a great deal of coverage to the film. *Pour Vous*, in its review, demonstrated something of the French critical consensus about the film. Somehow, sound seemed not to matter, and as great as the film was, it may have been better served by an older technology. In the first sentence of his discussion of the film, René Lehmann wrote, "In watching and listening to *Anna Christie*, I dreamed of the beautiful silent film that Clarence Brown could have made."[32] Listening to Garbo talk had little of the electricity of hearing Dietrich's voice, and signified nothing of the new potential of cinema.

Stardom and the Nation

Much more than silent film stars, whose nationality or regional affiliations could never be given away by their accents, both Dietrich and Chevalier were understood as national subjects, as German in the former case and French in the latter. But one of the signs of their success, of their special status as great stars of the new technology, was the possibility for a shifting national identity and for being understood and appreciated by fans in both local and international terms. Chevalier, of course, was known and advertised as the greatest of all French stars. When Paramount announced its coming film season in 1931 in *Les Spectacles*, the trade journal covering northern France, the studio began by praising the previous year's Chevalier "super-productions," *Parade d'amour* and *La Grande Mare* (*The Big Pond*; 1930). Then Paramount trumpeted both its American and French films, and exulted that "right next to the great stars of Hollywood, you will applaud . . . the elite stars of France," including Yvette Andréyor, Fernand Gravey, Marguerite Moreno, and, naturally, Chevalier, insisting on the fully national status of the performer who nevertheless had left France for the United States.[33]

Newspapers and trade journals in North Africa, even more than those in Paris or elsewhere in France, stressed Chevalier's "Frenchness," and so seemed to align audiences in the best cinemas in peripheral locations with those in the metropolitan centers of French culture. When Chevalier appeared in Algiers in person, in the 1930 revue *Un dimanche à New York*, *Les Spectacles d'Alger* asserted the star's importance as a French treasure while lovingly referring to him as the "celebrated national music hall star."[34] Three years later, when the film *Une heure près de toi* (*One Hour with You*; 1932) premiered there, the same newspaper claimed the French performer as theirs, informing readers that the film starred "our own" Maurice Chevalier.[35]

This claim of Chevalier's quintessential Frenchness, and of bringing that national quality to France's colonies, came at a time when, for French singing stars, the voice stood for both country and culture. When the greatest of all French music hall stars, Mistinguett, played Algiers, she made sure to bring France, or at least Paris, with her. In her 1930 appearance at the most important theatre in the city, the Majestic, she sang one song of purely local interest, "Bonjour Alger," but then began her revue, *Ça c'est Paris*. She came back two years later, this time in *Voilà Paris*.[36] The newspaper review for that performance acknowledged that "exporting Paris is no easy business," but noted that Mistinguett triumphed nonetheless. Through her voice and her singing, the chanteuse Mistinguett, like Chevalier, was able to bring France, as well as its greatest city, to places and listeners beyond its borders but nevertheless aligned emotionally and geopolitically with that country.

The French film press, however, always emphasized that Chevalier mostly made movies in the United States, and that he was a major star there as well. He had become so identified with his American work that, when he came back to France for a few months in 1930, newspapers reported the triumphant return of a national hero who one day might have his own museum in France, in the manner of Balzac or Victor Hugo.[37] These sources reported dutifully on Chevalier's importance in the United States, telling French fans, as *Cinéa* did, that *Parade d'amour* had played for fourteen weeks at the exclusive Criterion cinema in New York, and that, in an America that prized speed and informality over everything else, the great star, to his admirers there, was simply "M. C."[38] But there was also, always, the understanding of Chevalier's international importance, of his significance to a global community of movie fans. In Algiers, which seemed to have such a stake in affirming Chevalier's Frenchness as a means of asserting that of the audiences that attended the major cinemas there, the star's true status was fully understood. With the arrival of *Chanson de Paris* in North Africa, *Les*

Spectacles d'Alger wrote, simply, of the trajectory of Chevalier's stardom: Paris, America, the world.[39]

Like Chevalier's, Dietrich's international celebrity worked as a sign of the global importance of the Hollywood company that employed the star, Paramount. When that studio ran an advertisement in the film weekly *Hebdo* to stress its importance in Europe, images from three films appeared, and films that showed different approaches to Paramount's strategy for the continent: *Rien que la verité* (1931), which Paramount produced in French at its Joinville studio and intended only for French-speaking audiences; *Marius*, which Marcel Pagnol co-produced through his own company and Paramount, and which the American studio distributed in France and Europe and also some selected venues in the United States; and *Coeurs brûlés*, the film that appeared first in the advertisement, with an image showing Dietrich and her costar Gary Cooper, and which played throughout the United States, Europe, and the rest of the world.[40]

These three films in the advertisement together show Paramount's extensive industrial reach, in France, in Europe, and, in the case of *Coeurs brûlés*, to all of the countries where feature films might be seen. Typically, however, the emphasis in France fell on Dietrich's status as an international star of particular significance there. That was how *Cinéa* understood her when the magazine used her German/American film career to discuss the potential of the French sound film; that was also how Saint-Cyr described *L'Ange bleu* in *La Semaine à Paris*, as a film unimaginable in any language other than German, but that, in its nontalking French version, attained international status. It was also apparent in the ads for the film in French tabloids, which gave Dietrich billing over the imposing Jannings, and identified her as the great global star, "l'extraordinaire vedette mondiale."[41]

The French press took frequent pleasure in Dietrich's friendships with such homegrown performers as Suzy Vernon, and delighted in the diva's visits to sites of Parisian intellectual culture, for instance the office of the newspaper *L'intransigeant*.[42] Dietrich was so famous in France that journals taking no interest in film took an interest in her, in the manner of the professional journal *L'Association Médicale*, which in 1931 reviewed a new biography, *La Vie brûlante de Marlène Dietrich*, by Jean Lasserre. The capsule review touched upon the great star's discovery by director Josef von Sternberg and her move to Hollywood, but then insisted that the real measure of the biography came in its coverage of Dietrich's return to Europe and its speculation upon her future in Paris. According to Lasserre's book, Dietrich's stardom may have had its roots in America, but became notable for its full development in Europe broadly and the capital of France in particular.[43]

Over the course of her life and career, Dietrich almost certainly became much more associated first with Europe, because of her work there during World War II, and then with Paris, where she had lived for many years at the time of her death in 1992. The standard Dietrich historiography has it that her movie career declined after the disaster of her last film with Sternberg, *The Devil Is a Woman*, from 1935, and then revived after she refashioned her film persona in 1939 with *Destry Rides Again* for Universal, the less than prestigious Hollywood studio, but never regained the level of the early 1930s. This may just have been an American narrative, however, as Dietrich seems to have maintained a steady level of celebrity in France throughout the 1930s and 1940s, at least if we count as evidence her ongoing ubiquity in French film tabloids and other magazines from the period.

From World War II on, in France as well as the United States, Dietrich was as much defined by her voice as by her famous legs and figure, but in a fashion different from the era of her first sound films. During the war, with her adoption of the pacifist anthem "Lili Marlene," Dietrich became one of the most recognizable voices—on radio and recordings—for Allied soldiers, and then she spent much of the rest of her career as a cabaret singer giving live performances, invoking her success as Lola Lola in *L'Ange bleu*. She remained an international celebrity, but her status as an international film star had changed considerably, and certainly lessened, over the last fifty years of her life.

Chevalier's career changed even more quickly and dramatically than Dietrich's. After *Folies Bergère* in 1935 the star left Hollywood, perhaps because of contractual disagreements with his last employer, MGM, and did not return for more than twenty years, when he worked with Billy Wilder in *Love in the Afternoon* (1957) and then Vincente Minnelli in *Gigi* (1958).[44] Moreover the popular discussion about Chevalier in France in the mid- to late 1930s began to challenge both his international stardom as well as his status as a fully modern celebrity. In the film tabloid *Ciné France*, for instance, a 1937 gossip column full of short items announced that French tenor Georges Thil—nine years younger than Chevalier and representing a very different musical tradition, the opera—had arrived in Hollywood. As a means of celebrating Franco-American friendship, Thill sang "La Marseillaise," and the column hailed his performance. The column then added, when "Maurice Chevalier comes to Hollywood," even though the star seems not to have visited the United States anytime recently, "and for the same reasons sings 'La Marseillaise'... That's an execution."[45] In this apparently humorous notice, the movie star had been replaced by the opera star, and precisely in terms of who might best represent the nation while moving beyond national boundaries.

Chevalier frequently appeared onstage in North Africa during this period, and in 1938, when he came to Algiers, where he had always been so popular, *Les Spectacles d'Alger* referred to him, as always, as "our great national performer." The reviewer of Chevalier's act went on to comment, almost sadly, that despite the star's new repertoire, "he was obliged, at each show, to sing his old successes: 'Ma Pomme,' 'Prosper,' 'Valentine,' etc."[46] Just a few years removed from his successes in Hollywood, when he represented so many of the technological advances of cinema during the transition to sound, Chevalier—at least in Algiers—had turned into an icon of nostalgia seemingly forced to perform a familiar song list, a signifier for colonial audiences of the Parisian music hall of the 1920s and early 1930s rather than of the contemporary motion picture.

The timing of these shifts in Dietrich's and Chevalier's celebrity status makes it convenient to assume that, as soon as the transition to sound was complete and the use of sound in film had been fully standardized, movie stardom changed. It is important to point out, however, that stardom is not simply connected to, and determined by, film technology and production practices. Stardom itself is far too unpredictable. In just one example, by the end of World War II Chevalier's own national celebrity in France was fragmented by ideological preferences rather than industrial developments. He had been accused of wartime collaboration with the Nazis; the apolitical Chevalier, suddenly unpopular in his native country, then found himself championed by the French Communist Party, which typically opposed the political agendas of the various French "Purge Committees" that investigated collaborative activity.[47]

There are nevertheless periods when technological determinants override others in the construction of stardom, and this was particularly the case during the transition to sound. The importance of the shift has entered into the mythology of cinema; the belief that John Gilbert's unusually high voice, for instance, doomed the sound career of the silent film star. It seems undeniably true that the adoption of the new technology enabled the particular, international stardoms of Chevalier and Dietrich, among the first and most important such stars of the sound era. A close look at different periods of stardom, and at the various and sometimes overlapping levels of stardom—local, national, international—gives us a sense of how fans experienced movie celebrity, and also how that celebrity facilitated regional and global film distribution and exhibition. If sound represented a rupture for film companies in the United States and Europe, in terms of how films might be produced for international audiences, then Chevalier and Dietrich helped make possible the smooth functioning of a global industry while at the same time introducing audiences to new pleasures, based as much on the voice of the star as on the image.

4

Violence at the Cinema

1930–1944

For the Hollywood studios that had come to dominate global film distribution, Marlene Dietrich's stardom, as well as Maurice Chevalier's, eased the transition from silent film to sound. But, at least in Paris, that transition did not always go without incident. A case that demonstrates the point occurred on Sunday, December 8, 1929, during the early evening screening of *Fox folies* at the newly reopened Moulin Rouge cinema in the eighteenth arrondissement, just below Montmartre. "Donnez-nous des films français! Parlez-nous en français!" "Give us French films! Speak to us in French!" That's what the Parisian audience yelled during the movie, while some of the viewers tore the numbered, metallic plates off their seats and hurled them at the screen.[1]

The city and its suburbs, it would seem, were not always safe places for cinéphiles or casual fans. As a result, going to the movies in Paris might not be so simple as dipping into a ciné-club to hear a discussion or debate, or choosing to see a new Dietrich film rather than one showing in reissue. Throughout the 1930s and 1940s, one might at least occasionally pick out a film, settle into a seat, and find oneself suddenly a witness to, or participant in, a violence that we do not usually associate with spectatorship. Rather than violence onscreen, this brand was at the cinema itself. Politics typically seemed to motivate this violence, and these politics were almost always rightwing, sometimes carried out by the governing authority in and around Paris, sometimes by one of many fascist or fascist-leaning groups in France, and sometimes by a combination. At least one case, the 1930 *L'Âge d'or* screening at the Studio 28 cinema, has entered the canon of important historical events of French cinema. The others have remained mostly invisible, and hint at the possibility of still more that can never be documented.

Studying the occasional violent responses to movies in and around Paris moves us away from more rapturous viewings, when fans gazed at Greta Garbo, or the routine neighborhood pleasures of a film like *Nu comme un ver* moving around to various, peripheral cinémas des quartiers. These extreme instances tell us something more broadly about the importance of cinema, and about the significance, in Paris at least, not just of films but of the places where they were shown, and the cinema's day-to-day interaction with events that often, at first glance, might seem to have nothing to do with the movies.

The earliest such instance that I have found, if we begin with the sound period, was precisely about the movies, however, and particularly about the transition to new technology. This was the evening of *Fox folies* at the Moulin Rouge, a space that had been one of Paris's leading music halls since 1889, except for a six-year period after it burned down in 1915 and then was rebuilt for a 1921 reopening. The Moulin Rouge had occupied the same address on the boulevard de Clichy during all of that time, and just about everybody who was anybody in French popular music had performed there: Mistinguett, Max Dearly, Maurice Chevalier, Jean Gabin, and many, many others. The Moulin Rouge closed once again in 1929, but not because of any natural disaster like a fire. Rather, this time, the most famous music hall in Paris was being transformed into a cinema, to become part of the Pathé chain of exhibition sites in the city.[2]

This constituted a significant shift in the Parisian cultural landscape, and the press took notice. In November 1929, *La Rampe*, a weekly review of cultural events in Paris, let readers know that the Moulin Rouge would reopen for Christmas, completely transformed, with the latest American musical revue, *Fox folies*.[3] Of course, other sound films from Hollywood had played in Paris and had not caused any trouble, so there was no reason to believe that *Fox folies* would be any different.

In its coverage, *Les Spectacles* gushed that the city was being given the gift of "a large and luxurious cinema," and that the director of the Moulin Rouge had invited all of the best people in the city ("le tout-Paris") to the grand opening.[4] The weekly film journal *Cinéa* reported on the transformation of the Moulin Rouge and called it a "tour de force," and gave special praise to the new "American-style" mezzanine. Not all progress, however, was necessarily for the better. *Cinéa* also acknowledged the "justified irritation" of those in Montmartre who lamented such a major change and mourned the passing of the music hall.[5]

Opening night at the new cinema did not go well, and *Le Figaro* reported many of the details. The subtitles for *Fox folies* were "written in deplorable French." As a result, the "audience quickly tired of following a story it did not

Figure 4.1   The Moulin Rouge cinema, around the time of the premiere of *Fox folies*.

understand." They became unhappy, and the ensuing "ruckus" was such that the management called off the next show. The following day, Sunday, the same thing happened again, and that's when the audience started shouting at the screen, with those protests, according to the newspaper, becoming "something of a leitmotif" for the entire screening.[6]

In the interest of fairness, the reporter for *Le Figaro* talked to the management at the cinema. They said that the film already had been a big success in Marseille and Nice, where it went off without a hitch (*Fox folies*, apparently, was one of those rare films that opened elsewhere in France before coming to Paris). Even if the public had been unaware of those earlier screenings, they certainly knew, through advertisements as well as the posters at the cinema, that the film was from Hollywood, and that, anyway, there just weren't enough French sound films available to be shown (the first French film with recorded sound, *Le Collier de la reine*, had only opened two months before, in October 1929, and at the time of the incident at the Moulin Rouge only one other French sound film in addition to *Le Collier* was playing in Paris, *Les Trois masques* [1929]).[7]

This may have all seemed reasonable enough, but then the management fell back on a time-honored Parisian tradition; blame any problem on outside agitators. First, the management named a "cabal" to whom the current owners had refused to sell the Moulin Rouge, and who had paid off some members of the audience to cause trouble. Then they suggested that a few disaffected projectionists, who had quit just before the screening, may have been responsible for the unpleasantness. Finally, management claimed that the transformation of the Moulin Rouge into a cinema had infuriated the old music hall's orchestra members who suddenly were out of jobs and may have come to *Fox folies* looking to blow off a little steam.[8]

In its report on the "noisy and violent incidents," the Parisian fascist newspaper *L'Action française*, which always seemed ready to blame Jews or communists for any unrest in Paris, this time chose not to single out anyone from outside, or to place responsibility on outraged orchestra members. The newspaper devoted almost two full columns to the events at the Moulin Rouge, and gave the story a dramatic headline: "The Fall of *Fox Follies*" ("La chute des *Folies-Fox*"). The newspaper gave much more detail about the violence at the cinema than *Le Figaro* had, and it is here that we find the detail of spectators tearing the metal numbers from their seats and throwing them at the screen. The analysis in *L'Action française*, at least at the beginning, is surprisingly measured, and mostly placed the event within a nationwide context of a film industry unable to produce sound films as quickly and efficiently as the Americans. *L'Action française* claimed not to be surprised by any of this, and said that it had been warning readers for weeks that an influx of American films would cause problems. Making matters worse, a musical revue like *Fox folies* could only remind readers of what they had lost with the transformation of the Moulin Rouge, from music hall to cinema.[9]

After this, *L'Action française* reverted fully to form. The article complained not only of hearing only English rather than French, but to add visual insult to linguistic injury, *Fox folies* also showed "blacks and whites" ("noirs et blancs") on screen together. This was, according to the newspaper, more than viewers could take.[10]

The press kept the story going for some time. Not quite a week later, *La Renaissance*, a very serious weekly journal of politics and culture, headlined its article about the Moulin Rouge events, with no small amount of irony, "À Propos of Progress in the Cinema." *La Renaissance* explained that the audience was fully justified in its complaints, which also included shouts of "In French!" and "Shut up!" ("Ta gueule!"), and then, as viewers stormed out of the cinema and saw others standing in line for the next show, "Stay out!" ("N'entrez pas!").[11] As late as March 1930, the monthly—and very sober—French review *Europe* ran its own story, arguing that the sound film would undoubtedly evolve slowly, and that while *Fox folies* may have been enough to make Americans proud, it certainly wasn't sufficient, technically or aesthetically, for French audiences.[12]

Fox folies left the Moulin Rouge after a week or two and seems never to have played at another Parisian cinema. If this was indeed the case, it would have been extraordinary for a major American film to have such a brief run and then disappear completely, even if there were still relatively few Parisian cinemas wired for sound at the time. This certainly would not have been the original plan for the film, so French cinemas at the time must have been able to break contracts with distributors for Hollywood films, or had agreements that allowed them to cancel showings at fairly short notice. If this is what happened, it marks a rare occurrence of the French film industry responding quickly and directly to the apparent demands of its audience, demands that were vocal and violent and difficult to miss. At least in the very earliest months of the transition to sound in France, some Parisians literally refused to remain quiet about the films they wanted to see and hear.

The case of *Fox folies* tells us a great deal about the tensions that might work their way through a movie screening in Paris. In this instance, an innocuous American film agitated viewers to violence because, perhaps, of unwanted changes to a neighborhood venue, or a sense of American cultural domination, or the musicians' discontent over jobs lost as a result of the transformation of the Moulin Rouge, or outside agitators who were always looking to start trouble, or, if *L'Action française* is to be believed, because a movie implied that races might mingle. Different sources with different interests, from the Moulin Rouge management to journals across the ideological spectrum, were able to interpret the incident along varied but perhaps predictable lines. The incident itself, however, seems more or less benign, in terms of those that came after, and that directly involved the growing threat of fascism in France.

Fascists at the Movies: Some Background

The earliest and best-known instance establishes a pattern of behavior and introduces at least a partial cast of characters. Luis Buñuel's *L'Âge d'or* premiered at the Studio 28 cinema in December 1930. Studio 28, on the rue Tholozé in the eighteenth arrondissement, had opened in 1928 as a site for avant-garde films, although it also showed commercial movies as well as those that might hover between those two categories. A single week of screenings just a few months after the *L'Âge d'or* affair, and just as Studio 28 was reopening after dealing with the damage caused by the violence there, condenses all of the space's programming interests, and shows the fluidity in Parisian film culture at the time between the experimental and the conventional.[13] During the week of March 6, 1931, Studio 28 showed a short film by the great Franco-Russian stop-motion animator Ladislas Starevitch, as well as a 1930 Czech film directed by Karl

Anton, *Tonischka* (*Tonka Sibenice*), a reissue of the 1929 German film *Terre sans femmes* (*Das Land ohne Frauen*), a short 1930 film codirected by René Magritte, *Fleurs meurtriers*, and also the 1928 ethnographic documentary about cannibals (later exposed as a hoax), *Chez les mangeurs d'hommes*.[14] One of the feature-length films that week at Studio 28 almost certainly made no appeal to high art: the 1929 German version of the Sherlock Holmes novella, *Le Chien des Baskerville* (*Der Hund von Baskerville*). The other, however, was a film understood at the time to be both extraordinarily entertaining and a sign of the future of cinema, both popular and artistically important, René Clair's first sound film, *Sous les toits de Paris*, which had opened in Paris the year before. Given this typically eclectic mix of films as well as the practice of showcasing the experimental and the nontraditional, it made perfect sense for Studio 28 to stage the premiere of *L'Âge d'or*, and with no reason for this to seem anything other than business as usual.

The fascist group Jeunesses patriotes thought otherwise. A few nights into the run of *L'Âge d'or*, angered by what they perceived to be the film's anti-Catholicism and its decadent surrealist aesthetic, members of the group destroyed the screen while the film was playing, assaulted some members of the audience, and defaced artwork in the lobby of Studio 28. According to Georges Sadoul, the fascists shouted "Death to Jews" during their rampage. About a week later, and after a great deal of administrative hand-wringing, an alarmed Paris prefect of police, Jean Chiappe—who will return to this narrative of cinema violence—took it upon himself to shut the film down and ban further screenings.[15] This has become a familiar story and one told fairly often, perhaps because of the canonical status of the film and also as a sign of what has been called "Vichy before Vichy," the entrance of fascism into everyday life in France well before the war. But it also has served to obscure other acts of rightwing violence related to the cinema, and its dominance in the narrative of French film history has also worked to lessen our sense of the steady impact of fascism on Parisian popular culture during the years just prior to World War II.

From the occurrence at Studio 28 we can move to Paris *after* Vichy, to the first few weeks following the Liberation in 1944. Unlike the *L'Âge d'or* violence, we have only traces of an event involving the cinema, the first as a brief mention in the *Los Angeles Times*.[16] American newspapers were not always the most fastidious sources for information about Parisian violence at the movies, making this trace even more obscure. While the Jeunesses patriotes tried to prevent screenings in 1930, in 1944, according to the *Times*, trouble began because too many people tried to see movies, with police having to calm down "some 50,000 people milling" along the Champs-Élysées, trying to get into cinemas showing Liberation newsreels. "Many went home fearful of being crushed" by the crowd, the *Times* reported, and, apparently, these wild newsreel enthusiasts smashed store windows and fired guns in the air. All of this seems quite speculative. There was certainly a great deal of enthusiasm over newsreels about the Liberation, and I will write about that in a subsequent chapter. I have found just one Parisian report of this "combative joy," to use the *Times*'s term, and this one makes it difficult to accept at face value the *Times*'s sense of frightening violence. The Resistance newspaper *Combat* described the "enthusiasm, punctuated by gunshots" over the long-awaited reopening of Parisian cinemas, closed since the Liberation. *Combat* made the whole thing sound mostly playful, as it described not only the gunfire, but also mock duels with umbrellas rather than swords. The newspaper also insisted that, really, the crowds were smaller than might have been expected, because the metros leading to the Champs-Élysées had closed early that day.[17]

These events from 1930 and 1944, at the Studio 28 and along Paris's most famous thoroughfare, bookend those that most interest me here. Examining them provides us with the pleasure of the strange and perhaps unexpected aspects of spectatorship, but also helps us understand some of the particulars of Parisian film culture at the time. They tell us something about the relationship between the Far Right and popular culture, which is more usually discussed in far broader terms—fascist aesthetics in national cinemas or in mass gatherings like the Nuremberg Rally, for example.[18] In the instances from Paris and the suburbs from the period, the connection is more local and immediate, planned but also spontaneous, and linked more to neighborhoods than to the nation. These incidents also describe a form of spectatorial activity all too absent from discussions of the cinema. We are presented, here, with an extraordinarily active and dangerous spectator, one who is politically motivated and also mobilized by the events onscreen to act out in the public space of the exhibition site.

When French film historiography about the period concerns itself with what might broadly be called political rather than aesthetic issues, however, the emphasis tends to stay on governmental and industrial efforts rather than the activities of individuals or small groups or the risks of certain instances of film exhibition. Two foundational and important histories, one in English and one in French, typify this approach. Colin Crisp's *The Classic French Cinema, 1930–1960* remains fixed on import quotas imposed on foreign films, or the government's intervention in the 1934 Gaumont debt crisis, or the industry's development, a few years later, of the Fédération des chambres syndicales de la cinématographie française, intended to deter the state from intervening in the affairs of cinema.[19] Yann Darré maintains much the same emphasis in his *Histoire sociale du cinéma français*, at least in his discussion of the 1930s, as he moves from the Stavisky Affair to the Gaumont bankruptcy to the Herriot accords regarding imports as well as to other affairs of state and industry.[20]

The French cinema of the period, especially in Paris, also took up a different kind of place altogether in the political landscape. The events depicted onscreen, and the space of the cinema itself, might motivate actions by citizens and citizens' groups disconnected from government but hoping to achieve ideological goals. This version of politics and cinema had both macro- and microlevels, responding as they were to the various governing coalitions that rose and fell so quickly in France in the 1930s but also to specific neighborhoods, the activities of local political clubs, and even to modes of transit that facilitated movement through the city.[21] For some, and especially on the right, going to the movies in Paris during the 1930s came to be understood as engaging in political activity. The common debate about fascist cinema has been whether a fascist nation necessarily produces fascist films.[22] Fascism would not come to govern France, however, until the surrender to the Germans in 1940 and the subsequent Nazi Occupation of Paris and installation of the Vichy regime in the southern "Free Zone" of France. The events at cinemas in Paris and the suburbs in the 1930s, however, make us consider whether there are particularly fascist reception strategies at the movies, and fascist uses of cinema in general.

Part of the difficulty of assuming any such strategy overall is the problem of French fascism itself. During the 1930s, at least, there were any number of fascist groups, and although most of them emerged in response to the Franco-Prussian war and Paris Commune of 1870–71, or to the Dreyfus Affair at the end of the nineteenth century, or to the disaster of World War I at the beginning of the twentieth, they were marked as much by differences as similarities. There also have been longstanding debates as to whether or not we might even call these groups fascist with any assurance, and whether we might always consider them a reaction from the Far Right of the political spectrum rather than from the Left. At least since the 1990s and the meticulous work of Robert Soucy, among others, and at least in an American context, the argument has more or less been settled.[23] These groups indeed were fascist, and manifested an extreme rightwing version of French antiparliamentarianism and anticapitalism.

That the argument has existed for so long amply shows the difficulty of establishing all the relevant connections between these groups. As well, some of the most significant of these groups, like the influential and longstanding Action française, began at least somewhat respectably in the late nineteenth century, and only over time became more prone to violence and to paramilitary actions.[24] Thus, the contentious development of so many rightwing groups throughout the first few decades of the century, not only the Action française, but also Jeunesses patriotes, the Ligue des patriotes, the Union Nationale, the Ligue de la patrie française, the Ligue antisémitique française, and, among others, the Croix de feu. The latter group fully understood the importance of motion pictures, having established its own "Section ciné" for the production of propaganda films,[25] and was one of the largest fascist organizations in France by the early 1930s and one of the most significantly involved in the events from 1931 and 1937 that I will discuss in detail.[26]

These various groups did unite around a few core issues; their commitment to Catholicism and hypernationalism, a rejection of parliamentary forms of government, and also an embrace of antisemitism, antisocialism, and anti-Marxism, as well as their willingness to resort to violence.[27] All of these groups, and particularly the Croix de feu, sought to celebrate the veteran of World War I and especially an idealized veteran of the Battle of Verdun, which in the years after the war took on such mythic power in French culture. Just as the end of the war helped establish the democratic reforms of the Third Republic, and in doing so developed the possibility of the Popular Front in the 1930s, so too did it provide an important foundational moment for the modern French Right and also for French fascists.[28] While French fascist organizations might fight among themselves during the 1930s, they also made common cause with a range of rightwing groups, giving them at least a fair amount of political influence.[29] But for many years historians deemphasized the significance of these groups in France, largely because republican democracy remained stable there, precisely the opposite of Italy or Germany. Due to the significant levels of fascist terrorism in those two countries in the interwar period, historians have also, until recently, tended not to acknowledge fully the important place of violence in the organizational and political strategies of the French Far Right of the 1930s.[30] Urban political violence actually had a long and established history in Paris, from 1789 to the revolutions of 1830 and 1848 and on to the Commune of 1871. By the 1930s, the source of that violence had shifted fully from the political Left to the Right.[31]

That violence, in and around Paris, frequently targeted sites of film exhibition as well as other cultural venues, and just a few weeks after the events surrounding *L'Âge d'or* at Studio 28, there was a weekend of escalating disruption and violence in Paris cinemas. The connection between those events, while plausible, is also hard to pin down. At Studio 28 the actions seemed fully premeditated and associated with a significant faction of Parisian rightwing culture, the Jeunesses patriotes. Those later events appear perhaps more spontaneous, and more the work of individuals who may or may not have been members of fascist organizations. In each case, however, the images on screen became the immediate cause for action at the cinema.

They also took place in cinemas quite different from the independently owned Studio 28. The events a few weeks after the *L'Âge d'or* incident occurred at cinemas that were parts of the largest chains in Paris, the Pathé-Natan exhibition circuit and the one controlled by Gaumont-Franco-Film-Aubert. Gaumont and Pathé both had chronic money problems and would go bankrupt by the middle of the decade, but in early 1931 they were powerful, vertically integrated companies that produced films, distributed them around the world, and often showed them in cinemas that they owned. During the 1930s filmgoers in Paris, no matter where they lived, were almost of necessity habitués of cinemas in the Pathé and Gaumont chains.[32]

Even before these events at Pathé and Gaumont cinemas, and even before the *L'Âge d'or* violence, disturbances at exclusive cinemas were not unknown in Paris. There was, of course, the *Fox folies* incident at the Moulin Rouge. There also were others, where the evidence is spotty at best, for example a brief mention in early November 1930 in *Ciné-Comoedia*, a daily Parisian journal of cultural events, and a story seemingly deemed unworthy of note by every other journalistic source still available.[33] "Violent Demonstrations at a Cinema on the Boulevards," the headline claimed, with the location—on the boulevards—and the story about the effects of a film playing there, indicating that the unnamed cinema must have had some importance. The spectators, apparently unhappy with the film, became so agitated that the exhibitor called the police. As the result of a struggle either with another spectator or with the police, one of the viewers that night was wounded.

There were only two new films that week in Paris, *Toute sa vie* (1930) and *Nos maîtres les domestiques* (1930). The first was a Paramount film made in France and directed by Alberto Cavalcanti, playing at the Paramount cinema in the ninth arrondissement, while the second, produced by Jacques Haïk and made, in French, in Great Britain, also played in the ninth, at the Olympia. Neither seems compelling enough to generate such a heated response.[34] There were, however, several reprises opening that week playing at prominent cinemas. Buster Keaton's *L'Operateur* (*The Cameraman*; 1928), for example, played at the Raspail in the sixth and the Cambronne in the fifteenth. Most interesting, though, in relation to the events of just two months later, the

German director G. W. Pabst's silent film, *Le Journal d'une fille perdue* (1929), showed in the fifth arrondissement at the Ursulines cinema, which as I mentioned earlier specialized in experimental films and challenging commercial movies. *Le Journal d'une fille perdue* had opened in Paris the previous April, but had played for only one month, so it is possible to guess that many Parisians had not yet seen the film when it returned in November. Pabst's story of rape, illegitimacy, prostitution, and suicide indeed may have been just the thing to anger unsuspecting viewers.

Violence and the Sites of Parisian Popular Culture

A little more than two months later, on Saturday evening, January 17, 1931, spectators at the Mozart-Pathé in the sixteenth arrondissement whistled derisively when the image of Théodore Steeg appeared in a newsreel. Steeg had had a long career as a colonial official, and in December had been elected the head of a new (and, eventually, short-lived), leftwing French government, replacing that of the more moderate André Tardieu. The next day, during a matinee at the Gaumont-affiliated Aubert-Palace on the boulevard des Italiens in the ninth arrondissement, a group of young men tore up the movie screen, once again, it seems, when Steeg's image appeared, probably in the same newsreel that had played at the Mozart.

In all likelihood the patrons of neither cinema expected anything unusual that weekend, but this would have been particularly true for audiences attending the Mozart. That cinema tended to play innocuous films that had already shown in Paris, and the sixteenth had always been one of the most comfortable and well-heeled arrondissements in the city. Just previously the Mozart had played a Thelma Todd comedy from 1928, *La Petite dame du vestiaire* (*Naughty Baby*), and a week later the audiences watching the Steeg newsreel really had come to see *Atlantis*, a French-language version of a British film based on the story of the Titanic that had opened elsewhere a few months earlier, as well as a 1927 Laurel and Hardy silent short about World War I, *Les Gaietés de l'infanterie* (*With Love and Hisses*).

The angry young men at the Aubert the next day may have been more prepared for action than the viewers at the Mozart who hissed and whistled at Steeg. The Aubert audience had come to see a very different kind of film about the war from the Laurel and Hardy short. They were there for G. W. Pabst's *Quatre de l'infanterie*. This bleak antiwar film about four doomed members of the German infantry was a very big deal when it opened in Paris, exclusively at the Aubert in December 1930, just as *L'Âge d'or* began its brief run at Studio 28. Critics claimed that it was a fitting and important companion film to *À l'Ouest rien de nouveau*, which had premiered at about the same time at the state-of-the-art, newly opened Ermitage cinema in the eighth arrondissement on the Champs-Élysées.[35]

That film, based on Erich Maria Remarque's international antiwar bestseller, would play for months at the Ermitage, apparently in a silent version with music and sound effects. At the end of February, in an exhibition strategy typically reserved for only the most popular films, it moved to another exclusive engagement at the Impérial-Pathé on the boulevard des Italiens in the second arrondissement.[36] *Quatre de l'infanterie* did not cause quite the same excitement, but it did play at the Aubert for about three months, replaced on February 27 by the costume melodrama *Échec au roi* (1931), starring Françoise Rosay as the Queen of France and codirected (along with Leon D'Usseau) by international playboy (and former husband of Gloria Swanson) Henri de la Falaise. *Quatre de l'infanterie* moved immediately to thirteen cinemas throughout Paris, not quite the same trajectory as *À l'Ouest rien de nouveau* but still a probable sign of the movie's importance to film audiences in the city.[37]

A film moving to so many cinemas in Paris would seem to indicate that many filmgoers had no difficulty waiting to see a movie until it came to their neighborhood. But the months-long exclusive run of *Quatre de l'infanterie* at the Aubert also shows us that Parisians were willing to leave those neighborhoods and pay at least a little more for a film that particularly interested them. We have very little evidence with which to judge these filmgoing habits. Long after the evening of the torn screen at the Aubert, in 1947, the Société nouvelle des établissements Gaumont—the organization that owned the chain of Gaumont cinemas in France and throughout Europe—began polling the customers at the company's flagship cinema, the Gaumont-Palace in Paris's eighteenth arrondissement. That poll found that around one-third of all viewers came from the eighteenth, and another quarter came from the suburbs, and mostly those that bordered the arrondissement.[38] So more than half of this first-run cinema's clientele came from within easy walking distance, or were a short ride away on the metro—the Paris subway. Most of the rest of the viewers, though, came from other parts of Paris, and we might then assume that the same would have been true for other cinémas d'exclusivité during other eras.

On the day of the torn screen in 1931, police arrested two young men, both from working-class districts at least partially removed from the Aubert: a sixteen-year-old who lived on the boulevard Barbés in the eighteenth arrondissement and a twenty-nine-year-old accountant from the rue Capri in the twelfth. If either of them had just wanted to go to the movies, they would have had any number of choices within easy walking distance of their homes. In particular, the eighteenth arrondissement was full of cinemas, with seventeen showing programs that week. Nevertheless, transportation systems in Paris certainly brought neighborhoods closer and made it much easier to move across the city. The young man from the eighteenth would have had several metro choices on the street where he lived, the boulevard Barbès, all of them on the same line, and so he could have taken a long ride to the station at Réamur-Sébastopol, changed metros there, and taken a direct trip to the metro stop nearest the Aubert, the 4 Septembre station.[39] Coming from the twelfth arrondissement on the eastern edge of the city would have taken the other man arrested that day just a little longer, but still probably only involved one change of metro trains, at the Bastille station.[40] Thus the Paris subway—along with the elaborate bus system in the city—made it possible to go almost anywhere to see a movie, as well as for like-minded young people to meet and engage in a range of political activities.

A number of Parisian newspapers covered the events at the Mozart and Aubert cinemas that weekend, reporting on them together, with the newsreel images of Steeg serving as the link. Some reports refused to identify the men arrested for the crime at the Aubert, although at least one, in *Le Petit Parisien*, provided their names and addresses.[41] But only one source seems to have situated the men ideologically. According to the Communist newspaper *L'Humanité*, both men were fascists, just like the toughs who wrecked Studio 28 when *L'Âge d'or* played there. *L'Humanité* called them "troublemakers" (*troublions*) and "thugs" (*voyous*), probably belonging to the fascist youth group Camelots du roi. *L'Humanité* continued that they had been egged on by the newspaper that sponsored the Camelots, *L'Action française*, which had a long history of disrupting plays and other public events that the editorial staff considered unpatriotic.[42] Perhaps as further evidence of the political inclinations of the suspects, the eighteenth arrondissement, where the younger man lived, was one of those neighborhoods on the northeastern edge of the city that had become such significant areas of fascist sentiment and recruitment, in no small part as a reaction to all of the Eastern European Jews who had settled in these sections over the previous forty years.[43] *L'Humanité* then lamented that the men arrested at the Aubert would certainly be released soon from police custody. The newspaper likened the event at the cinema to the destruction of Studio 28, which had led to the decision to suppress further screenings of *L'Âge d'or*. According to *L'Humanité*, the fascists just kept winning.[44] Indeed, only five years later in February 1936, and making the Aubert eruption seem harmless by comparison, the Camelots du roi would drag newly elected

Socialist (and Jewish) Prime Minister Léon Blum from his car and beat him practically to death.[45]

The precise relationship between all of the incidents of December 1930 and January 1931 is difficult to determine. The same *voyous* at the Aubert may or may not have been at the Mozart the night before, and at Studio 28 a few weeks earlier. It also remains unclear whether any of them could have known which newsreel would be playing at the Mozart or the Aubert, because those short *actualités* tended not to turn up in the typical movie advertisements or listings. There is no question, though, that at least in the case of the violence at the Aubert, *Quatre de l'infanterie* alone was enough to attract a politically motivated crowd, from both the Right and the Left of Parisian politics.

In fact, in the weeks before the Aubert attack, in November and December 1930, the socialist Club du Faubourg held two apparently open conferences where the film would be featured. At the first, on November 8, speakers engaged in a "débat cinématographique" taking sides "for and against" the two antiwar films about to open in Paris, *À l'Ouest rien de nouveau* and *Quatre de l'infanterie*. The following month the club would be at it again, when a wide range of speakers from across the political spectrum, including leaders of women's groups and members of the military, discussed the possibility of a war in Europe while also focusing on "the horrors of chemical warfare" and "women against war," as well as the merits of the same two films. Both events received wide publicity, from periodicals like *La Semaine à Paris*, read, presumably, by everyone in Paris with an interest in the week's cultural events, to those with more specific interests, for example the Socialist Party's daily newspaper, *Le Populaire*.[46]

The Club du Faubourg met at 15 boulevard de Rochechouart in the eighteenth arrondissement, just a few blocks away from where the sixteen-year-old assailant at the Aubert lived, on the boulevard Barbès. It is easy to imagine that he might have been at one or both of the meetings, or certainly would have known about them, and would have had his interest piqued in a film so important to the Parisian Left. His presence at the club remains speculative, largely because after all of the initial excitement about the events of the weekend, both of the men arrested seem to disappear from the available public record, and so we can find out nothing about their activities before the screening. Perhaps *L'Humanité* was right, and they were quickly released and no charges were pressed. Certainly the rightwing Chiappe, the prefect of police who had banned *L'Âge d'or* the month before, would have sympathized with their politics if not with their actions. Or there may have been more compelling news

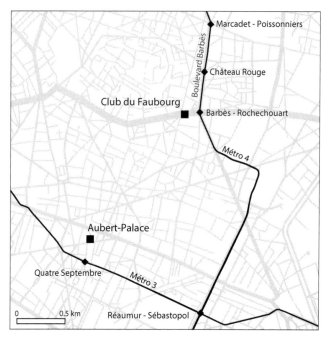

Map 4.1 The metro lines that may have taken one of the assailants from his home on the boulevard Barbès to the Aubert-Palace cinema located near the 4 Septembre station. The young man also could have gotten quite easily to the Club du Faubourg, where *Quatre de l'infanterie* had been discussed just a few weeks before the attack. Map by Michele Tobias.

to report, as there was no shortage of sensational murders in the Parisian press from the period.

Just a few days after the events at the Mozart and the Aubert, on January 22, 1931, Steeg himself was out of office after only five weeks as head of the government. *À l'Ouest rien de nouveau* and *Quatre de l'infanterie*, of course, continued to play in Paris, apparently without incident. But the events of December 1930 and January 1931 at three different cinemas in the city remain as reminders of the long history that links violence, and especially rightwing violence, to Parisian sites of leisure and popular culture.

Rightwing organizations targeted sites other than cinemas, and viewed much in the landscape of popular culture as dangerous. In the weeks just after the events at the Mozart and the Aubert, a fascist group made a more organized effort to disrupt Parisian entertainment venues than the young men who tore the screen during the Steeg newsreel. In mid-February 1931, the Théâtre Nouvel-Ambigu began presentations of *L'Affaire Dreyfus*. This was an adaptation of a German play about the most charged political and cultural event in France since the Franco-Prussian War, and one that, according to the press at the time, emphasized Dreyfus's innocence. The Ambigu was a distinguished theatre in Paris, in operation on 2 boulevard Saint-Martin in the tenth arrondissement since 1828. By the 1930s it was part of a significant entertainment district, just down the street from the Folies-Dramatiques cinema, which typically showed films that had just left their first-run, exclusive locations. The Ambigu would become a cinema itself in 1938, and then just a few years later reestablish itself as a theatre.[47]

The Croix de feu caused trouble at most of the performances, and by early March, the group's leader, the reliably anti-Dreyfusard François de La Rocque, had had enough. He wrote to Chiappe, the prefect of police, expressing concern that *L'Affaire Dreyfus* opened up old wounds that had "placed Frenchman against Frenchman for thirty years." La Rocque urged Chiappe to shut the play down, and seemed to threaten the possibility of more violent interventions if the group's concerns were not addressed. Chiappe, with his own Far Right politics, needed little convincing, and he followed La Rocque's instructions and closed the play. *L'Affaire Dreyfus* was replaced at the Ambigu by *L'Homme qui assassina*, based on a novel by Claude Farrère who, along with La Rocque, will return to this narrative of violence at the sites of popular culture.[48]

For good measure, that same week in March 1931, Chiappe also put a stop to an evening of classical music at the Théâtre des Champs-Élysées because the conductor would be the Austrian Felix Weingartner, who during the Great War apparently had cast aspersions on the French. Here Chiappe acted not on the advice of a rightwing group but on the orders of the fascist champagne mogul Pierre Taittinger, and apparently backed by threats by the Camelots du roi and the Jeunesse patriotes.[49] I mention these noncinematic events to give a sense of the many ways that the Right in Paris attempted to achieve political ends through manipulations of popular culture, manipulations that might be violent or at least involve the possibility of violence. In the years after the events at the Mozart, the Aubert, and the Ambigu, fascist groups only intensified these efforts, resulting in 1937 in one of the most violent events in Paris just before the Nazi Occupation, and one that particularly involved the cinema.

Three years earlier, in February 1934, French fascists staged an uprising in Paris that has been studied extensively but still remains somewhat mysterious, at least to the extent that we understand its motivating causes. Over a few days early in the month, fascist groups, and most notably the Croix de feu, stormed the Ministry of the Interior, the Place de la Concorde, and the presidential residence, the Élysée Palace. They were, ultimately, forced to withdraw after battling the Parisian police and French military authority. The uprising itself may have been a genuine attempt at a coup d'état by an emboldened coalition of rightwing groups. Or it may have begun as a protest over Chiappe having been fired as prefect of police, or possibly motivated simply because the many fascist groups in Paris joined forces so that none of them might be deemed weaker than any of the others.[50] Whatever the reason, when the Popular Front coalition of Radicals, Socialists, and Communists took over the Chamber of Deputies in 1936 and Léon Blum became prime minister, and with the 1934 rebellion still a very fresh memory, the new government outlawed all of France's Far Right groups.

The Battle of Clichy

With ground zero at the Place de la Concorde, those 1934 actions focused on the famous landmarks of Paris. But the violence of 1931 and 1937 dealt with the more modest and everyday aspects of Parisian architecture, the theatre and the cinema. After the Croix de feu had been outlawed, La Rocque legally reconstituted it as the Parti social français (PSF), and on March 16, 1937, around five hundred members met at the Olympia cinema in Clichy, a suburb just outside of Paris, for a screening of *La Bataille*. This was either the 1933 French film starring Charles Boyer or the 1934 British remake, which also starred the very popular French actor.

French fascists had mobilized at cinemas before. In May 1934, in the Parisian suburb of Drancy, the café manager at the Kursaal cinema had no interest in serving a group of fascists who obviously were looking to start a fight, and so he kicked them out. Sensing trouble, the Communist newspaper *L'Humanité* put the word out for leftists to converge on Drancy, and around twelve hundred answered the call. They sang "L'Internationale" as they moved through the suburb, and they shouted "Soviets everywhere!" as well as "Down with fascism!" and "Liberate Thaelmann!" (the imprisoned head of the German Communist Party who would be executed by the Nazis in 1944). They met with absolutely no resistance, as the fascists dispersed rather than challenge them.[51] Just a few days after the demonstration in Drancy, members of the fascist organization Solidarité française met at a cinema in Moulins, a town about 180 miles south of Paris, and this time there was violence. Local workers stormed the cinema, and the police, who would also protect the fascists at Clichy in 1937, fought them off. A few policemen were injured, and a number of workers were arrested and interrogated.[52] Still in May 1934, this time in the Parisian suburb of Cachan, fascists and the police combined once again, in what *L'Humanité* called an "état de siège," a state of siege. The Solidarité

Figure 4.2   The Kursaal cinema, in the Parisian suburb of Drancy, as it looked around 1934, when fascists tried to commandeer the café there.

française joined forces with another Far Right group, Action française, and about four hundred fascists overall, protected by around eight hundred members of local law enforcement, held a meeting at the Cachan-Palace cinema. Communists protested outside the cinema, shouting, as they did in Drancy, "Down with fascism!" as well as "Unity through action!" The police stood for none of this. Instead, they sent police cars and motorcycles crisscrossing through Cachan without stopping, to prevent any large gathering anywhere near the cinema. A number of protesters were injured; others threw rocks at the police. Meanwhile, the fascists were able to hold their meeting.[53]

In the leftwing, working-class Parisian suburb of Saint-Denis, and around the same time as the events in Cachan, fascists gathered in the Kermesse cinema. *L'Humanité* called that a clear provocation, and asked that "communists, socialists, and those not aligned with any party protest as vigorously as possible." Indeed they did, and they, too, used the spaces of popular culture as their headquarters. Rather than meeting in cinemas, they assembled in two of Saint-Denis's theatres, the Municipal and the Hénaff, and then took to the streets in a show of force that the fascists could do nothing about, because in Saint-Denis they apparently did not have the support of local police.[54] Then, in March 1935, the Redressement français (French Resurgence) scheduled a mass meeting at the Central cinema in Vitry, a southeastern suburb of Paris. Antifascists also gathered there to disrupt the meeting, but the police, in support of the Redressement, broke up the protesters and sent at least one of them to the hospital.[55]

In none of these instances was there much interest in watching a movie. Instead, the cinema functioned as a convenient space for a large gathering. We can see, then, that at least during the 1930s, in and around Paris, the typical cinema could be understood as a multiple-use space, ideal for movies, of course, but also for other things. In fact, in the working-class twentieth arrondissement of Paris, there was a cinema designed in just this way, the Bellevilloise, which as I mentioned earlier showed movies and also served as a community cultural center. There were also larger institutions with cinemas attached. While fascists gathered in Drancy, for example, the Fascistes slovaques, a Czech expatriate group, met at the cinema connected to the Maison catholique in Argenteuil, a northern suburb of Paris, where they were shouted down by workers who had come to protest.[56]

In 1937, at Clichy, the PSF seem to have bought out the cinema, and the audience included a number of women and children, as both the Croix de feu and the PSF had always emphasized family and family activities more than other similar groups and always welcomed women into their ranks.[57] Like so many gatherings of the Far Right in and around Paris during the 1930s, how-ever, this event was not simply planned as a chance to meet and mingle with like-minded ideologues. Communists had gathered around the cinema as a protest, and early in the evening, perhaps even before the movie started, fight-ing began between the fascists and police on one side and the Communists on the other. At least five were killed and many more were injured.[58]

It was no accident that La Rocque chose Clichy for his group's movie night. Clichy had long been a *banlieue rouge*, one of the "red suburbs" of Paris known for its Communist leadership.[59] La Rocque almost certainly hoped to embar-rass or intimidate Clichy's radicals on their own turf, and so tensions were already very high by the night of the screening. Members of the Comité du Front Populaire de Clichy (Popular Front Committee of Clichy) had put up posters throughout the suburb, alerting residents that La Rocque, "Chèf des Fascistes," and his followers would be coming to Clichy on March 16, with the committee calling for a counterdemonstration that very day.[60]

Knowing the details of the movie that night, and, really, knowing much at all about the cinema in Clichy, is extremely difficult. The available materials tell us very little about the Parisian suburbs from the period, with newspapers and other sources giving us only occasional information. Nevertheless, there are some things we can piece together. The Olympia cinema was on the rue de l'Union in Clichy, just at the back of the town hall, situating it perfectly for a political gathering that tried to pass itself off as a benign evening's entertain-ment. Clichy had a population of about fifty-five thousand in 1937, normally enough people to support three or four cinemas.[61] It is possible that, because of Clichy's proximity to Parisian cinemas in the neighboring seventeenth and eighteenth arrondissements, the Olympia was the only exhibition site in the suburb (even today, with about the same population, Clichy only has one cin-ema, the Rutebeuf).[62]

The Olympia served not only as the gathering place for the PSF but as a significant architectural presence in the battle. Newspaper reports indicate that the Clichy police, siding with La Rocque, placed themselves in formation behind the town hall, effectively making it impossible for the Communist protesters to go anywhere, blocked on one side by the police and on the other by the cinema. The police attacked, and there was little the trapped Communists could do.[63]

The movie that night, *La Bataille*, had had a long history in the area. The more prominent, at least in Paris, British version had premiered in the city in January 1934 at the very fashionable Marignan cinema in the eighth arrondissement, and then in March moved to the Max Linder cinema in

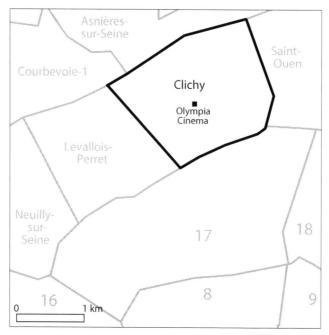

Map 4.2   The Clichy suburb just outside Paris, where the fighting at the Olympia cinema took place in 1937. Map by Michele Tobias.

the ninth for a further exclusive run. After that the film remained in fairly steady reissue, for instance at three important Parisian cinemas in July 1935 (the Majestic Brune, the Gambetta-Étoile, and the Mozart, the site of that evening of whistling at the newsreel), and at the glamorous Louxor in the tenth arrondisement later that same year, as well as at the Fério in the twelfth.[64] Charles Boyer, the star of the film, had a large following in Paris, and even while the PSF was gathering in Clichy, the Marignan and Max Linder cinemas once again were preparing for the premiere, in just a few days, of his latest film, the 1936 David O. Selznick production *Le Jardin d'Allah* (*The Garden of Allah*), which also featured Marlene Dietrich.[65]

For the fascists gathering in Clichy, however, Boyer was only one of the stars that night, making this the only instance I have found when the film itself, and not just the convenient space of the cinema, was particularly important, although it remains unclear whether a screening was part of the plan for the evening. *La Bataille* had been based on a novel by Claude Farrère, the same man who wrote the source material for *L'Homme qui assassina*, the play at the Théâtre Nouvel-Ambigu that replaced *L'Affaire Dreyfus* after the 1931 protest by the Croix de feu. In addition to being a well-known novelist, Farrère was also a fascist, a contributor to *Le Flambeau*, the newspaper of the Croix de feu, and someone who might give La Rocque's groups an imprimatur of cultural respectability at a time when fascist organizations liked to boast of having at least some adherents who were more literary than paramilitary.[66] *La Bataille* may not have had much of a political charge when it typically played in Paris or throughout France during the 1930s, but it certainly did that night in Clichy.

The violence in Clichy in March 1937 is well known to historians. The place of cinema in that violence tends to remain peripheral, if mentioned at all. This may in part be due to the difficulty of finding information about cultural events in the Paris suburbs at the time, or just to a general dismissal of the significance of popular culture to interwar French political movements. The events of 1929, at the premiere of *Fox folies*, show the possibility of aggrieved spectators resorting to protest and violence at the movies; and the uprisings in 1931 and 1937, and also the agitation around the screening of *L'Âge d'or* in 1930, make it clear that rightwing violence in and around Paris was often significantly connected to the cinema and other cultural venues. The incidents surrounding the Théâtre Nouvel-Ambigu and the Olympia cinema, no less than those in 1934 at the Place de la Concorde, demonstrate the dangers posed by the French Far Right and their understanding of the importance of a range of symbols of Parisian life, from the most elite to the fully mundane, and their willingness to stage violent disruptions there.

Just a few years later, during the Occupation, the cinema became an obvious space for Nazi surveillance of Parisians and for rounding up those thought to be threats to the Nazi authority.[67] Although evidence of these activities is hard to come by, as they typically went unreported in the collaborationist press, there are traces here and there. On September 2, 1941, the *New York Times* reported on a series of antifascist demonstrations in and around Paris, including an instance in a Parisian suburb where "in a cinema at Melun spectators left the house when a Fascist newsreel appeared on the screen."[68] According to the *Times*, "gestapo . . . agents drove the public back into the hall," with the German commandant of Melun, as a result, issuing a 9:00 p.m. curfew that went into effect the next day in this southeastern suburb of Paris.[69]

The *Times* article raises more questions than it answers. Were the gestapo typically policing Parisian and suburban cinemas, or did they just happen to be near that cinema in Melun?[70] Was there any risk of the crowd becoming violent, or were audiences simply refusing to watch the newsreel? How reliable was the *Times* article in the first place? Parisian newspapers provide no answers. The report in *Le Matin* said only that two Communists had been arrested because they had been circulating subversive tracts, perhaps inside the cinema, while other available newspapers seemed to be uninterested in the event.[71] Just a week later the Germans distributed an anti-Communist documentary, *La Face au bolshevisme*, to dozens of cinemas in Paris and the suburbs, including the Majestic cinema in Melun, and so, of course, we can imagine that the "Fascist newsreel" as well as other pro-Nazi films would be staples of the bills at cinemas during the period, even as the feature films might seem little changed from those before the war.[72]

We have come full circle, then, from the newsreel that incited protest and violence in 1931 to a newsreel that caused a walkout in 1941. In that first instance, of course, the fascists or fascist sympathizers objected to what they saw, and in the second, it was the fascist authority demanding that audiences continue viewing the film that so upset them. This state-sponsored violence at the cinema certainly had its antecedents in the seemingly more spontaneous uprisings at the Mozart and Aubert cinemas, while also drawing from the events at Clichy, when La Rocque and the PSF understood the cinema itself as a space of containment and control. Most of the available evidence during the period, from Paris especially, tells us about the feature films playing at cinemas, the times they played, and the ways those films moved through the city. There is a different kind of evidence, however, often barely visible, that tells us about what took place at those cinemas, and that tells us, as well, of the occasional and very serious political dangers in the 1930s and 1940s of going to the movies in Paris.

5

Occupied Paris

1939–1944, 2009

On January 1, 1941, the French newspaper *Le Matin* ran photographs of four movie stars in its section listing "les spectacles" in Paris. At the top of the page, Brigitte Horney in *Les Mains libres* (*Befreite Hände*; 1939), and below that, Marika Rökk in *Allö, Janine* (*Hallo Janine!*; 1939), Ilse Werner in *Bal masqué* (*Bal paré*; 1940), and Zarah Leander in *Marie Stuart* (*Das Herz der Königin*; 1940).[1] Even for the reliably rightwing and collaborationist *Le Matin*, this stands out as extraordinary, and would have been inconceivable less than a year earlier. Indeed, this display of some of the greatest divas of German cinema, just six months after the French surrender, points out how thoroughly German the French cinema had become, and how quickly. Of course, French actresses appeared in movies in Paris that week: Edwige Feuillère and Arletty, for example, along with such actors as Jean Gabin and Louis Jouvet. Nevertheless, this single page of movie ads, listings, and photos provides ample evidence of National Socialism's uses of German movie stars to produce a seemingly benign and celebrity-based cultural occupation of Paris and the rest of France.

How did this rapid and seemingly smooth transformation happen? We need to return to Paris, to the late summer and early fall of 1939, just after the beginning of the war. Had you been in the city then and wanted to get your mind off European affairs for just a few hours, your opportunities for doing so at the movies would have diminished considerably, from month to month and even from week to week, precisely because of the war. Just a few days before France surrendered to Germany in June 1940, only around 50 of the 230 or so cinemas in Paris still were showing movies, and by the time the Germans entered the city on June 14, all of the cinemas had closed.[2] The process had been a gradual one, with many businesses shutting down in the

Figure 5.1   Brigitte Horney, in the upper right, featured in *Le Matin*, January 1, 1941, along with, from the bottom to the top, Zarah Leander, Marika Rökk, and Ilse Werner. Source: Bibliothèque nationale de France, Paris.

first few months of the year as Parisians, confronted by the inevitability of the Nazi army, fled the city.[3] The closures of cinemas affected every neighborhood, but particularly those on the periphery of Paris and the smaller cinémas des quartiers there.

Many of the major cinemas already had closed in the days leading up to the surrender, although there were still a dozen open in the ninth arrondissement, always such an important area in Parisian exhibition. In the last available listings, for the week of June 5, 1940, just a little more than two weeks before the June 22 armistice between France and Germany, the Roxy cinema in the northernmost section of the ninth showed *Miss Manton est folle* (*The Mad Miss Manton*; 1938), with Barbara Stanwyck and Henry Fonda. The Paramount, on the southern end of the arrondissement, was in the fourth week of playing *Le Café du port* (1940), directed by Jean Choux and with slightly lesser French movie stars: René Dary and Line Viala, a singer making her only film appearance. In between those two cinemas, audiences in the ninth could see reprises of the Columbia film *Miss Catastrophe* (*There's Always a Woman*; 1938) or the British adaptation of Shaw's *Pygmalion* (1938) or the 1939 French film *Deuxième bureau contre kommandantur*, as well as other movies. In the working-class twentieth arrondissement, however, where there typically had been around twenty cinemas before the war, all of them showing subsequent-run films, only one remained in business, the Ciné-Bellevue, which showed a documentary that had come out before the beginning of hostilities but was titled, appropriately enough, *Le Monde en armes* (1939).[4]

As an occupying force, the Nazis hoped to provide Parisians, no less than the rest of Europe and the United States, with the certainty that the city was back to business as usual despite the French surrender. As Evelyn Ehrlich has pointed out in her study of National Socialist film policy during the war, when the Germans installed Philippe Pétain as the leader of Vichy and occupied the rest of France, they found an ideal but now unused film infrastructure— studio space and cinemas. They also understood the incentive for maintaining a French film industry that had a significant global presence and reputation, and could be used to help develop the face of benevolent German power. In October 1940 the Nazis formed their own movie studio, to make French movies in France and with a name so vague—Continental Films—that it could not really be associated with Germany.[5] They also banned, first, all British films, and then, between 1940 in the Occupied Zone and 1942 in Vichy, all American films as well.[6] Paul Virilio has described the shock of this embargo on Hollywood. "At a stroke," he wrote, "there would be no more American magazines, no more newspapers, above all, no more movies."[7]

The Nazis formed the Comité d'organisation des industries ciné-matographique (COIC), under the aegis of the Vichy regime, to administer this new, German-run film industry in France, and to try to convince French audiences that nothing had changed. To do so, and along with facilitating the bureaucracy of a vast entertainment industry, the Nazis understood the importance of regular news and publicity about the cinema, especially in Paris and aimed at the "average" fan. Of course, throughout the entire Occupation period, when the French read their newspapers, they were, in fact, reading news controlled by Germany.

In film journalism nothing signifies the French surrender in June 1940 more than the end of one publication and the beginning of another. *Pour Vous*, which has been such a valuable source for my study, had been perhaps the leading French film tabloid since its first weekly issue in 1928, with its broad view of the French film scene in general along with its focus on all the films playing in Paris in particular. Even though it was the sister publication of the rightwing newspaper *L'Intransigeant*, *Pour Vous* ceased to exist after the surrender. In its place, starting in early 1941, German authorities published their own French-language film weekly, *Ciné-Mondial*, providing much the same information as *Pour Vous* and other prewar movie tabloids, but with an emphasis on Franco-German cultural relations and on the place of German cinema in France. Just as with the name of the film studio—Continental—the very title of the magazine (in English, *Cinema World*) indicated a reach transcending national boundaries, a proposed international scope beyond the claim of *Pour Vous*, a name that seemed directed at the individual reader rather than a more global audience.

Much more than gossip and news about movies and movie stars, film exhibition would be vital to the German plan for the normalization of the film culture in Paris, and so the Nazis made sure that cinemas went back into business throughout the city. By the end of June 1941, just one year after the surrender and the closure of all of the cinemas in the city, around 150 of them had reopened. These cinemas would be concentrated in the most well-heeled parts of Paris, with the cinémas d'exclusivité in the second, seventh, eighth, and ninth arrondissements. At least ten of the cinemas that went back into business quickly were within just a few blocks of each other on the Champs-Élysées: the Élysées-Cinéma, the Ermitage, the Lord Byron, the Portiques, and the Normandie, among others, and also the Biarritz which, interestingly enough given the eventual ban on Hollywood movies, reopened in July 1940 with an American film, *They Shall Have Music* (1939).[8] Neighborhood cinemas, those cinémas des quartiers, also reopened, even in the more working-class eastern periphery of the city. In the twentieth arrondissement, the Pyrénées showed subsequent-run films, for instance during the week of June 28, 1941, when *Musique de rêve* (*Traummusik*; 1940), a German-Italian coproduction, played there.[9] Within just a few months there were even more cinemas in the twentieth, so that by September movie fans in the neighborhood could go to the Avron, the Cocorico, the Tourelles, the Gambetta-Aubert-Palace, as well as the Zenith to see movies that had long before left their opening engagements and were now making their way through the city.[10] The Nazis employed the same strategy in other neighborhoods, in the fourteenth, fifteenth, and nineteenth arrondissements, for example, which were all somewhat removed from the areas with Paris's most distinguished cinemas.

In fact, it seems as if reopening all of these cinemas as soon as possible was more important to the German Occupation project than having enough films to fill them. French movies, of course, dominated these screens, but there were far more reprises than new films while the production side of the German-controlled French film industry got itself up to speed. In the first year or so of the Occupation, the newest French films—and there weren't many—were playing at the most prestigious cinemas. *L'Enfer des anges*, for instance, from 1941 and directed by Christian-Jaque, played at the Ciné-Opéra on the avenue de l'Opéra in the second arrondissement in June 1941. Maurice Tourneur's *Volpone*, also from 1941 and with two great stars, Harry Baur and Louis Jouvet, showed at the Marivaux just a few blocks away on the boulevard des Italiens. Elsewhere in the second, where cinemas before the war had shown the most recent films from Europe and the United States, movie fans had to settle for reprises. They might go to the boulevard des Italiens to see Charles Boyer in *Orage* (1938) at the Impérial-Pathé, or Pierre Larquey in *La Griffe du hasard* (1937) at the Cinéac Italiens. On the boulevard Poissonière, they could watch Boyer yet again in Marcel L'Herbier's *Le Bonheur* (1935) at the Parisiana, or the 1937 Italian film *La Grande révolte* (*Condottieri*) at the Gaumont.[11]

At the same time, just one year after the surrender, German films naturally enough played throughout Paris. The great German star Zarah Leander appeared in two movies. *Première*, from 1937, showed in many cinemas in the city, at the Voltaire-Aubert-Palace in the eleventh arrondissement, for example, and also at the Montrouge-Aubert-Palace in the fourteenth, while the film she made with Douglas Sirk in the same year, *La Habanera*, was featured in cinemas all over the city. As one might expect, that 1940 homage to anti-Semitism, *Le Juif suss* (*Jud Süss*), played in Paris that June, at the Jeanne d'Arc in the thirteenth.[12]

Mostly, though, there were French films. Once again using the end of June 1941 as an example, many of those films were older and some of them quintessentially French, like Marcel Pagnol's *César* (1936). Or they starred popular French performers: Maurice Chevalier in Julien Duvivier's *L'Homme du jour* (1937) playing in the nineteenth arrondissement, or Danielle Darrieux, whose 1932 film *Le Coffret de laque*, an adaptation of an Agatha Christie play, ran in the tenth at the Folies-Dramatiques.[13]

The splashiest film event of the Occupation was the 1944 Paris premiere of the Technicolor extravaganza *Les Aventures fantastiques du Baron Münchausen* (*Münchhausen*; 1943), produced in Germany at UFA to mark the studio's twenty-fifth anniversary and starring a who's who of German cinema, including Hans Albers as the baron, Brigitte Horney as Catherine the Great, and Ilse Werner as Princess Isabella.[14] *Ciné-Mondial* ran articles about the movie and photographs from it for weeks in preparation for the film's opening at the Normandie cinema in early February 1944. The Normandie, at 116 avenue des Champs-Élysées, had closed in early February 1940 (the 1939 British film *Les Quatres Plumes blanches* had been the last film to play there), and its reopening, along with the other cinemas on the Champs-Élysées, had been, as we have seen, a priority for the Nazis. At least by early 1943 the Normandie had reopened with *Mariage d'amour* (1942), a French film from Continental.

Münchausen played at the Normandie through May 16, when it was replaced by the Continental film *La Vie de Plaisir* (1944), starring Albert Préjean. That three-month run counted as a long one for the Occupation, but not absolutely out of the ordinary. The week *Münchausen* began its run at the Normandie, *L'Inévitable M. Dubois* (1943), starring Annie Ducaux, was just finishing up a four-and-a-half-month appearance at the cinema next door, the Cinéma des Champs-Élysées. But leaving the Normandie did not mean leaving Paris. *Münchausen* appeared immediately and exclusively at the fashionable Caméo cinema at 32 boulevard des Italiens in the ninth arrondissement, and the film played there for more than two months, at least through the week of July 26, 1944. After that, listings for the next few weeks of the Occupation seem not to be available. In fact, it is possible that as the Allied army closed in on the city, and with a surge in fighting in the streets between the Resistance and the Nazis, often right in the center of Paris, cinemas began closing once again, just as they had four years earlier. The move to liberate Paris began in full on August 19, 1944, and the city was free by August 25.

Despite the premieres, the new French films, and the reopenings of so many cinemas, the film culture of the Occupation might only be considered normal, or similar to that of the prewar period, in relative terms. It certainly had more

Figure 5.2 The Normandie cinema on the Champs-Élysées, where *Les Aventures fantastiques du Baron Münchausen* opened in 1944, as it looks now. Photograph by author.

in common, for instance, with the period before September 1939 than it did with the early summer of 1940, when the cinema in Paris, really, ceased to exist. There were plenty of indications, though, of the strangeness of cinema during the Occupation. Regardless of location, none of the cinemas showed movies all week. Almost all of them were closed on Tuesdays, and many of them also opted for one other day to shut down, probably a result of the crippling shortages in the city, particularly of electricity.[15] The Nazis mandated that several exhibition sites have the label *soldatenkino* (soldiers' cinema), a cinema reserved for members of the German military and typically among the most important in the city, for instance the Marignan on the Champs-Élysées and the Rex on the boulevard Poissonière. Of course, drawing as they did crowds from across the city or from within neighborhoods, cinemas also functioned during the Occupation as ready-made locations for Nazi surveillance.[16] The cinemas of Paris, those prewar sites of escape, contemplation, or distraction, worked very much as an implementation of what Ronald C. Rosbottom has called the Nazis' determination to "reduce spatial freedom" for everyone in the city.[17]

Nevertheless, and as we will see, the Nazis tried to make Parisians think of the cinema as a refuge, and consider the spaces of cinema and the stars on-screen as signs of the benevolence of the occupying force. Film exhibition and the production of celebrity came to be central to the project of the German Occupation of Paris, and placing stars within certain exhibition contexts, those that signified the glamor of prewar French cinema, served a vital function in the strategy to place entertainment in the service of fascism. Indeed, one of the stars of *Münchausen* stands out as an ideal case study of so many of these aspects of Nazi film culture in Paris.

Nazi Stardom in Occupied Paris

We can return now to that January 1, 1941 issue of *Le Matin*, the one with the images of so many great German actresses. The most prominently featured of all of them, Brigitte Horney, serves as a particularly interesting instance of the Nazi star in occupied Paris. The period of her greatest celebrity coincided broadly with the history of National Socialism in Germany. She began making films in 1930, and in 1933, the first year of Hitler's chancellorship, she appeared in only her fifth film, *Heideschulmeister Uwe Karsten* (*The Country Schoolmaster*). In 1939, as the war in Europe began, she starred in no fewer than five films, including *Befreite Hände*, which, as *Les Mains libres*, opened on the Champs-Élysées in Paris at the end of 1940, an early demonstration of the importance of German melodrama on French screens during the war. Beyond her films, however, Horney's celebrity and star persona served National Socialism in a number of ways, and always as a means for establishing the logic of Nazi power in France and of a multinational European cinema controlled by Germany.

An extracinematic component to her biography makes Horney interesting as well. She was the eldest of three daughters of the feminist, neo-Freudian psychoanalyst Karen Horney. The information remains sketchy, but all of the sisters seem to have had vexed and emotionally distant relationships with their mother. As one biographer has written, "Karen Horney's approach to child rearing . . . resembled her approach to gardening: both were something she supervised and others carried out."[18] The Horneys were not Jewish, but Karen left Germany for the United States in 1932, before the ascendancy of National Socialism but with the handwriting, perhaps, already on the wall. She had her youngest daughter, Renate, with her when she arrived in Chicago, to begin work at the Institute for Psychoanalysis, and her middle daughter, Marianne, would join them a year later. Brigitte, having just begun a promising theatrical career, stayed in Germany.[19] During her subsequent work in film, and at least in the French context, Horney's connection to the preeminent feminist psychoanalyst seems never to have been mentioned. The various discussions of Horney, however, in film magazines or newspapers, certainly invoked those qualities that also might have been associated with her mother. News reports and features often stressed a sort of well-bred, intellectual cosmopolitanism that transcended national boundaries, and that made the actress as much at home in Paris as in Berlin.

The beginning of the war also hastened shifts in established celebrity and in the production of stardom. Lilian Harvey, one of the great German stars throughout the 1930s, left the country in 1939 and stopped making films entirely in 1940.[20] In France after the surrender, Michèle Morgan, one of the most popular of the country's movie stars, left for Hollywood and stayed away for the duration of the war, while the ban on American films deprived audiences in France of such longtime favorites as Jeanette MacDonald and Marlene Dietrich.[21] The wartime German film industry largely filled this void through films with established French stars who made movies for Continental and also through German stars, both longstanding, as in the case of Zarah Leander, and new, as with Horney.

By the time of the Occupation, Horney already had achieved at least the beginnings of an international reputation. In January 1935, for instance, *L'Afrique du Nord*, a weekly newspaper published in Algiers, announced on its movie page that UFA's *Le Diable en bouteille* (1935) had just completed production, and saw fit to mention that while Kate de Nagy acted the starring role in both the French- and German-language versions, in the latter Brigitte Horney would appear in place of Gina Manès.[22] That German version, *Liebe, Tod, und Teufel*, played in New York in May 1935, and the reviewer for the *New York Times* dutifully described Horney's character as a "shady local." In fact, that same critic (who signed reviews "H. T. S.") developed something of a fixation on Horney as her starring vehicles came to New York. He commented on her "rather indefinable allure" in *Verklungene Melodie* in 1938, described her as the "alluring wife" in *Der Gouverneur*, from 1939, and then the same year assured readers that she was "as alluring as ever" in *Ziel in den Wolken*.[23] But she was never remotely as well known to American audiences as such German actresses as Lilian Harvey, who had starred in movies made in Hollywood, or Dorothea Wieck, who also had worked in the United States after the international sensation of *Mädchen in Uniform* (1931), in which she had played the teacher, the object of all of the young girls' fascination. In France before the war, Harvey, Wieck, and other German stars, such as Anny Ondra, were significant draws at the box office, while Horney enjoyed only a very minor celebrity.

After the Germans took control of French cinema, they were determined to present Horney as an entirely new star to audiences in Paris and elsewhere in the country. In December 1940, newspapers started advertising Horney in *Les Mains libres*, her film from 1939, in which, to the extent that we can make out the plot from available materials, she plays a peasant who is also a brilliant sculptress, and who, after she comes to Berlin, ultimately chooses her art over the man she loves. *Le Petit Parisien* announced that this film "will reveal" to Parisians "the great star," Brigitte Horney.[24] Then, just two days later in its review of the premiere, the newspaper continued to discuss Horney in terms of dramatic disclosure rather than mere reintroduction, referring to the "revelation" of the film, "this unknown actress, Brigitte Horney," and assigning to her those traits that came to mark her in French journalism of the period: intelligence, sobriety, truth. Underscoring this description, and under a photograph of Horney in the film, a caption asserted "une révélation."[25]

Le Matin agreed, and in precisely the same terms, but now extended to the nation rather than only the capital. Anticipating the opening of *Les Mains libres*, *Le Matin* claimed that the film "will reveal" to "all France . . . an artist of the first rank, Brigitte Horney."[26] This revelation of the great star coincided with the reopening of a significant exhibition site, the Cinéma des Champs-Élysées on Paris's most famous avenue in the very fashionable eighth arrondissement. With only around 450 seats, the Cinéma des Champs-Élysées had never been among the largest exhibition sites in Paris, but it had long been among the city's prominent sites for seeing films.[27] In just one example among many, *Anna Christie*, Greta Garbo's first sound film and a major cultural event in Paris, had opened there in 1931.[28] During the gradual closing of Parisian cinemas in the lead-up to the surrender in June 1940, the Cinéma des Champs-Élysées seems to have stayed open until the middle of January, when it showed *Ennuie de ménage*, a title lost to us now but apparently the French name for a foreign film.[29]

Thus the presentation of the new star and the newly reopened cinema coincided, each one contributing to the significance of the other. With Horney, the Germans showed all Paris the National Socialist gender ideal, the romanticized eternal feminine of her character's peasant upbringing, and also the new woman who feels completely at home in densely urban Berlin.[30] The space of this presentation, the Cinéma des Champs-Élysées, assured Parisians about the reestablishment of pre-Occupation French culture, but, of course, fully thanks to the efforts of the occupying authority. We are used to the Nazis' ideologically charged architecture: Albert Speer's Reich Chancellery, his stadium at Nuremberg, and his plans for a sort of Haussmannization of Berlin. The Cinéma des Champs-Élysées indicates yet another architectural mode, one that acknowledges the usefulness of buildings from before the war restored to prewar use, in this case the showing of films. That space, however, would come to be co-opted by the Nazis as a showpiece for the new, wartime German film industry in France, and as the site for the creation of one of that industry's chief commodities, the movie star.

The film opened as a fully multimedia event, one that stressed the film industry's development of celebrity, the architectural space of the culture of the Occupation, and also the relationship of both to the collaborationist journalism of the period. When *Le Petit Parisien* announced the premiere, and in its subsequent advertising for the movie, the newspaper took credit for presenting the film.[31] The exact link is unclear and remained unacknowledged in other newspapers, but it seems evident that Parisian movie audiences must have understood that Horney's "new" stardom indicated direct links and cooperative efforts between visual and print media and the spaces of leisure and entertainment.

This linkage helped establish a standard practice for the German occupying authority. Less than a year and a half later, for example, for Easter, at the Théâtre des Champs-Élysées on the avenue Montaigne in the eighth arrondissement, the media corporation Radio-Paris, in cooperation with two film magazines— *Ciné-Mondial* and *Film Complet*—staged a "grand gala" of stars of radio, theatre, and cinema, all of them introduced by Vichy officials.[32] The event was more overtly ideological than the opening of *Les Mains libres*. While that film may have depicted Horney as the female model of National Socialism, the Easter gala, in the words of the Vichy bureaucrat who opened the event, announced itself specifically as a celebration of the families that trained children to be heads of households, and especially girls to be mothers. To underscore the message, the famous theatre and film star Jean Tissier appeared onstage with Anne Mayen, who had played a supporting role in Renoir's *La Règle du jeu* (1939), and so too did composer Raymond Legrand, with various stars of French radio.

The Easter gala seems to follow directly from the opening of *Les Mains libres*, both of them using significant theatrical spaces and emphasizing the political role of celebrity while connecting film with other media industries. It should be pointed out, however, that French film culture during the war might also seem little different either from before the Occupation or from the installation of Philippe Pétain in Vichy. When *Les Mains libres* opened in December 1940, a revival of Julien Duvivier's 1937 film, *Un carnet de bal*, played at one of Paris's most famous cinemas, the Ursulines, in the fifth arrondissement. Another reprise from 1937, *Pépé le Moko*, showed as well, at the Folies-Dramatiques in the tenth arrondissement. Other, now forgotten, French films from before the surrender played throughout the city: *Quartier latin* (1939), *Bécassine* (1940), and *Circonstances atténuantes* (1939), for example.[33] Thus Parisian audiences, at least, might see not only Brigitte Horney along with other German stars, but such quintessentially French performers as Fernandel, Junie Astor, Sylvia Bataille, Michel Simon, and, of course, Jean Gabin. Indeed, until 1944, when the German authorities realized that Gabin, who had left for Hollywood, had no intention of returning to France and so banned all of his films, several of the great star's prewar movies—*La Belle Équipe* (1936) and *Le Jour se lève* (1939) in addition to *Pépé le Moko*—were a frequent presence in French cinemas during the Occupation.[34]

We can see here the back and forth of French cinema during the period, at least in those locations—usually urban, such as Paris—where we have sufficient information. Familiar French films, many of which would never be taken for Nazi propaganda, playing alongside French films made by Continental, the German film company, or films from studios in Germany that either clearly espoused a party line or, like *Les Mains libres* (a Tobis production), might be shown in ideologically overdetermined contexts. Shortly after the premiere of Horney's film at the Cinéma des Champs-Élysées, however, *Les Mains libres*, like other first-run films, made its way through the rest of Paris and, probably, France as well. By the middle of January 1941, the film had moved to another posh cinema, the Français on the boulevard des Italiens in the ninth arrondissement, where viewers could see the dubbed French version (the information is unclear, but the film that opened in Paris probably was subtitled, rather than this subsequent, dubbed "version française"). The ads for the film still stressed Horney as an "incomparable artist whose talent lights up this simple story" and also emphasized the atmosphere of the cinema itself ("what a wonderful ambiance"). But *Les Mains libres*, as well as Horney, had shifted from an exhibition context indicating the connections between popular media, architecture, and National Socialism, to one that stressed the conventionally smooth machinery of film distribution throughout a major city.[35]

During the war, stars appeared not only in movies, and not just at special events in Paris. Rather, the Germans mobilized movie stars and other celebrities, French as well as German, as entertainers and ambassadors, and sent them to locations important to the war effort. The Germans also enlisted something of an intellectual star system in their efforts, rounding up famous, and willing, French novelists and journalists, for example, to attend the Congress of European Writers in Weimar in October 1941. When those writers met at the conference, or visited Goethe's home, even they became movie stars of a sort, as their activities were duly recorded by the *Actualités mondiales* newsreel cameras and then shown to French audiences as proof of a new, modern, international community of philosophers, artists, and writers produced under the auspices of National Socialism.[36]

It would be celebrities from the entertainment industry who performed most conspicuously for the Germans. When German stars came to France, they invariably met publicly with French celebrities, as was the case one evening in 1942 when Marika Rökk, the Hungarian-born German film actress, shared a stage at the Casino de Paris with the greatest of all icons of the French music hall, Mistinguett. *Ciné-Mondial* duly reported on the event, and stressed both the internationalism of the meeting by referring to the stars as "European" rather than as one particular nationality or another, as well as the quintessential Frenchness of Mistinguett, labeled as "our Miss National."[37] French stars, of course, also went to Germany. In 1942 a who's who of French celebrities—including, once again, Raymond Legrand as well as the great chanteuse and actress Fréhel—traveled to Germany to entertain the French workers there. In the most famous trip of all from the period, Maurice Chevalier arrived in Berlin in 1941 and then performed nearby at the Alten Grabow prisoner-of-war camp, where he himself had been held after his capture in World War I, and where many French soldiers from the current war still were incarcerated.[38]

What was almost certainly the most extensive official trip to Germany began in March 1942, when the "train of stars" left the station in Paris for a tour of Berlin, Munich, and Vienna, with Brigitte Horney ultimately playing a significant role as an ambassador for Franco-German relations. The eight French participants included some of the most significant stars of European cinema, including Danielle Darrieux, Junie Astor, Suzy Delair, and Albert Préjean, and they were accompanied by the screenwriter André Legrand (no relation to Raymond) and film journalist Pierre Heuzé. The participants came ostensibly in the name of the cinematic arts, invited by Carl Froelich, the president of the Reichsfilmkammer, the organization that held significant control over the German film industry during the period, as well as by Alfred Greven, an executive at Continental Films. Darrieux, Préjean, and the others brought French films with them to show in Germany and also planned on visiting German film studios. The event had enough significance as Nazi propaganda that it was front-page news in *Le Matin* and a cover story in *Toute la vie*, which from its first issue in August 1941 became one of the more important weekly French magazines during the war, while *Ciné-Mondial* enlisted Heuzé to report on the trip over a two-month period.[39]

For the French movie fan, this kind of visit and its place in the popular film tabloids were nothing new. Other major stars had gone to Germany before, typically to make films, and the press covered those visits as well, and in a manner that prefigured the 1942 trip, as signs of the French cinema's place in Europe broadly and of the possibility of cooperative filmmaking efforts. As early as 1931, and over a two-week period, *Pour Vous* covered the trip Annabella took to Berlin, where she planned to make films. Emphasizing the role of the French film star as a cinematic emissary, the same tabloid in the same year wrote of the Franco-Romanian star Pola Illéry, who had appeared in *Sous les toits de Paris*, bringing that film herself to Düsseldorf for a special presentation.[40] Naturally, in 1942, the collaborationist press failed to report on levels of coercion. Darrieux, for instance, took part in the tour as a means of protecting her companion at the time, Dominican diplomat Porfirio Rubirosa, who had been imprisoned by the Nazis when his country sided with the Allies.[41] In other words, in much the same way that *Ciné-Mondial* resembled *Pour Vous* and other prewar French film journals, and in much the same way that the celebrity of Darrieux, Préjean, or Astor seemed unchanged by the war, the 1942 trip to Germany may have seemed like nothing unusual within the French film culture of the period.

One of the early reports from the trip isolated the ideological project of the tour: to humanize Nazi officials on the one hand and to support the geopolitics of a Nazi-controlled Europe on the other. Titled "Better than a Dream . . . the Reality of the Future," this dispatch from Heuzé has the actress Suzy Delair exclaim to one of the accompanying German officials—Fritz Dietrich, the chief of the ss—"But you are so elegant!" Then Heuzé moved from the personal to the poetic, and claimed that, at night, as the train moves across the countryside, "it seems as if one great land stretches out before us; it's Europe!," with this singular land mass, without national boundaries, precisely that which was "better than a dream, perhaps the reality of the future."[42]

Heuzé's subsequent dispatches in *Ciné-Mondial* followed the same pattern. When the travelers arrived in Berlin the streets appeared to be larger than those in Paris, but the people looked the same and all of them seemed to be saying "Bonjour! Bonjour!" The always happy Junie Astor smiled at them, but both Viviane Romance and Danielle Darrieux had tears in their eyes, in anticipation of this "great adventure."[43] At various stops along the way they had wonderful conversations with Nazi officials, who spoke "with heart, and with the echo of humanity." They met with Carl Froelich, who had been one of the producers of *La Nuit est à nous* (1930), which Heuzé identified incorrectly as the first French sound film. Thus the inextricable linkage between German and French film history, and the blurred boundaries between one and the other, just as the different European nations all seemed the same from the train that carried the emissaries of French cinema.[44] All of the travelers and their hosts spoke the "universal language" of cinema. "Is it German?" Heuzé asks. "Is it French?" These conversations produced a "veritable spiritual communion." Despite all the ways that cinema transcended national difference, though, Darrieux seemed nervous before presenting her most recent film in Germany, according to Heuzé the first French film shown there since the beginning of the war. Darrieux had no reason to be jittery, as the screening quickly resulted in a "miracle." Parisian audiences were known to be extraordinarily critical, but the German viewers "abandoned themselves" to the film, thereby giving evidence that, eventually, France and Germany will experience "a great reconciliation . . . under the sign of cinema."[45]

At the party after the screening of Darrieux's film, the visitors met with painters, sculptors, writers, musicians, and movie stars, and Heuzé marveled that he could also speak with German boxer Max Schmeling, with whom he discussed the famous French fighter from the 1920s, Georges Carpentier. Schmeling marked the low-culture end of this broad spectrum of elites brought together under the aegis of National Socialism. The next day, when the "little caravan" traveled to the UFA studio in Babelsberg, Brigitte Horney counted for the high-culture end.[46] As the group sat down for a meal with a

Figure 5.3   Danielle Darrieux, Brigitte Horney (center), and the journalist Pierre Heuzé meet at the UFA studio. Photo from *Ciné-Mondial*, May 8, 1942. Source: Bibliothèque nationale de France, Paris.

number of German stars and filmmakers, Heuzé singled out Horney for special attention. Horney sat next to him and the two engaged in a multilingual conversation. "We exchanged confidences half in French and half in German," Heuzé wrote, "and we each used a little Latin, when there were gaps in our vocabularies."[47] Their brief relationship across languages stands in for the ideological possibilities of rapprochement between France and Germany, one of the ongoing tropes of Heuzé's dispatches. That relationship might have had some difficulties—those moments when neither French nor German seemed to work—but remained possible nonetheless because of a shared educational upbringing, one that prepared them both to speak in Latin.

Horney here emerges as emblematic of one of the contradictions of National Socialism. At least since the beginning of World War II, Western politicians as well as scholars have written of the German rejection, during the period, of the "cosmopolitan character" of the ruling European aristocracy. No less a diplomat than George Kennan, who served in so many US State Department positions during the war, viewed that cosmopolitanism as one of the last hopes for restoring a democratic Europe.[48] As others have pointed out, though, the remnants of this "aristocratic cosmopolitanism" also created a formidable rightwing support of Nazism.[49] If it is possible to collapse these ideological issues onto the uses of celebrity, then we can see how Horney functioned, at least on this tour of French stars and filmmakers, as one of the signs of the benefits of the cosmopolitan, something she could share with the French stars and particularly with the writer Heuzé. Her ease in different languages, including her proficiency in Latin, showed the possibilities of a postwar confederation of European countries, controlled by Germany but respectful of all the old lines of class, education, and culture.

At least in the extant, German-controlled French sources, the period from the Parisian opening of *Les Mains libres* to her meeting with the representatives of the French film industry marks the height of Horney's celebrity and, apparently, of her usefulness to the cultural aims of National Socialism. In March 1942, just before that trip to Germany began, *Ciné-Mondial* ran a story on Horney and her new film, *La Tempête* (*Das Mädchen von Fanö*; 1941), and celebrated the naturalness of the actress's "face without makeup" and her "heart full of light." In discussing Horney, the author of the article, Pierre Leprohon (who would become one of postwar France's leading film historians), claimed that nothing was more important to her than the cinema: "If you asked Brigitte Horney what art meant to her, she undoubtedly would respond that it was her life."[50] Toward the end of 1942, Horney's film *Illusion* (1942) opened, and that, too, marked an occasion to extol the naturalness of her beauty and her art: "There is nothing artificial about her—from the lashes that fringe her eyes to the feelings expressed by her lips."[51] These two films opened in two of the most fashionable cinemas in Paris, the Marivaux in the second arrondissement in the case of *La Tempête* and the Biarritz on the Champs-Élysées for *Illusion*. Just as in the case of *Les Mains libres*, here Horney's apparently fully natural elegance and acting combined with the grandeur of Paris's best cinemas to produce a cinematic experience showcasing the various forms of Franco-Aryan truth and beauty.

Horney's next appearance, and her last during the war, would be in *Münchausen*. The ample French publicity about the film that is still available to us, however, both before the film's opening in Paris and after, rarely mentioned Horney, despite her role as Catherine the Great. Usually, the French press covered the production details of *Münchausen*: the color process used to film it, the exorbitant costs, the length of the film. Readers also learned about the historical importance of the film, which linked German cinema to the French tradition, as the great Georges Méliès himself had made a version of the baron's adventures when the cinema was still "hesitantly" coming

Figure 5.4   Brigitte Horney as Catherine the Great in *Les Aventures fantastiques du Baron Münchausen*.

to life.[52] Largely because of its rococo Technicolor fantasy, *Münchausen* has come down to us as ideologically neutral, and Horney has seemed an actress whose films, either narratively or stylistically, did little to advance the party line, unlike Zarah Leander, perhaps, or Kristina Söderbaum. Nevertheless, *Münchausen* served precisely ideological functions in the French collaborationist press, which typically claimed that the international success of the film proved to a skeptical Europe that Germany did not simply dwell on the war, and might "forget about combat now and then in order to pursue more interesting projects."[53]

After *Münchausen*, Horney disappeared from French movie screens and also, practically, from the French press. That disappearance tells us something about the vagaries of stardom in general, but also provides information about the status and development of national cinema during extraordinary periods dominated, in this case, by war and by occupation. It is altogether possible that, despite the best efforts of the French press and the splashy reopening of the Cinéma des Champs-Élysées, *Les Mains libres* failed to attract large crowds in Paris or elsewhere in France, and the same may have been true for Horney's next films, *La Tempête* and *Illusion*. In that case, then, Horney's career paralleled that of so many performers in France, Germany, the United States, and elsewhere whose stardom may have lasted only a few years. Indeed, while not discussing specific films, Evelyn Ehrlich has pointed out that attendance at the German films playing in France dropped considerably during the first years after the surrender.[54]

The political realities of the war and the approaching defeat of Germany also almost certainly affected Horney's status as a celebrity. In early June 1944, *Le Matin* announced that "*Au bout du monde* (*Am Ende der Welt*) with Brigitte Horney" had just finished shooting. In perhaps a sign of the changing cultural landscape from wartime to postwar France, the same issue of *Le Matin* announced the coming premiere of Albert Camus's first theatrical piece, *Le Malentendu*.[55] The following month, *Ciné-Mondial* ran a story on *Au bout du monde* with pictures of Horney, whom the magazine called "one of the most engaging and original stars of the German screen."[56] Just one month later, in August, the Allied forces liberated Paris and were pursuing the Germans throughout the rest of France. *Au bout du monde*, the last film Horney made under National Socialism and the occasion of the last references to her in the German-controlled French press, did not premiere in Germany until 1947.

The press coverage of the last year or two of the war, in *Le Matin* as well as *Ciné-Mondial* and other sources, and also the details of film production, indicate another possibility for the apparent decline of Horney's stardom, and another way of understanding European national cinemas from this period under the shifting pressures of war. The opening of *Les Mains libres* in 1940 certainly was one of the signs of the German takeover of French film in the first months after the surrender. In the long lead-up to the liberation of France in August 1944, however, the French cinema—and French film culture broadly—seems to have become much more French and much less German.

Colin Crisp has noted that, while the French film industry had been "paralyzed" after the surrender, film production by French companies increased over the course of the war, in part because the Germans realized they could not simply flood the French market with their own films and expect enthusiastic audience response. In the occupied north of France, for instance, filmmaking activity went from nothing in the aftermath of the surrender to forty-three films being produced in 1941, and more still in 1942 and 1943, and there were increases, as well, in the Vichy-controlled south.[57] Although it had no oversight over the films made by Continental, COIC controlled most of the rest of this production activity, and the extraordinarily complicated legal and economic relations between that organization, French production companies, and German authorities have been detailed most notably by Jean-Pierre Bertin-Maghit and Jean-Pierre Jeancolas, as have the frictions and co-operative activities between such wartime centers of French film production as Paris, Nice, and Marseille.[58] It is important to point out that increased activity by French production companies was not at all antithetical to the aims of German officials, who typically sought to exploit French cinema as a sign of Nazi benevolence and commitment to cultural uplift. Nevertheless, over the course of the war, French cinema came to be centered increasingly in France rather than in Germany, and under the purview of French rather than German production companies.

Precisely because of these complex relations, agreements, and coercive actions, and because of shifts in production and financing, the French cinema of the war has proven difficult for historians to label with any certainty. This cinema marks either a departure from anything that came before or after, or business as usual with some variations, or a combination of both.[59] As it had before the surrender and as it would after the fighting had ended, the French press emphasized performers. During the final stages of the war, publicity increasingly went to French rather than German stars. Ciné-Mondial, which had so championed Franco-German cooperation early in the war with its photos and stories about French and German stars meeting on stage or in studios, stressed French star photos and publicity in its final stages of publication. One of the weekly's last issues, from late May 1944, provided a cover photo of Odette Joyeux as well as an article about her, and photographs and news briefs about Georges Marchal, Maddy Breton, Annie Ducaux, Fernandel, Charles Trenet, and a back cover image of Liliane, while mentioning only one German star, Jenny Jugo.[60] In another issue from the same year, when the journal wondered what "today's anointed stars" would be doing if the cinema had never existed, the inquiring reporter asked only French performers: Raymond Bussières, Madeleine Sologne, Jean Marais, Gisèle Pascal, Michel Marsay, and Junie Astor.[61]

During the same period, and throughout 1943 and 1944, Le Matin ran photographs of movie stars and other celebrities every week, in a combined Saturday and Sunday issue, and with just a few exceptions they gave readers images of French actors and actresses. They ranged from some of the most famous of all French stars, for instance Pierre Fresnay and Arletty, to popular performers from the period, such as Gaby Morlay and Odette Joyeux, to those who seem to have had a brief celebrity but are more or less unknown to us now: Maurice Baquet, Michèle Alfa, Josseline Gaël. German stars rarely appeared. A random search through 1944 found only Olly Holzmann, who enjoyed a brief vogue as a leading lady in German movies toward the end of the war.[62] Just as it would have been unthinkable, a few months before that 1941 issue with its photographs of Horney, Leander, Rökk, and Werner, for *Le Matin* to publicize so many German stars, so too does it appear to have been impossible for the newspaper to let German performers dominate the movie page as the war wound down.

The temptation may be to read the declining presence of German films in French cinemas, as well as Horney's disappearance and that of other German stars from French film journalism, solely in terms of the changing fortunes of war and of the impending liberation of Paris and the rest of France. But the shift toward increased French production, and an emphasis on French stars, also came as part of Germany's desire to support French filmmaking as the sign of Nazi cultural broad-mindedness, and demonstrated Germany's practical understanding that French audiences preferred French movies and personalities. Of course, Continental, the German studio, produced many of these French films, while COIC, run by Vichy, controlled most of the others. Moreover the French stars themselves did not simply stand as the unproblematic antifascist binary opposites of Horney and other National Socialist performers. Several had gone on that 1942 tour of Germany that included a meeting with Horney. In another case, Arletty endured postwar imprisonment for her affair with a German officer.[63]

Instead, we can use the shift as a means of understanding some of the determining factors on stardom. During what we might refer to as "typical" periods, stardom can be bound up in so many things: audience preferences, genre cycles, the relative strength of certain film companies, and so on. There are also periods when more isolated causes may have an overdetermined effect on the creation of stardom. The transition to sound, which I described earlier, in the late 1920s and early 1930s probably hastened the demise of Emil Jannings as an international star, because his thick German accent made it difficult for him to work in Hollywood, while the new technology launched the film careers of Maurice Chevalier, Marlene Dietrich, and others.

In the case of Brigitte Horney in France and particularly in Paris, the exigencies of war and German control worked together to create her stardom. These efforts to make her a star may have failed, and in any event her French celebrity was short-lived. Much more significantly than Horney's films, German film policy during the war produced Horney's celebrity itself, and used it to facilitate ideological ends in ways that her films probably never did. Horney's stardom may well have been more significant as an aspect of the French press than the French cinema, and so her celebrity functioned broadly

Figure 5.5   The card game at the café in *Inglourious Basterds*.

in film culture and somewhat negligibly in the films themselves. Horney's importance came as a representative of German cosmopolitanism during that tour of Germany, as a sign of a rebuilt French film industry, albeit under German control, with her film reopening one of the most important cinemas in Paris, and as a symbol of the Nazi feminine ideal not just in her movies, but in the ways that she and her films were written about in newspapers and film magazines.

After the liberation of France and the subsequent German surrender, Horney became something of a lesser, local celebrity, appearing in films and television shows in Germany from the late 1940s to the mid-1980s. She died in Germany in 1988, and there are no obituaries in French sources, or at least none that are readily available. Only scant evidence of her stardom remains today, in various reconstructions of *Münchausen*, for example, and in one contemporary film that investigates the cinema of the Occupation as well as international film celebrity.

In Quentin Tarantino's *Inglourious Basterds* (2009), there is just a trace of Horney, and really only of her name. In a small bar in the Occupied Zone, not far from Paris, a German major, a British officer posing as a German captain, his two colleagues, and a German actress working for the Allies play a party game, before the typical Tarantino carnage that kills everyone in the bar except the actress. As the major explains it, "The object of the game is to write the name of a famous person on [a] card . . . Real or fictitious, doesn't matter." Cards are passed to the right, and the players moisten the cards without looking at them and stick them to their foreheads. They then ask questions about the names on their foreheads and guess what is written there.

The five names on the cards are indeed famous, both real and fictitious, and four come from the movies. There is the explorer Marco Polo; then Brigitte Helm, the actress known for her role as Maria in *Metropolis*, who appeared in many other German films; G. W. Pabst, the director who fled fascism for the United States and France but then returned to make films in Nazi Germany; and King Kong. The major, who initiated the game, writes "Brigitte Horney" on his card, and passes it to the British officer on his right.

The card is visible for only a few seconds in just a few shots, while the major asks a series of questions that allows him to guess that the card on his forehead says "King Kong." But in this movie that so lovingly, and violently, details the importance of cinema during the war, to the Germans, to the French, and to the Americans, the brief reference to Horney and her status as a "famous person" tell us a great deal about her celebrity. This scene, of course, takes place outside of any cinema and is devoid of images of any of those named on the cards. It is the major, the only Nazi at the table, who writes down Horney's name. That her name should appear on a card at all, along with such iconic figures as Pabst, Helm, and King Kong, indicates something of her importance to wartime cinema. The play between legibility and invisibility—her name is both easy to see and also hidden, offscreen or difficult to read—seems to work as a metaphor for the fleetingness of her stardom, and also for the way that it might linger in memory and in national culture.

Liberation Cinema, Postwar Cinema

1944–1949

In 1944 Parisians celebrated the Liberation of their city from Nazi control by going to the movies to watch Deanna Durbin in *Eve a commencé* (*It Started with Eve*; 1941). Brigitte Horney had appeared in Parisian cinemas at least until just before the August 1944 Liberation, as *Münchausen*, according to the last available listings, continued to play in multiple cinemas.[1] Just a few months later, though, this Nazi star of the Occupation gave way to the young woman with the grown-up lyric soprano when *Eve a commencé* was the first "new" American film to play in the recently freed French capital and Durbin became the first great symbol from Hollywood of liberated Paris. This shift from one actress to another, however, gets us just a little ahead of the story of the film culture of Paris after the Germans surrendered the city.

Even before the end of the Occupation, a group of filmmakers associated with the French Resistance—Jacques Becker, Jean Painlevé, and others—had been making plans for a new, postwar French cinema, one that would reject the fantasy excess of *Münchausen*, that sought to reclaim French cinematic sovereignty from Continental Films and German control, and that planned to reeducate an all too often collaborationist, or at least acquiescent, French population. To facilitate their project they formed the Comité de la libération de cinéma français, the CLCF, and in their first "bulletin official" from October 1944, the founders claimed, "We have an ideal: the cinema, and through cinema, France."[2] Nevertheless, despite the nationalist, heroic rhetoric, things still moved slowly in bringing the film culture of Paris, let alone the rest of France, back to anything resembling the vibrancy of the prewar period. For the first two months after the Liberation, film enthusiasts in Paris had only limited opportunities for going to the movies, as the cinemas in the city could show films only two nights a week, almost certainly because of ongoing shortages of electricity and other essentials for operation. As a sign of some progress, that same CLCF bulletin for October 1944 announced that cinemas now would be authorized to show movies five days a week, all except Tuesday and Thursday, and instead of just a single evening screening at 9:30, cinemas now were allowed to show one matinee on Saturday and two on Sunday.[3]

Assessing the last few weeks of the Nazi Occupation and the first few months following the Liberation remains extraordinarily difficult. The evidence is thin at best, and is often nonexistent. To the extent that information is available, it appears that, during the Occupation, there was no significant damage to the city's exhibition sites. In fact, despite the fighting in the streets of the last days before the Liberation, between Resistance forces and the Germans, Paris was left more physically intact than other European cities that had been centers of ground combat and aerial bombardment, and that had not been occupied by the enemy. While the cinema infrastructure remained intact, there were other obstacles to a fully functioning film culture. Immediately after the Liberation, for example, the hundreds of barricades that had gone up throughout the city during the street fighting were almost certainly still in place, inhibiting movement around Paris. There were also administrative standoffs between various groups seeking some control over the city, Gaullists and Communists, for instance, as well as smaller bureaucratic and military units, such as the Commission d'action militaire, or the Conseil national de la Résistance, or the Comité parisien de la Libération. All of this, along with crippling shortages of electricity and other necessities, no doubt slowed the development of Parisian post-Liberation cinema.[4]

The available primary materials tell us that by the end of July 1944, some forty-five cinemas remained open in Paris.[5] Just three weeks later, around the middle of August, with German control of the city weakening, that number had gone down to three: the Normandie on the Champs-Élysées in the eighth arrondissement and two other cinémas d'exclusivité in the eighteenth, the Palais-Rochechouart and the Gaumont-Palace.[6] During this period, these three cinemas seem mostly to have been screening documentaries, and within just a few days the Gaumont-Palace would be closed. Cabarets were closing as well, and so were theatres, and those of the latter that remained open often presented their shows only in the daytime ("jouant à la lumière du jour"), probably to save on the electricity that was in such short supply in the city.[7]

BULLETIN OFFICIEL DU C.L.C.F.

(Comité de Libération du Cinéma Français)

23 OCTOBRE 1944 — N° 1

CE QUE NOUS VOULONS

Il y a deux mois, les Allemands occupaient encore Paris. Aujourd'hui, sur tous les fronts, nos Alliés se battent. Les glorieux F.F.I. débarrassent la France des derniers îlots de résistance.

Pendant ce temps, nous, nous parlons de Cinéma. Pour le moment c'est notre humble tâche. Demain, s'il le faut, nous reprendrons les armes.

Pendant ce temps aussi, sur les Champs-Elysées, dans les bureaux des maisons de Production, l'inquiétude règne. On échange des propos malveillants, parce qu'on n'est pas renseigné. On essaie même d'amorcer des campagnes, pour le moment simplement verbales. Il y aura toujours des égoïstes, des êtres pour lesquels l'intérêt particulier prime l'intérêt général. Il y a aussi des faiblesses impardonnables.

Nous, rien ne pourra nous décourager. Nous avons un idéal : le Cinéma, et, à travers lui, la France. Nous irons jusqu'au bout.

Tant pis pour ceux que notre action gêne. Il n'y a pas, comme on voudrait le faire croire, de fossé entre ceux qui ont participé à la résistance et ceux qui n'y ont pas participé. Le problème est plus simple : d'un côté les Français, ceux qui veulent que la France reprenne sa place et sa souveraineté, ceux qui luttent avec le général de Gaulle ; de l'autre côté, ceux qui ont toujours vécu de compromissions, ceux qui se sont enfermés pendant quatre ans dans leurs coffres-forts pour ne pas entendre les cris de douleur de la France, ceux qui ont peur de l'inévitable révolution qui secoue le monde entier.

En ce moment, il n'est pas question de jouer ou de spéculer. Il faut lutter, comme nous l'avons fait pendant l'occupation, lutter surtout contre nous-mêmes, contre tout ce qui pourrait nous entraîner vers des solutions faciles mais négatives.

Le Cinéma Français existe. Il vit. Il l'a prouvé.

Il nous appartient de le faire grand. A nous de lui donner une impulsion telle que la France puisse avoir la place qu'elle mérite dans les échanges internationaux. Sachons voir loin, et ne menons pas une politique d'épiciers. N'ayons pas de complexe d'infériorité. Unissons-nous, ouvriers, auteurs, techniciens et producteurs dignes de ce nom. Unissons-nous, pour que fraternellement, dans le monde de demain, nous participions avec nos Alliés à l'épanouissement de cette culture et de cette liberté pour lesquelles tant d'êtres sont morts et meurent encore aujourd'hui.

Louis DAQUIN,
Secrétaire Général du C.L.C.F.

LE COMITÉ DE LIBÉRATION DU CINEMA FRANÇAIS est dirigé par un Comité présidé par Pierre BLANCHAR et qui comprend les membres suivants : BECKER, DAQUIN, metteurs en scène ; MAURETTE, MERE, assistants metteurs en scène ; Pierre BOST, auteur ; LEMARE, opérateur ; LAROCHE, assistant opérateur ; MERCANTON, chef monteur ; HOUDET, PROTAT, électriciens ; PIGNAULT, machiniste ; Germaine BERGER, COUTY, ouvriers ; DAGUEST, employé de laboratoire ; KNABEL, projectionniste ; O'CONNEL, SENAMAUD, JAY, SEGARD, DESFONTAINES, producteurs ; DANIAUX, directeur de laboratoire; DERVOUX, SCHOUBRENNER, distributeurs ; AUBIN, PHILIPPOT, exploitants ; BARDONNET, pour les Cinés-Clubs.

L'activité et les buts du C.L.C.F.

Le Comité de Libération du Cinéma Français réunit les représentants des différents Groupements de Résistance, qui ont existé dans le cinéma sous l'occupation allemande et qui étaient en contact bien avant la libération de Paris, à savoir : Le Front National, l'Union des Syndicats, les Milices Patriotiques, les Comités Populaires d'entreprises, les Employeurs Patriotes, le Mouvement des Prisonniers et Déportés, les Communistes du Cinéma, — tous ces groupements étant rattachés au COMITE NATIONAL DE LA RESISTANCE.

On connaît l'action clandestine menée pendant de longs mois par le Comité de Libération du Cinéma, action qui s'est exercée aussi bien dans la préparation de l'insurrection, que dans la propagande, au moyen de journaux clandestins, tels que « L'ECRAN FRANÇAIS » et « LA CINEMATOGRAPHIE FRANÇAISE », et de tracts envoyés à tous les membres de la profession.

Au premier jour de l'insurrection, le 19 août, le Comité de Libération s'installait au siège du C.O.I.C., 92, avenue des Champs-Elysées, et, en même temps qu'il se préoccupait de rassembler immédiatement les forces vives de la profession, il entreprenait la réalisation des Actualités ; de cette première réalisation du C.L.C.F. est né le Journal filmé de « FRANCE LIBRE », dont nous parlons plus loin.

* * *

Il n'est nullement question, pour le C.L.C.F., de prendre la gestion et la direction du cinéma ; nous voudrions qu'il n'y ait pas la moindre confusion sur ce point.

La Direction du Cinéma est assurée par Jean PAINLEVE, chargé de mission à ce titre par le Ministère de l'Information ; chaque branche de la profession aura auprès de lui des représentants qualifiés, désignés par les différents syndicats que groupe l'industrie cinématographique.

Toutefois le Comité de Libération n'entend nullement disparaître.

Il aura d'abord, pendant plusieurs semaines, à assumer le fonctionnement de la Commission d'Epuration. Lorsque cette Commission aura terminé son travail, il y aura un contrôle permanent à exercer : la cinquième colonne n'est pas morte, au contraire : ceux qui se sont terrés aujourd'hui essaieront de reparaître dans quelques mois. A ce moment, le Comité de Libération pourra et devra in-

Figure 6.1 The first issue of the *Bulletin official du CLCF*, October 23, 1944.
Source: Bibliothèque nationale de France, Paris.

On August 25, 1944, the Germans surrendered Paris. As difficult as it is to find information about the cinema there in the weeks just before the Liberation, it is, apparently, impossible for the five weeks that followed. By October 1, at least five cinemas had opened: once again the Gaumont-Palace and the Normandie, but also the Savoie in the eleventh arrondissement, the Ciné-Batignolles in the seventeenth, and the Paramount in the ninth. Audiences did not have much choice, however, about what they saw. All of those cinemas showed the same film, *France libre*, a compilation of actuality footage made by the CLCF that documented the Liberation of Paris.[8]

At least seven cinemas had opened by October 15, and audiences had by then a limited range of films from which to choose. The 1939 World War I melodrama starring Junie Astor and Léon Mathot, *Deuxième bureau contre kommandantur*—which, as I mentioned earlier, had been released initially just a few days before the 1940 French surrender and so probably never had played widely in France because of its anti-German sentiment—showed at two cinemas, the Aubert-Palace and the Club des Vedettes, both in the ninth arrondissement. At two cinemas just a couple of blocks apart on the boulevard des Italiens in the second arrondissement, a new French film, *Coup de tête* (1944), premiered at the Marivaux, and Jean Delannoy's *Pontcarral, colonel d'empire*, from 1942, was in reissue at the Impérial. Just two weeks after *France libre* blanketed the city, the only real reminder of the war played at the Normandie, a documentary that became something of a hit in Paris, *Un jour de guerre en URSS*, a 1941 Soviet film detailing a single day of the war.[9]

Eve a commencé is the film that provides the most compelling information about post-Liberation film distribution in Paris, and also exposes the limits to what we might find out, at least given the evidence available to us. Durbin's film, the first Hollywood movie in Paris since 1940, also played in two of those seven cinemas, just like *Deuxième bureau contre kommandantur*: in the second arrondissement at the Rex, one of the largest cinemas in Paris and that, as a soldatenkino, had been reserved for members of the German military during the Occupation, and also at the Avenue cinema in the eighth arrondissement.[10] Why was it Durbin's film that had this particular significance in Parisian film history, and how had it gotten to Paris in the first place?

Film historians have been aware for a long time of Durbin's incredible celebrity in the United States and Great Britain, especially among teenage girls and young women, the fans who were around the same age as the actress when she was at the peak of her popularity in the late 1930s and early 1940s.[11] At the same time, Durbin was also extremely popular in France and France's colonies. In October 1937, the film journal *Ciné France* ran a photo of Durbin across half of its front page, with the caption "new star, new singer, and the new ingenue who triumphs" in *Deanna et ses boys* (*One Hundred Men and a Girl*; 1937). That same year, the daily newspaper *Le Petit Parisien* also put a photo of Durbin on its front page, and in fact ran a double column practically down the length of the page to advertise a long story about the performer the newspaper called "the great new star from the Hollywood sky." A year later, again in *Ciné France*, an article compared the teenager to the great new French star Michèle Morgan, herself only eighteen, and predicted a global trend toward ever younger actresses. That article referred to Durbin in a mixture of French and English as "la child-woman," who "knew how to cry and laugh through her tears, and who was one of the most gracious stars" of cinema. French radio played Durbin's recordings throughout the country, and her celebrity reached the colonies and the French expatriate community, with the Saigon newspaper *Le Nouvelliste d'Indochine*, for example, profiling her in a January 1938 column on "Stars from Hollywood."[12]

Still, there were other Hollywood stars who were just as famous, if not even more well known, and whose films made during the Occupation might seem even more appropriate for breaking the embargo on Hollywood movies that had been imposed by the Nazis. The historical importance of Durbin's film almost certainly had more to do with the vagaries of international film distribution during wartime than with the preferences of Parisian audiences. Of course, the Nazis had banned American films in the Occupied Zone, including Paris, in 1940, and then in southern France, in Vichy, in 1942, bans that would stay in effect until the Allies drove the Germans out of France in the summer and fall of 1944. French North Africa, however, where there seems never to have been a significant Nazi embargo on American films, had been liberated by early 1943, and movies from Hollywood played steadily in major urban areas like Algiers very shortly after that. By August 1944, *Eve a commencé* was showing there, at the Mondial cinema and then at the Royal.[13]

It would make things convenient to be able to say that Durbin's film simply moved from Algiers to Paris when cinemas began to open after the Liberation, but following that run at the Royal, *Eve a commencé* came back to Algiers, playing at the Caméo cinema at precisely the same time as it showed in Paris, in mid-October 1944.[14] Those two prints *of Eve* showing in Paris, along with the other one at the Caméo in Algiers, probably indicate that there were several copies of the film in North Africa when Paris was liberated, making it easy to move to the French capital while also staying in colonial cinemas.

Because of the scarcity of exhibition information, it remains difficult to know if this was the standard procedure for the period just after the Liberation, with films going to major North African cities and then to Paris, reversing the usual route. There were films, though, that ran truer to prewar form. Another of the first America films to play in Paris after the Liberation, *Un américain pur sang* (*Joe Smith, American*; 1942) opened there about the same time as Durbin's film did, in October 1944, and then premiered in Algiers at the Bijou about six weeks later.[15] So it seems possible that American film companies established their Paris distribution offices, or at least their methods for getting films into Paris, within just a few weeks of the Liberation.

Opening as it did a new era in Parisian film culture, *Eve a commencé* generated a great deal of excitement. *Combat* headlined its movie page "Les Premiers films étrangers à Paris" ("The First Foreign Films in Paris"), and then went on to discuss Durbin's film and also *Un américain pur sang* (which as far as I can tell had not yet premiered). The reopening of Parisian cinemas had brought huge crowds, so many that exhibitors "thought they were dreaming." Then *Combat*, founded as a Resistance newspaper and hardly known for its sentiment, itself went on dreamily about Durbin, viewing her as the perfect symbol of a new beginning but also of what was lost during the Occupation. This wonderful reopening of cinemas "was also cruel for us," because "it reminded us how we had aged." *Combat* continued that when Parisians had last seen Durbin (this was probably in *First Love*, from 1939, or *That Certain Age*, from 1938), she was "just a little girl," and now "we find her almost a woman."[16] This aging appears to be less a reference to films that were made, really, only a couple of years apart, but rather to not having seen Durbin at all, or any American films, for the four years of the Occupation.

Eve a commencé seems to have been reviewed in every Parisian newspaper of every political persuasion: *Temps présent, Figaro, Jeunesse, Carerefour, Libération, Ce soir, Front National, Les Lettres françaises, L'Humanité, Populaire,* and others.[17] As well, some of the most distinguished critics in Paris weighed in on the film. Roger Leenhardt, who would begin a significant career as a filmmaker in a few years, praised Durbin in *Les Lettres françaises*, but then acknowledged that the film could not stand up against the great American prewar comedies directed by Frank Capra, *L'Extravagant Monsieur Deeds* (*Mr. Deeds Goes to Town*; 1936) and *Monsieur Smith au Sénat* (*Mr. Smith Goes to Washington*; 1939). The journalist Jeander, who as we have seen lectured on film history in Nazi ciné-clubs in Paris during the war, called the film "charmante" in *Libération*, which had begun in 1941 as a newspaper of the Resistance. Paul Barbellion, who worked as Robert Bresson's assistant director on *Les Dames du Bois du Boulogne* (1945), also wrote about *Eve a commencé*, and so, too, did André Bazin, for *Le Parisien libéré*, which had begun publication only two months before (Bazin would remain a critic there until his death in 1958).[18]

Bazin used the occasion of the film—after first calling attention to Durbin's great beauty—to comment on the state of American cinema, and comedy in particular. For Bazin, the film proved how Hollywood comedies had become more and more standardized, and in such a way that it was impossible to be bored while watching them. Nevertheless, the conditions of the screening also needed to be standardized. As proof, Bazin moved to a recent viewing at the Madeleine cinema in the eighth arrondissement of a revival of Ernst Lubitsch's great 1938 comedy, *La Huitième femme de Barbe-Bleue* (*Bluebeard's Eighth Wife*). That experience was ruined for Bazin because the film had been dubbed. He wrote that he didn't understand a word of English, but nevertheless subtitles would allow any viewer's imagination to become perfectly oriented to the story, and that one would soon forget that the film was in a foreign language.[19]

Eve a commencé may seem like a negligible film to us now. At the time of the Liberation, however, after years of waiting for American films, which themselves would signal the end of German control of Paris, Durbin's movie was anything but inconsequential. *Eve a commencé* certainly tells us something of interest about international distribution during the period, but also shows how little we can actually know, and how difficult it is to assess how films came not only to conventional cinemas just after the Liberation and after the end of the war, but also to ciné-clubs and other sites. In this case, we are left, then, simply with Deanna Durbin, "toujours aussi jolie" ("always so pretty") according to Bazin,[20] and the extraordinary impact that she had on Parisian audiences in October 1944, an impact that could only lessen as more cinemas opened and more American films came to the city.

By early November, in fact, around thirty cinemas showed films, including the posh Biarritz in the eighth arrondissement (with the Paris premiere of Julien Duvivier's 1942 Hollywood film, *Six destins* [*Tales of Manhattan*]) and also, in the second arrondissement, the Ciné-Opéra, one of three cinemas in the city showing the 1941 Alfred Hitchcock film *M. et Mme Smith* (*Mr. and Mrs. Smith*), which was playing in Paris for the first time. As typically had been the case in prewar Paris, there were also important reprises: *L'Extravagant Monsieur Deeds* at the Cinéma des Champs-Élysées, and perhaps most significantly given the recent Liberation, Jean Renoir's celebration of the French Revolution, *La Marseillaise* (1938), at the Moulin Rouge in the eighteenth arrondissement.[21]

By the end of 1944 more than fifty cinemas had reopened in Paris. They showed new French films (Jean Delannoy's *Le Bossu* [1944] at the Vivienne in the second arrondissement), Russian movies (*L'Arc-en-Ciel* [1944] at the Max Linder in the ninth), a range of American films from before the war (*Âmes à la mer* [*Souls at Sea*; 1937], at the Gaité-Clichy in the seventeenth), and Hollywood films that had been kept out of Paris because of the Occupation (John Stahl's comedy *Mme et son clochard* [*Our Wife*; 1941], at the Ermitage in the eighth). One such Hollywood film playing at the time stood out as perhaps the most eagerly anticipated movie event of the immediate post-Liberation period, René Clair's *Ma femme est une sorcière* (*I Married a Witch*), from 1942, showing at both the Biarritz in the eighth and the Caméo in the ninth.[22] The popular press at the time typically understood Clair as the father of modern French cinema, and a Clair film that Parisians had to wait more than two years to see caused even greater excitement than a new film by the master.

Along with the much-anticipated opening of Clair's film, the event that marked the return of Parisian film culture was certainly the Grande Quinzaine du cinéma français (the Great Fortnight of French Cinema). We tend to think of the 1946 Cannes Film Festival, held for the first time after the war put the 1939 planned opening on hold, as the sign that French cinema had regained its prominence. As important as that may have been on an international scale, on a more local level the Grande Quinzaine marked Paris once again as a film capital. For two weeks beginning on December 4, the Normandie cinema on the Champs-Élysées, always one of the most important exhibition sites in Paris, screened fourteen "grandes productions" made between 1940 and 1944.[23] These films played in addition to the newly released movie showing exclusively at the Normandie throughout December, the Annie Ducaux vehicle *Florence est folle* (1944). A film schedule for the Quinzaine seems no longer to exist, but it is safe to assume that nothing shown there would have been made by Continental, the German studio that produced so many French-language films during the war. Available sources provide just one film in the festival, Jacques Becker's rural melodrama *Goupi mains rouges*, from 1943 celebrated for its critique of the Vichy regime's idealization of peasants. Les Films Minerva, a company that began in the 1930s, well before the war and so without any direct links to the Occupation, produced Becker's entry in the Quinzaine.[24]

We can find other, less elevated signs of the film culture of Paris having returned to something resembling its pre-Occupation place, as well as indications of the demilitarization of the city in general. Also in December, just as the Quinzaine got underway at the Normandie, the major cinema chains in

Paris announced an end to the post-Liberation policy of giving French soldiers discounted admissions to Saturday and Sunday screenings.[25]

Postwar

A little less than a year later and just a few months after the war had ended, things had changed considerably. The evidence is still scant for the modern researcher, but a new movie weekly, *Cinévie*, began publication in October 1945 and typically ran complete listings for Paris as well as articles that give us a sense of film culture in the city in the immediate postwar period. At the time, there were around 275 cinemas in Paris. About forty of them would be considered cinémas d'exclusivité, the most important cinemas in the city and mostly in the "best" locations, in the eighth arrondissement, for instance, on and around the avenue des Champs-Élysées, or on the boulevard des Italiens in the second and ninth arrondissements. Some, like the Gaumont-Palace in the less chic eighteenth arrondissement, were simply among the very largest cinemas. These locations showed the newest films and, with foreign movies, in subtitled rather than dubbed prints just as they had before the war. The other sites were those cinémas des quartiers, many still in the better parts of Paris but others that were farther away from the center and from the more affluent districts. These locations tended to show films only after they had shown *en exclusivité* for at least a week, and then frequently showed dubbed versions of foreign films. The distinctions between these two brands of exhibition sites were not, however, always absolute.

Cinévie listed not only the addresses, metro stops, and feature films at cinemas in the city, but also which days they would be open for business. Paris still faced a shortage of electricity in fall 1945, the "régime des restrictions d'électricité" according to *Cinévie*, and this utility problem was the great equalizer among cinemas.[26] Most of them only showed movies on Sundays, or perhaps also on Saturdays, and practically all of them were only open for one afternoon screening and one in the evening, usually at 8:00 or 8:30, a restriction apparently mandated by law. Only a few cinemas ran films every day, and none of them was a cinéma d'exclusivité. In the fourth arrondissement, the Rivoli and the Saint-Paul stayed open "tous les jours," as did the Fantasio in the eighteenth arrondissement and just a very few others, while the Alésia-Palace in the fourteenth added a third evening, Thursday, to its Saturday and Sunday offerings. By the end of November 1945, *Cinévie* announced that because electricity was now in somewhat better supply, cinemas would be allowed to schedule one or two extra screenings, depending on the length of the program, between 2:00 p.m. and 6:00 p.m.[27]

A year later, at the end of 1946, some cinemas started their programs as early as 10:00 in the morning and some had final screenings after midnight. During the final week of the year, for example, the Marignan on the Champs-Élysées had its last screening of Marcel Carné's *Les Portes de la nuit* (1946) at 12:30 in the morning. Nevertheless, most cinemas still were only open on weekends. The Delambra cinema, the Denfert, and the Univers-Palace, all in the fourteenth arrondissement, now were open every day, as was the Nouveau-Théâtre in the fifteenth, all of these neighborhood cinemas more or less on the periphery, geographically and otherwise, of Parisian film culture. Some cinemas had schedules that make no sense to us now, unless they were intended to decrease demand on electricity in certain areas. In the nineteenth arrondissement that same week in 1946, the Belleville held screenings on Saturday, Monday, and Thursday, while the Éden, also in the nineteenth, opened on Monday, Wednesday, and Thursday, and the Renaissance in the same neighborhood showed movies on Monday, Tuesday, Thursday, and Saturday.[28]

If we return to the end of October 1945, twenty-six films were playing in the thirty-five exclusive cinemas that reported their listings to Cinévie. There were American films made during the war that now appeared in Paris for the first time, such as Alfred Hitchcock's *L'Ombre du doute* (*Shadow of a Doubt*; 1943) at the Triomphe cinema at 92 avenue des Champs-Élysées, and *Prisonniers de Satan* (*The Purple Heart*; 1944), with Dana Andrews, at the Biarritz just across the street. Parisians might also see new French films like *La Route du bagne* (1945), with the great star Viviane Romance, or *La Cage aux rossignols* (1945) featuring Noël-Noël. These major cinemas did not just show new films, however, and there were also some reprises of movies with stars who had large followings in Paris. The most notable that week was *Drôle de drame* (1937), directed by Marcel Carné and featuring two iconic performers, Louis Jouvet and Michel Simon. Throughout the rest of Paris, in the neighborhoods, around 120 films were playing, and most of them were either American or French. Many of these were reprises of older movies, and some of them were films that had recently been showing en exclusivité. As might be expected, given his consistent status as one of the most significant of all French directors, René Clair was well represented, with films in the best cinemas as well as the neighborhoods during this period, while other movies demonstrated the typical range in Parisian film culture, from low- to highbrow.[29]

Firmly in the former category, various parts of the twelve-episode, low-budget Republic Pictures serial *Les Vautours de la jungle* (*Hawk of the Wilderness*; 1938) played throughout Paris at the end of 1945, featured at cinemas, at various times, in the ninth, tenth, eleventh, and thirteenth arrondissements, and so too did Universal's African adventure serial, *Richard le Téméraire* (*Tim Tyler's Luck*; 1937). At the other end of the scale, however, Robert Bresson's *Les Dames du Bois du Boulogne* had just opened in Paris at two cinémas d'exclusivité, the Ermitage on the Champs-Élysées and the Rex on the boulevard Poissonière. This was only the director's second feature-length film and perhaps the most accessible of all his works, but it is a Bresson film nevertheless, and we might not think of it today as a possible commercial hit. Yet *Les Dames* played exclusively throughout the late summer and early fall of 1945, and then moved immediately and systematically to cinemas in the neighborhoods. During the week of October 31, and after having left its exclusive engagements, the film showed in seven cinemas, including one of the larger locations in the city, the elegant, Egyptian-style Louxor-Pathé in the tenth arrondissement, and also two cinemas each in the sixteenth and seventeenth arrondissements. A week later, *Les Dames* had left the Louxor, and its run had contracted to three cinemas, all of them different from the week before. Showing, perhaps, the logic of Parisian distribution, Bresson's film moved that week from one edge of the eighteenth arrondissement to the other, from the Sélect cinema on the avenue du Clichy on the western edge to the Capitole on the rue de la Chappelle on the eastern border. The following week, the film had crossed the eighteenth arrondissement again and gone back to the western side at the Métropole cinema, and opened at four cinemas in the seventeenth and two in the sixteenth, as well as one in the third.[30]

Les Dames du Bois du Boulogne has come down to us as a significant critical and commercial flop, mostly because of François Truffaut's 1975 retrospective on the movie's reception, when the filmmaker wrote that the public came to see *Les Dames* only to smirk, and that the producer "was ruined."[31] This indeed may have been the case.[32] The evidence in *Cinévie*, though, seems to indicate that Bresson's film found an audience just after the end of the war, in Paris if not the rest of France, and this apparent success perhaps indicates the possibility for a film with significant artistic pretensions having a place in the everyday film culture of the city. There also may have been a broader economic incentive to the way *Les Dames* made its way through Paris, as it seems to have been part of a distribution package of films with high aspirations, paired with *Sérénade*, a 1940 Franz Schubert biopic starring Louis Jouvet and the great German actress Lilian Harvey, who had left Germany and her career as a Nazi star just the year before. At each of the cinemas where *Les Dames* had played in the week of October 31, *Sérénade* appeared the following week. The films had been made by different, and very small, production companies, but their apparent combination here does seem to hint at the project of

Figure 6.2   The faux-Egyptian Louxor cinema in the tenth arrondissement, where
Les Dames du Bois du Boulogne played in 1945, as it looks today. Photograph by author.

larger distribution firms handling films like these, renting them in packages to neighborhood cinemas.

Other films show the differences between exclusive showings and those in the neighborhoods, and also that these locations were not in absolute opposition one to the other. Charles Chaplin's *Dictateur* (*The Great Dictator*; 1941) had opened in Paris in the spring of 1945, and by the fall of that year was still playing en exclusivité at the Avenue cinema in the eighth arrondissement, although it is unclear whether this was a continuation of an extended opening run or a return engagement. At the same time, however, the film also played at the Royal-Haussmann in the ninth arrondissement, and over the next few weeks the neighborhood engagements would extend to other arrondissements. As a result, Parisians might choose the most convenient neighborhood to see the film that counted as one of the great cultural events in the city that year. But they could also make an aesthetic and technological choice. At the Avenue, *Dictateur* played in *version originale*, that is, subtitled, but throughout the rest of Paris, the movie could only be seen *doublé*, or dubbed.[33]

As I have mentioned, dubbed films were typically the case in the neighborhoods, but not always. That same week, just a short metro ride away from the Royal-Haussmann and still in the ninth arrondissement, audiences could have seen Humphrey Bogart and the Dead End Kids dubbed into French in *L'École du crime* (*Crime School*; 1938) at the Delta cinema, or French actors speaking for Conrad Veidt and Valerie Hobson in Michael Powell's *Espionne à bord* (*Blackout*; 1940) at the Cinécran. But just as close by and in the same arrondissement, another British film, *Sublime Sacrifice* (*Pastor Hall*; 1940), as well as *Gung Ho* (1943), with Randolph Scott, played with French subtitles.[34]

Throughout this period, in exclusivity and in the neighborhoods, subtitled and dubbed, there were René Clair films. *Cinévie* wrote about the French master throughout the last few months of 1945, calling him "much more than a well-known director," and indeed "a great Frenchman," in an article with a title that seemed to sum up a nation's gratitude: "Merci, Monsieur René Clair."[35] A few months after this, in March 1946, the magazine ran an article assuring readers that, in Clair's own words, "I count on coming back to France" after having spent most of the war in Hollywood.[36] At the end of the year, *Cinévie* wrote about his next film, Clair's first French film since before the war, which would unite the great director with the great French star, Maurice Chevalier, in *Le Silence est d'or* (1947). Finally, Clair could return from Hollywood and make films back at home.[37]

In early October 1945, two Clair films played at exclusive cinemas.[38] Parisians could go to the Marbeuf cinema in the eighth arrondissement to watch *C'est arrivé demain* (*It Happened Tomorrow*), a 1944 Hollywood film that naturally had not played during the Occupation. They could also go to the Normandie cinema, one of the most prestigious in Paris, on the Champs-Élysées to see Clair's 1935 British film, *Fantôme à vendre*, which had shown extensively in Paris on its initial release a decade earlier, had been reprised a number of times, and had been a staple of ciné-club screenings. For any Clair film, apparently, there was always an audience, even one that may have seen the movie a number of times.

Those two films ran at the Marbeuf and the Normandie for about a month, and *Fantôme* would return in early 1946, this time at the Panthéon cinema in the fifth arrondissement.[39] During this time, another Clair film, *Ma femme est une sorcière*, which as we have seen had opened in Paris to much fanfare in 1944, played throughout the neighborhoods (at four cinemas, for example, in mid-November 1945), and also back en exclusivité at the Agriculteurs cinema in the ninth arrondissement.[40] In the immediate postwar period, it seems as if the surest sign of a return to "normal," pre-Occupation Parisian film culture was the omnipresence of Clair throughout the city.

There were other returns to Paris practically as triumphant as Clair's. At least since the mid-1930s, Jean Gabin's movies, either new or reprised, had been a constant of Parisian film culture. When it became apparent that the great star would not leave Hollywood and return to France during the war, the Nazis banned his films. After *Remorques* in 1941, Gabin did not make another French film until *Martin Roumagnac* (1946). Following the war, however, his films once again played throughout Paris. A quick and random look through the *Cinévie* listings seems always to show an available Gabin film. In October 1945, *Pépé le Moko*, with Gabin in perhaps his most iconic role, began making its way through Paris, first in the fifth arrondissement and then in the sixteenth.[41] In early January 1946, *Pepé le Moko* played once again, at the Cardinet in the seventeenth, and so too did *Remorques*, in the tenth.[42] The next month, *Les Bas-Fonds* (1936), which Gabin made with Jean Renoir, played at the Sebastopol-Ciné in the second, and a year later, while *Martin Roumagnac* played exclusively at the Normandie cinema on the Champs-Élysées and the Olympia on the boulevard des Capucines, *La Bête humaine* (1938), another collaboration with Renoir, showed at the Royal-Haussmann in the ninth arrondissement.[43] There also would be showings of *Quai des brumes*, the 1938 film that Gabin made with Marcel Carné, and which turns up very early in the available *Cinévie* listings, at the end of October 1945 at the Paris-Ciné in the tenth arrondissement.[44]

From its original release, *Quai des brumes* has come down to us as among the great star turns in French film history, introducing audiences to Michèle Morgan, who would become one of the legendary figures in European cinema. Indeed, *Quai des brumes*, with Morgan holding her own against the formidable Gabin, did indeed make an extraordinary impact on Parisians in the summer and fall of 1938 at least until the beginning of 1939, when the film played continuously in Paris at several of the city's best cinemas.[45] Even before this, the actress had begun to impress audiences. She made a few films before *Quai des brumes*, including, when she was only seventeen, a costarring role opposite another monumental French actor, Raimu, in *Gribouille* from 1937. Morgan worked constantly during this period, and made two more films with Gabin, *Le Récif de corail* (1939) as well as *Remorques*.

Morgan then left France for Hollywood until the end of World War II, a self-imposed exile that, however professionally expedient it may have seemed at the time, was also an act of resistance to the Nazi Occupation of Paris and the rest of the country. Indeed, the Nazis understood that getting Morgan back was a major part of their project of making French and Parisian culture seem just as it was before the war began. When Morgan refused to return, the Germans threatened the safety of her family, who had stayed in France, threats that came to the attention of the United States Department of State.[46] Because Morgan still would not come back, the Nazis seem to have given up their efforts to force her return and banned her films in France, just as they did with Gabin's. After an up-and-down career in Hollywood, Morgan came back to France, but her first new French film, *Symphonie pastorale*, would not appear until 1946.

Well before that, however, *Cinévie* heralded her return from the United States as one of the surest signs that the war really had ended. Throughout the last few months of 1945 and the beginning of 1946, the magazine focused on stars who now could come back to France. When Simone Simon returned to France and then to the capital, in December 1945, *Cinévie* announced that "Paris was Simone Simon's Christmas gift." Later that month, the magazine began a series bylined by Simon herself about her stay in the United States, "America in Five Episodes."[47] In the case of Sessue Hayakawa, who had been a great celebrity in Paris since the sensation of *Forfaiture* (*The Cheat*; 1915), it was not so much his own return to France as it was the return of the actor's work to Parisian cinemas. Hayakawa had made a few French films that had appeared after the surrender to Germany, but perhaps had played only sporadically, because according to *Cinévie* in 1946, it had been "six years since we have seen" the great star, and now, finally, the public would get to watch him in his latest French movie, *Le Cabaret du grand large* (1946).[48]

Always and above all others, there was Morgan. In January 1946, the magazine began the multipart series "Five Years in America, Told by Michèle Morgan," which included stories about her love life and her work.[49] When *Cinévie* reported that "A New Michèle Morgan Was Born ... in a Hair Salon," the magazine ran sketches of four hairstyles that the star had rejected, and then a photograph of the fifth one, "the best."[50] In April, Morgan appeared on the cover of *Cinévie* with her costar Pierre Blanchar, in a publicity photo from the long-awaited *Symphonie pastoral*.[51] Certainly there were other stars who were celebrated in *Cinévie*, stars who had stayed in Paris during the Occupation: Edwige Feuillère, for instance, as well as perhaps the greatest of all French actresses at the time, Danielle Darrieux, whose third marriage required a cover photo and a multipage spread of photographs and stories.[52] For the French film culture of the immediate postwar period, however, and at least in the one movie magazine that is available to us today, it is the triumphant return of exiled French stars, and especially Morgan and Gabin, that signified the end of the war and of German control.

UNE NOUVELLE MORGAN EST NÉE...

Les nattes ont été éliminées. Elles faisaient ressembler Michèle à une héroïne de film russe.

Quoique moins apprêtée, la coiffure reste dure et pour cette raison ne sera pas retenue.

Nattes ou diadème, le style « vamp » demeure et convient peu à la jeune aveugle du film.

Ici perce une pointe de jeunesse, mais les ondulations prouvent trop que la coiffeur est proche.

La 5e esquisse est la meilleure. Le nœud de velours ajoute la note jeune qui manquait.

...dans un salon de coiffure

Des cinq croquis qu'a faits le dessinateur, un seulement a été jugé bon. Ce n'est pas à la légère qu'aura été fixé le nouveau type de coiffure de Michèle.

Midi. A deux pas de la Concorde, chez un des coiffeurs les plus réputés de Paris, Michèle Morgan, anxieuse, attend de savoir comment sera la coiffure qu'elle portera dans La Symphonie Pastorale. Depuis deux jours, un dessinateur crée des coiffures pour elle. Déjà, elle a surpris plusieurs croquis où son aspect « femme fatale » ne lui dit rien qui vaille, et elle tremble à l'idée que les Français, eux aussi, après les Américains, vont vouloir la changer. Mais voici qui est plus à son goût ; sous le crayon du dessinateur, elle aperçoit un visage triangulaire, encadré de cheveux flous et surmonté d'un nœud. L'affaire est donc réglée et Michèle, avec un soupir de soulagement, abandonne sa chevelure au soin de l'homme de l'Art.

DES ROBES 100 % GOUT FRANÇAIS

Ce ne sont pas ses compatriotes, mais les Suisses, qui pourront juger les premiers de sa transformation. Le soir même, à 22 h. 30, elle prend un train qui l'emmènera à Genève où, le lendemain, en soirée, elle prête son concours à un gala pour lequel on lui a demandé de vendre et de dédicacer ses photos. Les courses qui lui restent à faire avant l'heure du départ sont innombrables. Pour mettre en valeur ses yeux turquoise, elle a jeté son dévolu sur deux robes en velours noir pailletées d'or. L'une d'elles, qui est longue et très habillée, sera as « tenue de gala ». Pour elle aussi, on a créé un modèle chaud et très amusant, avec lequel elle pourra affronter le voyage et les neiges helvétiques. C'est un manteau de velours noir, ...

blanche et qui s'agrémente d'un bonnet et de gants assortis.

Si l'Amérique l'a conquise sous bien des rapports, elle ne cache tout de même pas sa joie de porter à nouveau tous ces modèles de goût français, à l'exception peut-être d'un drôle de couvre-chef. Elle emporte aussi tout un assortiment de parfums. Si son rôle d'aveugle de la Symphonie Pastorale va, pendant la durée du film, la priver de bien des plaisirs visuels, du moins ceux de l'odorat lui resteront-ils. Elle a passé sa dernière journée parisienne à faire des achats. Son premier jour de travail ressemble à un premier jour de vacances.

RÉVEIL EN SUISSE

C'est donc trois grosses valises qui quittent avec elle le domicile familial. Dans une quinzaine, trois semaines au plus, Michèle sera de retour. Les extérieurs la feront rester en Suisse, juste le temps d'un voyage d'agrément. Avant de retrouver l'ambiance du studio de Neuilly, où Delannoy continuera son film, elle aura visité le canton de Vaud, séjourné et tourné au fameux château d'Oex et fait des sports d'hiver. Si, il y a quelques années La Piste du Nord l'a initiée aux joies de la neige, en Amérique, la débutante est devenue une sportive émérite. Le train va partir. Michèle Morgan, qu'aucun membre de sa famille n'accompagne, retrouve à la gare la productrice du film, avec qui elle va voyager. Déjà, elle s'installe, comme si le trajet devait durer longtemps, ouvre ses valises, sort des photos. En dernière en France, c'est en Suisse, demain, qu'elle se réveillera.

NOËL COWARD quitte l'écran ... « BRIEF ENCOUNTER »
mais on verra son dernier film...

(de notre correspondant à Londres)

Noël Coward va se retirer pour un an du monde théâtral et cinématographique. Il va partir pour sa propriété de Douvres-Cottage, et écrira une suite d'anecdotes qui seront la suite de « Présent indicatif » qui était une sorte d'autobiographie qui s'arrêtait avant 1939.

Et peut-être retrouvera-t-on des anecdotes sur son passage dans les théâtres aux armées, dont il fut un des animateurs. Connaissant fort bien notre langue, il a chanté des chansons d'Edith Piaf et dit des vers d'Anna de Noailles.

Pourtant si Noël Coward ne travaille plus pour le cinéma, nous verrons sa dernière production « Brief Encounter », que la critique anglaise a qualifiée de meilleur des films de l'année. C'est le thème de « Voyage sans espoir ». On y retrouve cette femme partagée entre deux amours. Celui du mari qui lui est attaché depuis longtemps et celui de l'homme qu'au cours d'une brève rencontre elle aime. Tout ceci enveloppé dans l'atmosphère d'une gare londonienne et de ses abords.

Les seuls extérieurs du film de Noël Coward sont cette scène sur la Tamise.

Notre correspondant est allé rendre visite à Noël Coward qui lui confie ses intentions.

Figure 6.3 "A New Michèle Morgan Was Born . . . in a Hair Salon," *Cinévie*, January 23, 1946. Source: Bibliothèque nationale de France, Paris.

French authority over its own cinema might be marked in other ways. The cinemas themselves could indicate a national patrimony interrupted by the Germans but certainly not ended by the Occupation. In March 1946, *Cinévie* announced a new Parisian cinema in the ninth arrondissement, this one called the Méliès in honor of one of the first and certainly one of the greatest French filmmakers, Georges Méliès, whose films almost half a century before had reached a global audience.[53] The location itself seemed predetermined for a cinema that honored the great magician of the movies, the man who made *Le Voyage dans la lune* (1902) and so many other films full of astonishing sleights of hand. The Théâtre Robert-Houdin, founded by the great magician Houdin himself, and which Méliès had owned for a few years, had been on that site from the late nineteenth century until its demolition in the 1920s. The film that inaugurated the new cinema was American rather than French, but seems to have been perfectly suited to the occasion, *Le Magicien d'Oz* (*The Wizard of Oz*; 1939). In this case, then, the location of film viewing rather than the film itself, and the history of the exhibition site, asserted the continuity of French cinema and Parisian film culture.

What is most noticeable about that film culture is the astonishing availability of films, with the entire city providing a sort of vast film repertory. To fill the demands of all of the cinemas in the city, films kept coming back, and might well play, at any one time, throughout Paris. In the immediate postwar period, for instance, there seem to have always been any number of options for seeing films made by Max Ophüls. *De Mayerling à Sarajevo* (1940), which starred Edwige Feuillère, played throughout the city in 1945, at five cinemas the week of October 10, at nine different cinemas the following week, and then at twelve new locations two weeks later.[54] Ophüls's *Yoshiwara* (1937), with Sessue Hayakawa, appeared in one cinema for one week only beginning on October 31.[55] Frank Capra's films apparently were as popular as Ophüls's, with reprises during this same period, in the neighborhoods and at exclusive cinemas, of *Vous ne l'emporterez pas avec vous* (*You Can't Take It with You*; 1938) at the Ursulines cinema, *Monsieur Smith au Sénat* first exclusively at the Biarritz and then at the Cinéac-Madeleine in the eighth arrondissement, and *L'Extravagant Monsieur Deeds* playing for one week in the fifteenth arrondissement.[56]

As we move into 1947 and farther away from the war, the evidence of the film culture of Paris becomes scanter. *Cinévie* may have ceased publication by this time, or, at the very least, issues after 1946 are unavailable to the historian working in the United States. My evidence in this instance comes from a lucky discovery at the now long-gone magazine store I mentioned in the introduction to this book, Archives de la presse in the fourth arrondissement. Among

Figure 6.4   The wedding photo of Danielle Darrieux on the cover of *Cinévie*,
January 16, 1946. Source: Bibliothèque nationale de France, Paris.

a bunch of issues of the film magazine *L'Écran français*, there was one that still
had a four-page insert listing all of the films playing in Paris, and at which cinemas, for the week of January 15, 1947.[57] By then there were just over three hundred cinemas in Paris and another fifty or so in the nearby suburbs. There were
about 150 films showing in Paris, and by my count seventy of those came from
Hollywood, mostly made after the French surrender in June 1940 and before
the Liberation in August 1944, the period during which the Germans banned
Hollywood movies throughout the Occupied Zone of France. Now Parisians
could see everything they had missed: *Hantise* (*Gaslight*; 1944), playing at
the Max Linder in the second arrondissement as well as at the Ermitage; *Le
Tueur à gages* (*This Gun for Hire*; 1942) at the Broadway in the eighth; Walt
Disney's *Fantasia* (1940) showing at the Empire in the seventeenth; the Marx
Brothers in *Chercheurs d'or* (*Go West*; 1940) at the Ciné-Opéra in the second;
and *Citizen Kane* (1941) at the Artistic in the ninth.

At least for this very brief postwar period, the French cinema held its own
against the Hollywood product. During this same week in January more
than sixty French films showed in Paris, and around thirty of them had been

released in 1946 or 1947. Jean Cocteau's *La Belle et la Bête* (1946) continued its exclusive run at the very chic Madeleine cinema in the eighth arrondissement, and Marcel Carné and Jacques Prévert's *Les Portes de la nuit* showed at the Marivaux in the second. There was also Duvivier's *Panique* (1946) at the Olympia and at the Normandie in the eighth arrondissement, René Clément's *Le Père tranquille* (1946) at the Club cinema in the ninth, and Marc Allégret's *Pétrus* (1946), with the great star Fernandel, at the Studio Universel in the fourth and the Panthéon in the fifth, to name just a few of the new French films from the period. Indeed, 1946 would be a terrific year for French cinema, at least in terms of numbers, with the production of anywhere from 100 to 120 feature films (depending on the source reporting the figures), four or five times the total from 1944.[58]

In addition to all of the new French films, there were also standards showing in the neighborhoods: Marcel Pagnol's *César* at the Florida in the twentieth arrondissement, for instance, as well as his *La Fille du Puisatier* (1940) at the Abbesses in the eighteenth. As an ongoing signal to postwar audiences that the Occupation really had ended, Jean Gabin's films continued to play in Paris. During that week in January 1947, his 1936 film *La Belle Équipe* showed in the eighteenth, at the Myrrha.

The film culture of Paris in those first years after the Liberation, however, did not completely repudiate the memory of Nazi control. One of the films playing in the city that week in January 1947 had been made by Continental Films, the Nazi company founded during the war to produce "French" movies. *Pierre et Jean* (1943), directed by André Cayatte and starring Renée Saint-Cyr and Noël Roquevert, appeared at the Gloria cinema in the seventeenth arrondissement and the Stéphen in the eighteenth, neither one a prominent site. From just a week's worth of evidence, it is difficult to tell whether Continental's movies commonly showed in Paris at the time, or just filled in here and there, given the exhibition demands of the Parisian film market. Perhaps predictably, there seems not to have been much of a market for any German films in Paris. Only one played that week, at the cinema that had received so much publicity in *Cinévie* when it opened, the Méliès in the ninth arrondissement. That film was *Symphonie inachevée* (*Leise flehen meine Lieder*), a 1933 period drama about Franz Schubert, significantly removed from any aspect of the war, and that had attracted large crowds to the Studio de l'Étoile in the eighth arrondissement when it played there, possibly in its Paris premiere, for six weeks in the summer of 1936.[59]

There was, in fact, little presence of any other foreign films besides those from the United States. Ten or eleven films from Great Britain played in Paris that week, including David Lean's *L'Esprit s'amuse* (*Blythe Spirit*; 1945), along with *Le Septième voile* (*The Seventh Veil*; 1945) and *Elephant Boy* (1937). There were only about a half dozen other foreign films, with Roberto Rossellini's *Rome, ville ouverte* (*Roma città aperta*; 1945) the most prominent and playing in multiple cinemas. *Ordet* (1943), from Sweden, and directed by Carl Theodor Dreyer, also showed, as did *Il était une petite fille* (1944) from the Soviet Union. Even the ciné-clubs that week concentrated on French and American films. At Ciné-Art, audiences could watch another Continental Films production, the Henri-Georges Clouzot classic *Le Corbeau* (1943). Two groups featured the work of Marcel Carné, the Club-Boulogne-Billancourt screening *Hôtel du Nord* (1938) and the Club universitaire showing *Jenny*. Both the Ciné liberté club and the Club Jeanson de Sailly showed Renoir's *Le Crime de Monsieur Lange* (1936), and the Club Poissy played *Pépé le Moko*, with Jean Gabin. Fans of American films that week might go to the Ciné-Club for *La Chevauchée fantastique* (*Stagecoach*; 1939) or the Ciné-Club de Paris for *Murder My Sweet* (1944). Only two clubs showed movies that had not been produced in France or the United States: the Ciné-Club Renault with Luis Buñuel's *Terre sans pain* (1933), produced in Spain although filmed in French, and the Moulin à Images, which showed Fritz Lang's German classic, *Metropolis*.

Nevertheless, the postwar development of French—and especially Parisian—ciné-clubs indicates as much as anything else the return of a familiar film culture and the repudiation of the cinema of the Occupation. In terms of the films shown at the postwar clubs and the discussions that took place there, as well as the seemingly immediate development of a national administrative bureaucracy of affiliated clubs, the ciné-clubs of 1947, 1948, and 1949 would have felt comfortably familiar to club habitués of the prewar period. The national scope of the club movement was marked by the Fédération française des ciné-clubs, which began publishing its own newspaper, *Ciné-Club*, in October 1947. This is the source that we can use now, to chart the growth of the postwar ciné-clubs as well as their programs and speakers.

In March 1948 the Ciné-Club universitaire, on rue Yves-Toudic in the tenth arrondissement of Paris, hosted a series of speakers mostly from the French film industry. Georges Van Parys, who had composed the music for the 1934 Josephine Baker/Jean Gabin film *Zouzou*, addressed his audience on "La musique de film." Nicholas Hayer, the cinematographer of *Le Corbeau* and many other films, discussed "Le role de l'image," and screenwriter Denis Marrion, whose *Le Secret de Monte-Cristo*, starring Pierre Brasseur, would open in Paris later in the year, lectured on that perennial ciné-club favorite, René Clair.

More than three-quarters of a century later, however, the talk that most of us would have wanted to hear was about Jean Renoir, and delivered by a film critic and avid ciné-club enthusiast rather than a filmmaker, André Bazin.[60] There were any number of events like this in Paris at the time, and throughout France as well. In fact, Hayer seems to have been on something of a junket, having just given another talk at a conference at the ciné-club in Alès in southern France.

Ciné-Club always provided details of groups throughout France. At the end of 1947, for instance, filmmaker Jean Painlevé visited clubs in Annecy, Saint-Hilaire du Touvet, Chambéry, Tournon, Besançon, and Vesoul. Claude Autant-Lara screened two of his films, *Douce* (1943) and *Le Diable au corps* (1947), at the club in La Rochelle in southwestern France.[61] In early 1948, the Ciné-Club de Chartres hosted Renoir and the screenwriter Pierre Laroche for talks about comedy, while at around the same time the club in Dijon screened Eisenstein's *Alexandre Nevski* (1938) and sponsored a talk by Georges Sadoul, while Charles Spaak screened the film he cowrote with Julien Duvivier, *La Belle Équipe*, at the club in Versailles.[62]

There was also much talk of the new clubs in France, of clubs in Nemours, Privas, Roubaix, and Boulogne-sur-Mer, that had their first screenings at the end of 1947. There was discussion, too, of the incredible success of groups even in the least populated areas of the country, with the club in Poissy claiming 1,800 members despite a population of only 15,000.[63] In addition, affiliated clubs had been created throughout Europe, in Belgium, Switzerland, Italy, Portugal, and Romania. The Fédération française des ciné-clubs took special interest in colonial North Africa, announcing in October 1948 the formation of the Fédération nord-africaine des ciné-clubs and the opening of five clubs in Algeria—two in Algiers and others in Tiemcen, Oran, and Bône, as well as one in Saïda, in France's former colony, Lebanon.[64]

Closer to Paris, there was a flourishing club culture in the suburbs, one that hasn't received much attention from historians. In those banlieues that formed a dense ring around the city, there were clubs in Argenteuil, Asnieres, Bagnolet, Colombes, Corbeil, Gennevilliers, Neuilly, Saint-Ouen, Saint-Germain, Saint-Cloud, and elsewhere.[65] Mostly, of course, there were clubs in Paris. By March 1949 there were at least a dozen or so affiliated clubs there (and perhaps many others, such as Francois Truffaut's Cercle cinémanie, that were not connected to the federation). During the 1930s the ciné-clubs were concentrated in the more affluent sections of Paris, with many of them meeting at the Marignan cinema on the Champs-Élysées. After the war the clubs were scattered throughout the city. Two of them took their names from their arrondissement, the Ciné-Club du 13ème on the rue Cantegrel and the Ciné-Club du 11ème on the rue Basfroi. Three clubs met at the Musée de l'homme in the sixteenth arrondissement, and two others—the Ciné-Club universitaire and also the Ciné-Club Vendredi, which dated from before the war—held screenings and talks in the same place on the rue Yves-Toudic. The Ciné-Club de la chambre noire met at the elegant Sevres-Pathé cinema in the seventh arrondissement, and the Ciné-Club 46 screened films at the Delta cinema on the boulevard Rochechouart in the ninth.[66]

New clubs formed frequently, sometimes with very specific audiences in mind or with particular sponsorship agreements. December 1948 marked several openings. The Ciné-Club volontaire catered to foreigners who had volunteered for French military service, while the club D. W. Griffith, which met at the Michodière cinema in the second arrondissement, had been formed through an American and French consortium.[67] All of the Parisian clubs met from once a month to once a week, and a look at a random month of club activity gives some sense of the screenings. In January 1949, the Ciné-Club 46 showed Roberto Rossellini's *Paisà* (1946), René Clément's *Bataille du rail* (1946), and then an evening of films by G. W. Pabst. The Ciné-Club de l'APA held only one screening that month—apparently outdoors, at a playground in a boys' school in the eighteenth arrondissement—Marcel Carné's 1939 film *Le Jour se lève*, and the Ciné-Club Renault showed Dreyer's *Jour de colère* (*Vredens dag*; 1943).[68]

There also seems to have been some movement of the same films between the clubs. Two weeks before screening *Jour de colère*, for example, the Ciné-Club Renault staged a one-night Buster Keaton retrospective. That same retrospective played at the Cinéum ciné-club that month (as part of a three-week film festival that also featured nights dedicated to Charlie Chaplin and Harold Lloyd), and, indeed, *Jour de colère* also played in January at the Ciné-Club de la chambre noire. René Clair's *Le Million* played at two clubs that month, the Ciné-Club du centre universitaire and the Ciné-Club Vendredi.[69] In fact, there appears to have been a well-organized distribution system between French clubs in general. Still in that same month in 1949, Frank Capra's *L'Extravagant Monsieur Deeds* showed at the club in Bourges in central France, and then quite probably the same print of the film traveled the 150 miles or so to the Parisian suburb Levallois-Perret for a screening two weeks later, and then went back out again to the club in Le Havre for a screening on January 26. Just one week later, on February 3, *Deeds* played at the Rialto cinema for the club in Tourcoing in northern France, about two hundred miles up the coast from Le Havre.[70]

While we can well appreciate today these incredible opportunities to see a range of films, some of the other events at the clubs seem even more tantalizing than the movies. Jacques Prévert and Jean Painlevé were tireless participants (the latter served as honorary president of the Fédération française des ciné-clubs) and gave constant talks at clubs throughout the country.[71] Or with just the scant information provided in the periodical *Ciné-Club*, we can only wonder about the program for the conference on "Cinéma et télévision" at the Ciné-Club Jean Vigo in Fontainebleau, about an hour outside Paris, in June 1948.[72] Of course, when we think of Paris and its status as one of the film capitals of the world, we think of the most extensive and well-financed film "club" of all at this time, the Cinémathèque française, which had reopened in 1944 and which apparently had no connection to the Fédération française. But while it might be more prosaic than Henri Langlois curating the extraordinary screenings at the famous Cinémathèque, or the young François Truffaut and Jean-Luc Godard watching Hitchcock films there, perhaps nothing better indicates a nationwide postwar culture of cinephilia than the vast network, from Paris to Poissy, of urban, suburban, and provincial ciné-clubs.

From the evidence of the commercial cinemas during the late 1940s and even from the ciné-clubs, the temptation might be to conclude that the Parisian cinema immediately after the war was less varied, less cosmopolitan, than it had been just before, when there typically would be a far wider schedule of foreign films. The available evidence might be suggestive, but is just too incomplete to claim anything so definitive. Still, from just that one week's worth of evidence in *L'Écran*, and from the information available in *Ciné-Club*, we might see the signs of a surprisingly vibrant exhibition industry in Paris if not the rest of France, a fleeting golden age of French film production, and the ongoing, and no doubt increasing, domination of Hollywood.

Indeed, in 1946 France signed the Blum-Byrnes agreements with the United States, agreements aimed at rebuilding all aspects of the French economy, and that specified the relation of American to domestic films in France's cinematic marketplace, and always to the great advantage of the former. Many in the French film industry lobbied the government for protection against the reopening of the national market to foreign films, and especially those from Hollywood. The agreement, though, signed by Léon Blum, representing the French government, and US Secretary of State James F. Byrnes, placed virtually no restrictions on the import of American films to France, and few, as well, on the exhibition of those films. Blum-Byrnes thus guaranteed that American movies would soon come to dominate Parisian cinemas and also those in the rest of the country. Of course, any agreement like Blum-Byrnes, covering so many aspects of commerce between France and the United States, would be densely complex. In its defense, the French government pointed to the nationalization of large exhibition chains, which were freer than other cinemas to show French rather than American films. Nevertheless, about a year and a half after the agreement had been signed, more than half the films in circulation in France would come from Hollywood.[73]

Largely because of this, and at least in French popular understanding, the agreements guaranteed the decline of French cinema and the triumph of American cultural imperialism, the "légende noire," in Jacques Portes's terms, of postwar relations between France and the United States.[74] These agreements and their effects over the next few years mark a fitting end to a study like this one, as much as the founding of *Cahiers du cinéma* in 1952, or the new filmmaking practices of the New Wave a few years later, or the government's adoption of its new film financing program ("avance sur recettes"), indicate a significant break with the past. For typical filmgoers, however, who had been going to the movies for the last two decades or so, the cinematic geography of the city must have looked comfortingly familiar. There were still the great cinemas on the Champs-Élysées, as well as the Paramount, the Normandie, and the Rex as landmarks in different neighborhoods, and hundreds of cinémas des quartiers tucked away in the neighborhoods.

One example of film journalism from the period demonstrates this link between eras and the unaltered attitudes about film history and stardom. After the war, Air France, the official French airline carrier, published a monthly magazine, *Terre et ciel* (*Earth and Sky*), for its employees. The June 1947 issue, on the "Arts and Culture" page, ran a review of the great Mexican film *María Candelaria* (1944), which had played at the recent Cannes Film Festival, as if to emphasize the international scope of Air France as well as that of French film culture.[75] On the same page there was an announcement of the new "ciné-club Air France," aligned with the Fédération française des ciné-clubs and coming to cinemas in Paris and elsewhere.[76] Along with this corporate endorsement of French cinephilia, there was, as well, a review of the new René Clair film, *Le Silence est d'or*, which referred to Clair as "le plus français de nos réalisateurs," the most French of our directors.[77] That sentiment echoed so much of the previous twenty years of French film journalism, with Clair typically emerging as the most important of the country's filmmakers and one of the most significant subjects of critical scrutiny. *Terre et ciel* also ran a photograph from the film and of its star, Maurice Chevalier. Recently acquitted of all charges of wartime collaboration, stemming from his 1941 performance for French soldiers held at the Alten Grabow prisoner-of-war camp in Germany,[78]

Chevalier once again might signify the best of classic French cinema, providing an assurance of a connection to the past, to the coming of sound, to all of the film magazines that always extolled Chevalier's career, to the star's upbringing in the working-class twentieth arrondissement and his triumphs in the theatres and cinemas around the Champs-Élysées. For the cinéphile or even for an average movie fan walking through Paris in the 1930s, an encounter with Chevalier—his films or photos or stories about him—was practically unavoidable. Now, in the late 1940s, the commercial airline, a mode of movement not nearly so earthbound, might also present the great star to the film enthusiast, and provide some of the same pleasures of going to the movies in Paris from before the war.

A Final Stroll

1948–1954, 1980–2016

In 1947, had you gone to the movies at the Gaumont-Palace, you might have been asked to fill out a questionnaire. As I mentioned in the introduction, this cinema in the eighteenth arrondissement was one of the grandest in all of Europe, and the showpiece of an international empire for its parent company, the Société nouvelle des établissements Gaumont (SNEG). That company, always in and out of financial difficulty, hoped to find out more about the patrons of the Palace, perhaps to have a better sense of the immediate postwar Parisian film marketplace, perhaps to know how best to serve customers at the Palace, or perhaps because this was simply the way companies did business in the late 1940s. The pertinent details about the audience for the Gaumont-Palace were compiled by SNEG in 1948, in the *Étude du comportement des spectateurs du Gaumont*.

Eight hundred viewers from Paris and the surrounding suburbs participated in the Gaumont project. Answers were itemized by gender ("par sexe"), by age ("par âge"), and by where respondents lived ("par habitat"), in order to get as nuanced a sense as possible of favorite stars and movies, and attitudes about going to the Gaumont-Palace in general. Because of this, we know that 13 percent of female viewers considered Ingrid Bergman their favorite actress, while 10 percent preferred Danielle Darrieux. Around seven out of ten viewers came from Paris, and about one-quarter from the suburban banlieues. Reasonably enough, almost a third of the cinema's audience lived in the eighteenth arrondissement, the neighborhood that housed the Gaumont. Very few viewers made the trip to the Gaumont from the working-class twentieth arrondissement at the eastern edge of the city, but there were also relatively few filmgoers at this cinema from the much more well-heeled fifth, sixth, and seventh arrondissements.

There certainly would have been a racialized as well as a classed component of these audiences, especially from the deeply stratified banlieues, typically the home, in just one example, of the Algerian Muslims who moved to the country in such high numbers during the ten years following the war, and which in part led demographers at the time to claim for Paris the status of "city of migrants."[1] But Gaumont considered the Parisian suburbs only in broad, regional terms. The poll revealed that the most frequent audiences for the Palace from just outside the city came from the north, northeastern, and northwestern banlieues (those nearest the cinema), but it remains a mystery how many, as well as their composition, came from the working-class, heavily immigrant and nonwhite Boulogne-Billancourt, for instance, and how many may have come from the far more affluent and homogenous Neuilly-sur-Seine.

In all cases, and beyond the percentages from each region, the survey really was concerned not so much with the demographics of the suburban audience but rather with how they came to the Gaumont, by bus, by metro, or by train.[2] Once they got there, the poll asked if they would just go to another cinema if the queue at the Gaumont was too long. About 20 percent said they would. Did they prefer American and British films to be subtitled or dubbed? A full 60 percent expressed a preference for dubbing. How much were they willing to pay to see movies? Most respondents thought they might pay as much as 110 francs (around 30 cents in relation to the US dollar). Did they go to the Gaumont during the week, right after work? About half of the respondents answered in the affirmative.[3]

Most of the questions, naturally enough, dealt with reasons for going to the Gaumont-Palace in the first place, and how customers might act once they got there. In 1947, the Gaumont had shown new French films but also a number of American movies that had been produced during the war and were only just coming to France. The preferred films, at least for those who went to the Gaumont, all came from Hollywood, and ranged from solidly middlebrow to unmistakably lowbrow. Gaumont audiences' favorite film of that year had been the Hemingway adaptation *Pour qui sonne le glas* (*For Whom the Bell Tolls*; 1943), followed by William Wyler's rich social document *Les Plus Belles Années de notre vie* (*The Best Years of Our Lives*; 1946) and Esther Williams and Red Skelton in *Le Bal des sirénes* (*Bathing Beauty*; 1944), a film of far simpler pleasures. Audiences then cited *Casablanca* (1942), and only after that a French film, *Le Mariage de Ramuntcho* (1947), which may have been rated so favorably because it was the first French feature-length color film.

If the Gaumont-Palace audiences provide any broader indication, tastes had changed over the course of the decade. Of the major films to play there, among the least favored were *Miroir* (1947), with Jean Gabin in only his second French film since spending the war in the United States, and *La Taverne du poisson couronné* (1947), which starred Michel Simon. The apparent shift from two prewar movie icons, Gabin and Simon, to Red Skelton, may well tell us something about changing notions of masculinity in post-Liberation Paris.[4]

Just a few years later the French government got into the act, concerned that fewer and fewer people in France were interested in the cinema. The result of all of this worry appeared in 1954, in a fifty-page study of the French film market overseen by economist Paul Degand and published by the Centre nationale de la cinématographie (CNC), *L'Étude de marché du cinéma français*. We can find the principle reason for the brochure in the title of chapter 2, "Les Français qui ne vont pas au cinéma." Degand and the rest of the CNC wanted to find out precisely who these people were "who don't go to the movies."[5]

The French government had formed the CNC after the war, as a reconfiguration of COIC, the Comité d'organisation des industries cinématographique, that had been instituted by the Nazis after the French surrender. Like its predecessor, the CNC administered the film industry in France.[6] The experts at CNC had come to question the motives, desires, and practices of the French film audience, so much so that they believed that a crisis confronted the French cinema during this first decade following the war. The CNC's analytical tool for examining this crisis would be the poll, as was the case with the Gaumont inquiry, but this would have a national rather than a purely Parisian reach.

The government had assessed the challenges facing the French film industry at least once before. From December 1936 until May 1937 the French Parliament, having created the Groupe du cinématographe, convened fourteen sessions for "a vast inquiry into the actual situation of the film industry in France." The speakers who came to Parliament included "the principle producers, directors, actors, distributors, and critics," all those who "interacted with the seventh art." The hearings and the problems they addressed were significant enough to merit publication in a single volume called *Où va le cinéma français?* (*Where Is French Cinema Going?*), and received a significant amount of coverage in the popular press. The testimony from industry executives, eminent filmmakers such as Marcel L'Herbier, and the man who had the last word at the last hearing, Louis Lumière, tended toward the nonscientific and the anecdotal, and Paris often occupied a central position.[7]

There were helpful numbers provided during this inquiry. Around four hundred films per year were released in four thousand French cinemas, about 120 of those movies coming from French companies, with the average French film taking only two weeks to make—with quality sacrificed for speed—and perhaps returning between F800,000 and F1.2 million. Mostly, however, the experts complained, often about the audiences in Paris, the cinemas in Paris, and also about the rest of the country not being Parisian enough. They lamented that some of the best cinemas in Paris—those around the Champs-Élysées—typically refused to play French films, favoring those from the United States and Germany (a charge that was, in fact, true), and scorned the taste of Parisian filmgoers ("Le goût du public!" as one witness, occasional screenwriter Pierre Wolf, exclaimed to the members of Parliament). Of course, the taste of audiences in the provinces seemed to be even worse. They rejected films without the biggest stars, Gaby Morlay and Harry Baur, for example, or, even worse, demanded only those films that starred the great French comic actor and everyman, Fernandel.[8]

The 1954 government inquiry adopted a more scientific tone and methodology. For purposes of the study, the government divided the French public into four economic and social classes: the *grande bourgeoisie* and industrialists at the top; followed by a middle class of proprietors and functionaries; then a laboring, artisanal, and agricultural class; and finally workers and small pensioners at the bottom. The age ranges were fifteen to twenty-four, twenty-five to thirty-nine, forty to forty-nine, and those aged fifty and older, with children understood to be a significant part of the film audience but typically following the movie tastes of parents or older siblings. Slightly more than half the respondents were women. Region presented the most complicated category, with the government recognizing ten distinct areas, including large spaces such as Alsace-Lorraine and the Mediterranean coast, and those as small as Paris, with the capital nevertheless accounting for almost 12 percent of respondents.[9]

So what, exactly, did the government find out about the French who went to the movies or stayed home? First, the mythically movie-crazy French actually attended the cinema far less frequently than fans in Italy, Germany, or the United Kingdom, going only eight or nine times a year as opposed to a dozen times in Germany and about twenty-five times in the UK. At least in Paris, the music hall, which typically has come down to us as a form of popular entertainment aligned with the period from before World War I, and which often yielded its stars to the cinema (think of Maurice Chevalier), actually had made recent and significant gains in popularity while enthusiasm for the cinema had decreased.[10]

Throughout the country women made up only 45 percent of the movie audience, and the same held true regionally, with men forming the largest part of the audience in Alsace-Lorraine, for instance, as well as in Paris.[11] These men attended in greater numbers even though they were far more susceptible to new media technologies such as television, which itself seemed to appeal more to those who went to the movies frequently rather than less often.[12] For the women who did go, the cinema provided particular pleasures beyond the movies themselves. More often than men, women purchased food and other items at concession stands, and they often imagined a trip to the cinema as a "night out," when they might "laugh," "joke," or "show off clothes and hairdos." Women tended to enjoy an "entire cinematic spectacle," which was "something other than a hasty trip into a room to watch a film."[13]

Only around two-thirds of the French public went to the movies at all, and most of the one-third that did not go had simply given up the habit.[14] Those younger than twenty-five made up the largest audience for movies, and were typically middle class and living in big cities. As a result, cities stood out as the most significant targets of the report, both in terms of governmental approval and the need for development. Paris, of course, was a model. The capital had the most cinemas of any city in France, at 357, and also the most cinema seats, a number of far more value than that of exhibition sites. Paris also seemed to have the most astute fans. Nationally, only those in the upper classes chose their films according to the critics they read in newspapers and magazines. In contrast, that was the norm among Parisian movie viewers across classes. Lower-brow fans in other cities and in the provinces made decisions based on the photos and posters outside the cinemas, word of mouth, or because a film might belong to a favorite genre.[15]

Perhaps surprisingly, Lille and Metz had even more enthusiastic audiences than those in Paris, and they attended their far fewer cinemas even more often than the Parisians.[16] These smaller movie-mad cities seemed to indicate the possible future of cinema in France far more than did Paris. The CNC report understood that the French cinema and the cinema marketplace were national phenomena but of still varying regional significance. The report hoped that understanding the individual spectator, and spectators in places such as Paris but also Lille and Metz, might extend French film to those places (and especially cities) of weak interest, such as Limoges or Nantes.[17] Thus for the CNC, one of the significant problems of the French film market was that it was insufficiently national. There might be differences among filmgoers in Paris, or those in Lille. Most importantly, however, "la psychologie du spectateur" differed dramatically from city to city, and from cities to more rural areas.[18] The project for the French cinema would be to turn the filmgoer in Paris or Lille or Metz into a national film enthusiast, and to move from the individual or the city to the nation.

Just who were the French who disliked the movies, the "lost spectators," or "les spectateurs perdus" in the words of the report?[19] They came disproportionately from the middle and lower-middle classes, and many of them were between twenty-five and thirty-nine years old. They tended to live on the Mediterranean coast and in the southeast and southwest of France, but also, troublingly, in Paris, the most important market in the country. More often than not they cited a lack of time, the demands of family life, and the cost of attendance as reasons for staying away.[20] These were personal, domestic reasons. But the CNC also imagined France, and the French city, as a sort of Darwinian space of leisure activity. Rather than finding relations and alliances between these activities, and seeing how one might lead to the other, the CNC report understood clearly that the various bars or cafés, or the card game belote or the possibility for playing boules, each constituted a "veritable spectacle" equal to and competing with motion pictures.[21] The cinema existed in a cutthroat marketplace of leisure, and had found it increasingly difficult to hold its own against other forms of relaxation and escape.

All of the science and exactitude, and even the hand-wringing so evident in the 1954 national poll, seem to remove us from looking mostly at Paris, and moving through that city to examine the options for seeing movies there and the changes over time as well as the consistencies in film culture. These were the concerns and interests that motivated this project, and those with which I began this book. I mentioned being a film studies graduate student in Paris from 1980 to 1981; I went to the movies all the time that year, and the opportunities to do so seemed almost limitless. I lived in the fourth arrondissement, something of a ground zero for film viewing because at that time the Cinémathèque française had a screening room there, in the recently opened Centre Georges Pompidou. I kept a log of all the movies I saw that year, but not always where I saw them. I also kept a few mimeographed pages of schedules, which was one of the ways the Cinémathèque distributed its listings back then, so I know that, on January 18, 1981, I walked over to the Centre Pompidou to see René Clair's 1937 British film *Fausses nouvelles* (*Break the News*), which starred Maurice Chevalier, Jack Buchanan, and June Knight. The next day, I went to the Pompidou once again, for Eric Rohmer's *Le Signe du lion* (1959).

Of course, I saw movies elsewhere in Paris: at the main Cinémathèque screening space at the Palais de Chaillot in the sixteenth arrondissement,

LA CINÉMATHÈQUE FRANÇAISE

SALLE BEAUBOURG - Centre G.Pompidou (5° Étage) Rue Rambuteau-Téléphone 278 3557-PARIS 3°

MERCREDI 29 AVRIL 1981
15H00 - L'AVENTURE EST AU FOND DE LA MER (Under the Caribbean) de Hans HASS   R.F.A. 1954
        Dr Hans Hass, Lotte Hass, Dr Georg Scheer, Dr von Eibesfeldt
                                CINEMA DU REEL 1981
17H00 - PRISONERS OF CONSCIENCE de John WILLIS (VOSTF)   G.B. 1980
      - ECOUTEZ JEANNE HUMBERT de Bernard BAISSAT   FRANCE 1980
                30 ANS D'UNE REVUE : "LES CAHIERS DU CINEMA" 1951/1981
19H00 - LE TROU de Jacques BECKER, d'après l'oeuvre de José GIOVANNI   FRANCE/ITALIE
        Michael Constantin, Jean Keraudy, Philippe Leroy, Raymond Meunier   1960

JEUDI 30 AVRIL 1981
15H00 - LE MYSTERE DU CAMP 27 (Portrait of Life) de Terence FISHER   G.B. 1948
        Mai Zetterling, Robert Beatty, Guy Rolfe, Herbert Lom
                                CINEMA DU REEL 1981 *
17H00 * GUBER, LES TAILLEURS DE PAVES de H.V. SCHLUMPF (VOSTF)   SUISSE 1980
      * THE LIFE AND TIMES OF ROSIE THE RIVETER de Connie FIELD (VOSTF)   U.S.A. 1980
                - - - - - - - - - -
19H00 - NEUF JOURS D'UNE ANNEE (Deviat Dnei Odnovo Goda) de Mikhail ROMM   URSS 1962
        Alexeï Batalev, Innokenty Smoktounovsky, Tatiana Lavrova,N.Plotnikov

VENDREDI 1er MAI 1981 : R E L A C H E

SAMEDI 2 MAI 1981
15H00 - LA PORTE DE L'ENFER (Jigoku-Mon) de Teinosuke KINUGASA   JAPON 1952
        Kazuo Hasegawa, Machiko Kyo, Isao Yamagata, Y.Kurokawa
                                CINEMA DU REEL 1981
17H00 - STATIONS OF THE ELEVATED de Manny KIRCHHEIMER   U.S.A. 1980
        CROSS AND PASSION de Kim LONGINOTTO et Claire POLLAK   G.B. 1980
                30 ANS D'UNE REVUE : "LES CAHIERS DU CINEMA" 1951/1981 *
19H00 * LE SIGNE DU LION de Eric ROHMER   FRANCE 1959
        Jess Hahn, Van Doude, Michèle Girardon, Jill Olivier, Jean Le Poulain
                - - - - - - - - - -
21H00 - LILIOM de Fritz LANG, d'après la pièce de Ferenc MOLNAR   FRANCE 1934
        Charles Boyer, Viviane Romance, Florelle,Madeleine Ozeray,Mila Parely
        Robert Arnoux, Alcover, Roland Toutain, Alexandre Rignault,Antonin Artaud

DIMANCHE 3 MAI 1981
15H00 - LES SOEURS DE GION (Gion No Shimai) de Kenji MIZOGUCHI   JAPON 1936
        Yamada Isuzu, Unemura Yoko, Shiganoya Benkei, Shindo Eitaro, O.Fumio
                                CINEMA DU REEL 1981
17H00 - N!AI, THE STORY OF A ! KUNG WOMAN de John MARSHALL et Adrienne MIESMER
        (Prix du Festival 1981 "Cinéma du Réel") VOSTF   U.S.A. 1980
      - DES GOUTTES D'EAU, DES CHOSES VRAIES de Anne-Marie MASQUIN (Mention)   FRANCE 1980
                30 ANS D'UNE REVUE : "LES CAHIERS DU CINEMA" 1951/1981
19H00 - TIREZ SUR LE PIANISTE de François TRUFFAUT, d'après le roman de
        David GOODIS "DOWN THERE", Musique de Georges DELERUE   FRANCE 1960
        Charles Aznavour,Marie Dubois,Michèle Mercier,Albert Rémy,N.Berger
21H00 - LE BEL AGE de Pierre KAST   FRANCE 1960
        Alexandra Stewart, Loleh Bellon, Françoise Brion, Anne Collette,
        Ursula Kubler, Jean-Claude Brialy, Françoise Prévost,Marcello Pagliero

LUNDI 4 MAI 1981
15H00 - UNE PAGE FOLLE (Kurutta Ippeiji) de Teinosuke KINUGASA   JAPON 1926
        Masao Inoue, Yoshie Nakagawa
                                CINEMA DU REEL 1981
17H00 - QUELQUE CHOSE DE L'ARBRE, DU FLEUVE ET DU CRI DU PEUPLE de Patrice
        CHAGNARD (Prix du Festival 1981 "Cinéma du Réel")   FRANCE 1980
      - BEKOIDINTU, TOUTE MAISON VAUT MIEUX QUE LA MIENNE (Bekoidintu : Elk
        Huis is Beter dan Het Mijne) de Emile Van ROUVEROY (VOSTF)   HOLLANDE 198

Figure C.1   The mimeographed schedule, beginning April 29, 1981, for the
Cinémathèque française at the Centre Georges Pompidou.

and also at cinemas throughout the city. Mostly I saw reprises of American and European films, at Action Écoles and the Cluny Palace in the fifth arrondissement, at Saint André des Arts and Action Christine in the sixth, at the MacMahon in the seventeenth. I went to only four or five new films that year, three of them within a two-week period in April 1981 when I saw *Fame* (1980), *The Elephant Man* (1980), and *Raging Bull* (1980), the last two, I think, in large, luxurious cinemas on the Champs-Élysées.

In subsequent trips to Paris, I saved at least some complete movie listings. An issue of *Pariscope*, a weekly listing of cultural events in the city, from August 1989 has programs for 129 cinemas.[22] The largest concentration of exhibition sites was in the fifth arrondissement, with fifteen cinemas, and the sixth, with eighteen. By then, the twentieth arrondissement on the eastern edge of the city, which had been so packed with cinemas fifty years before, had only one, the Gambetta on the rue Belgrand. By contrast, cinemas filled the Parisian suburbs in 1989, with more than 150 combined in Seine-et-Marne, Yvelines, Essonne, Hauts-de-Seine, and elsewhere, while during the 1930s and 1940s, at least according to the sketchy information available, audiences from just outside the city often had little choice but to come to Paris to see movies. Even this apparently complete listing from *Pariscope*, however, still leaves so much out, certainly the museums and other institutions that often showed films and, on the other side of the cultural divide, the adult cinemas that still could be found throughout the city.

A quarter century later, in 2015, there were two cinemas in the twentieth, but only 82 in the city. Many of these sites had multiple screens—the Paramount in the ninth arrondissement, the Danton in the sixth, the Gaumont Champs-Élysées in the eighth, and so on—but the shift in the cultural geography of Paris nevertheless had been significant. On a walk through the city in 2015, many of the spaces that had been cinemas twenty-five years before yielded little information about the past. The great Cinéma des Champs-Élysées, for instance, where Brigitte Horney's *Les Mains libres* premiered in 1940, had become a Mercedes-Benz dealership, and a smartphone store occupies the space of the Ermitage cinema a few blocks away. The Corso-Opéra in the second, a 350-seat cinema that, as I have mentioned, specialized in silent films throughout the 1930s, had turned into a Pizza Pino Italian restaurant, and any number of cinemas seem to have been repurposed into Monoprix stores, the ubiquitous retail spaces in modern Paris. There are also, of course, old cinemas that have been torn down and others that are now just empty, such as the old Novelty-Palace on the avenue Ledru-Rollin in the twelfth arrondissement.

Figure C.2　The Mercedes-Benz showroom that now occupies the site of the Cinéma des Champs-Élysées. Photograph by author.

Paris still has cinemas that have been showing movies for eighty years or more: the Balzac in the eighth arrondissement, the Rex in the second, the Hôtel de Ville cinema in the fourth. There are several that have been nothing if not resourceful, changing with the times, with their clientele, or with their ownership. In the sixth arrondissement, there is still the MK2 Parnasse, which opened in 1930 and after a few years moved from showing conventional French and American movies to specializing in Yiddish films to concentrating on newsreels and then moving back to products from France and Hollywood. Along the way, the name has changed from the Studio-Paris to the Studio-Parnasse to the *Ce soir*-Parnasse to the 14 Juillet Parnasse to the MK2 (with several others undoubtedly in between).

Clearly, Paris is not a cinema ghost town, and, in fact, there have been some extraordinary renovations. The faux-Egyptian-style Louxor cinema in the tenth arrondissement had been one of the most imposing exhibition sites in Paris, from its opening in 1921 through the 1960s, but difficult years followed and the cinema closed in the early 1980s. The city of Paris bought the building in 2003 and began a renovation, and the multiscreen result has been spectacular.[23] In 2016, the Gaumont company, which for so many years operated so many cinemas in Paris and the rest of France, opened the Fauvettes in the thirteenth arrondissement, on the site of an old music hall, where audiences at the multiscreen location can see restored films. By the end of the Fauvettes's first year of operation, those films ranged from *L'Atalante* (1934) to *Harry Potter et la chambre des secrets* (*Harry Potter and the Chamber of Secrets*; 2002), and from *Madame de . . .* (1953) to *Bridget Jones's Baby* (2016).[24] The Cinémathèque française also still shows films. While I might miss the intimacy of the old screening room at the Pompidou Center and the slightly rundown opulence of the Cinémathèque space at the Palais de Chaillot, the new location in the thirteenth arrondissement presents viewers with a wonderful architectural space for seeing movies.

I hope this book provides a sense of the astonishing film culture of Paris from the 1930s until around 1950, something that still seemed very much a part of the city when I first visited in 1980, and that might seem largely absent today. But there is continuity as well. I began the first chapter of this book by writing about the seemingly endless—and daylong—possibilities for seeing films in the ninth arrondissement in 1933. On my last trip to Paris in 2015, there were some thirty films playing in the four cinemas in the ninth, and many screens showing them all day. Of course, rather than strolling through the neighborhood going from cinema to cinema, I simply could have stayed in the multiscreen interior space of the Gaumont Opéra cinema on 2 boulevard des Capucines, the site of the old Paramount cinema, watching movies from morning until night. Nevertheless, I could still feel a kinship to that imaginary cinéphile of 1933, starting the day with *Un soir de réveillon* at 9:30 a.m. and ending with *Tire au flanc* at 3:00 the next morning.

NOTES

Introduction: A Walking Tour

1 Richard Abel, *The Ciné Goes to Town: French Cinema 1896–1914* (Berkeley: University of California Press, 1994), 9–58; Abel, *French Cinema: The First Wave, 1915–1929* (Princeton, NJ: Princeton University Press, 1984), 251–60; Christophe Gauthier, *La Passion du cinéma: Cinéphiles, ciné-clubs et salles specialisées à Paris de 1920 à 1929* (Paris: Association Française de Recherche sur l'Histoire du Cinéma, 1999); Annie Fee, *Male Cinephiles and Female Movie-Fans: A Counter-History of French Cinephilia, 1918–1925* (PhD diss., University of Washington, 2014).

2 Jean-Jacques Meusy, *Paris-Palaces, ou, le temps des cinémas (1894–1918)* (Paris: CNRS Éditions, 1995); Meusy, *Écrans français de l'entre-deux-guerres, volumes I et II: Les Années sonores et parlantes* (Paris: Association Française de Recherche sur l'Histoire du Cinéma, 2017).

3 For an examination of the shift in film studies from an emphasis on texts to an interest in audiences, see my introduction, "The History of Film History," in *Looking Past the Screen: Case Studies in American Film History and Method*, ed. Jon Lewis and Eric Smoodin (Durham, NC: Duke University Press, 2007), 1–33. See also Kathy Fuller-Seeley, "Introduction: Spectatorship in Popular Film and Television," *Journal of Popular Film and Television* 29, no. 3 (2001): 98–99. Annette Kuhn writes of the spectator "constructed by the film text" in *Dreaming of Fred and Ginger: Cinema and Cultural Memory* (New York: NYU Press, 2002), 3–4.

4 Christian-Marc Bosséno, "La place du spectateur," *Vingtième siècle: Revue d'histoire* 46 (April–June 1995): 143–54. See page 143 for the shift from the "screen" to the "cinema" and page 144 for the list of questions.

5 Emilie Altenloh, "A Sociology of the Cinema: The Audience (1914)," trans. Kathleen Cross, *Screen* 42, no. 3 (2001): 249–93; Kathryn Fuller-Seeley, ed., *Hollywood in the Neighborhood: Historical Case Studies of Local Moviegoing* (Berkeley: University of California Press, 2008); Lee Grieveson, *Policing Chicago: Movies and Censorship in Early-Twentieth-Century America* (Berkeley: University of California Press, 2004); Ben Singer, "Manhattan Nickelodeons: New Data on Audiences and Exhibitors," *Cinema Journal* 34, no. 2 (2001): 5–35; Gregory Waller, *Main Street Amusements: Movies and Commercial Entertainment in a Southern City, 1896–1930* (Washington, DC: Smithsonian Institution Press, 1995).

6   The three case studies come from Melvyn Stokes and Richard Maltby, eds., *American Movie Audiences: From the Turn of the Century to the Early Sound Era* (London: BFI, 1999). See Judith Thissen, "Jewish Immigrant Audiences in New York City, 1905–14," 15–28; Leslie Midkiff DeBauche, "Reminiscences of the Past, Conditions of the Present: At the Movies in Milwaukee in 1918," 129–39; and Gregory Waller, "Hillbilly Music and Will Rogers: Small-Town Picture Shows in the 1930s," 164–79.

7   For details about the Finsbury Park as well as Greta Garbo's popularity in London and the system for films to play in cinemas there, see John Sedgwick and Clara Pafort-Overdun, "Understanding Audience Behavior through Statistical Evidence: London and Amsterdam in the Mid-1930s," in *Audiences: Defining and Researching Screen Entertainment Reception*, ed. Ian Christie (Amsterdam: Amsterdam University Press, 2012), 96–110, in particular pages 96 and 99.

8   Renaud Chaplain, "Les Exploitants des salles de cinéma lyonnaise: Des origins à la seconde guerre mondiale," *Vingtième Siècle: Revue d'histoire* 79 (July–September 2003): 19–35; Pierre Berneau and Jeanne Berneau, *Le Spectacle cinématographique à Limoges de 1896 à 1945: Cinquante ans de culture populaire* (Paris: Association Française de Recherche sur l'Histoire du Cinéma, 1992); see also Jean A. Gili's preface to the volume (7–13), which cites studies of such places as Marseille, Toulon, and Nice; Sylvia Rab, "Le Cinéma dans l'entre-deux-guerres; une politique culturelle municipal impossible? L'exemple de Suresnes," *Le Mouvement social* 184 (July–September 1998): 75–98.

9   For a discussion of new approaches to national cinema, see my essay "American Madness," in *America First: Naming the Nation in US Film*, ed. Mandy Merck (London: Routledge, 2007), 65–82. For a full rethinking of national cinema, and particularly in terms of internationalizing our notion of the term, see Andrew Higson, *Waving the Flag: Constructing a National Cinema in Britain* (Oxford: Oxford University Press, 1995); and Ruth Vasey, *The World according to Hollywood, 1918–1939* (Madison: University of Wisconsin Press, 1997).

10   Michel de Certeau, *The Practice of Everyday Life*, trans. Steven Rendall (Berkeley: University of California Press, 1984). See in particular chapter 7, "Walking in the City," 91–110, and page 100 for the "rhetoric of walking."

11   Walter Benjamin, *The Arcades Project*, trans. Kevin McLaughlin (Cambridge, MA: Harvard University Press, 2002); Theodore Reff, "Manet and the Paris of Haussmann and Baudelaire," in *Visions of the Modern City: Essays in History, Art, and Literature*, ed. William Sharpe and Leonard Wallock (Baltimore: Johns Hopkins University Press, 1987), 135–67; Deborah Epstein Nord, "The City as Theater: From Georgian to Early Victorian London," *Victorian Studies* 31, no. 2 (1988): 159–88.

12   Jean-Michel Renaitour, ed., *Où va le cinéma français?* (Paris: Éditions Baudinière, 1937), 99. For information about sound technology in various European exhibition industries, see "Le Nombre des cinémas en Europe et la proportion des salles sonorisées," *Livre d'or du cinéma français*, January 1931. Germany at the time had converted 27 percent of its just over five thousand

cinemas to sound, while Great Britain had converted 65 percent of 4,200. In France, which had the same number of cinemas as the UK, the conversion rate was just 14 percent.

13 "Les Présentations," *Le Figaro*, October 25, 1931, 8.

14 Charles O'Brien, in *Cinema's Conversion to Sound: Technology and Film Style in France and the U.S.* (Bloomington: Indiana University Press, 2005), discusses the "sound" categories of films in France at this time. Besides the *film parlant*, there was also the *film sonore*, that is, the film that "had been shot silent and then supplemented with a separately recorded soundtrack." See pages 68–69.

15 *Le Figaro*, October 31, 1931, 9. The advertisement referred to Capra's film as the "grand film Américain parlant français."

16 For a discussion of film journalism in France between the late teens and early 1930s, see Colin Crisp, *The Classic French Cinema, 1930–1960* (Bloomington: Indiana University Press, 1997), 216–22. Crisp discusses the founding of *Pour Vous*, and Bailby's interest in cinema, on page 220. Abel, *French Cinema*, 245–50, also examines film journalism from about the same period.

17 *Pour Vous*, January 22, 1931, 15.

18 *La Semaine à Paris*, January 16, 1931, 52.

19 *Pour Vous*, January 22, 1931, 15. For news of *À l'Ouest rien de nouveau*, see, for instance, Morienval, "Toutes les horreurs de la guerre dans *Quatre de l'infanterie*," *La Semaine à Paris*, December 19, 1930, 60–61.

20 For news of the radio show in Nantes featuring music from *Mon coeur incognito*, see, for example, issues of *L'Ouest-Éclair*, from February 24, 1931, 10; March 10, 1931, 14; and March 14, 1931, 9. For the film's play dates in Nantes, see *L'Ouest-Éclair*, September 8, 1931, 5.

21 For *Les Quatre Plumes blanches* in Paris, see *La Semaine à Paris*, May 9, 1930, 76. For the film in Marseille, see "Aux quatre coins de la France," *Pour Vous*, July 17, 1930, 15.

22 Henri Hugault, "Au Moulin-Rouge: Le public manifeste contre la projection d'un film sonore américain," *Le Figaro*, December 9, 1929, 3.

23 For the movement of *J'étais une espionne* through Paris, see *La Semaine à Paris*, November 17, 1933, 33; December 15, 1933, 43; January 5, 1934, 39; January 28, 1934, 36; February 16, 1934, 37; and April 10, 1934, 38.

24 *La Revue de l'écran*, May 11, 1934, 7.

25 François Garçon, in his book *La Distribution cinématographique en France 1907–1957* (Paris: CNRS Éditions, 2006), discusses the dominance, by 1950, of Hollywood through the example of the Paramount studio, which that year distributed at least one hundred films in France. See page 194.

26 Crisp uses the term in the title of his book, *The Classic French Cinema*. See also the conclusion, "The Classic French Cinema and the New Wave," 415–22.

27 Frédéric Hervé, "Encombrante censure: La place de la Commission de contrôle des films dans l'organigramme de la politique du cinéma (1959–1969)," in *Le Cinéma: Une affaire d'état 1945–1970*, ed. Dimitri Vezyroglou (Paris: Comité d'histoire du ministère de la Culture et de la Communication, 2014), 123–32.

28 Garçon, *La Distribution cinématographique*, 124–25.

29 Garçon, *La Distribution cinématographique*, 105.

30 SNEG, *Étude du comportement des spectateurs du Gaumont* (Paris: Societé nouvelle des établissements Gaumont, 1948).

31 Renaitour, *Où va le cinéma français?*; Claude Degand, *Étude de marché du cinéma français* (Paris: Centre national de la cinématographie, 1954).

32 For a more extensive discussion of cinema chains in Paris, see Garçon, *La Distribution cinématographique*, 98–104.

33 Admission prices are very difficult to determine from the available sources. See, for example, *La Semaine à Paris*, March 31, 1931, and the listing and advertisement for the Rex cinema on pages 39 and 41.

34 For historical information about the Gaumont-Palace, see Wikipédia en français, s.v. "Gaumont-Palace," accessed September 24, 2016, https://fr.wikipedia.org/wiki/Gaumont-Palace; and also Xavier Delamare, "Gaumont Palace," Cinema Treasures, accessed September 24, 2016, http://cinematreasures.org/theaters/6787.

35 "L'Équipement et l'outillage; Une date dans les annals du spectacle; La réouverture du Gaumont-Palace," *Les Spectacles*, July 24, 1931, 4.

36 "Supplément du #81," *L'écran français*, January 15–21, 1947, 4.

37 Lorenz Jäger, *Adorno: A Political Biography* (New Haven, CT: Yale University Press, 2004), 62.

38 *Le Petit Parisien*, March 27, 1938, 7.

39 *Paris-Soir*, March 17, 1938, 13.

40 As just one example among many, the daily newspaper *Le Petit Parisien* gave *L'Impossible Monsieur Bébé* a featured review. See André Le Bret, "Cinéma," March 21, 1938, 8.

41 "Autour d'Alger," *L'Echo d'Alger*, June 20, 1939, 4

42 "Aujourd'hui," *L'Ouest-Éclair*, June 13, 1940, 3.

Chapter 1: The Cinemas and the Films

1 "Voici les films qui passent à Paris," *Pour Vous*, October 12, 1933, 15.

2 For a discussion of the development of the Champs-Élysées in the 1920s as a location for shopping and going to the movies, see Meusy, *Écrans français, vol 2*: 120.

3 In 1931 the population of the eighteenth arrondissement was around 290,000, while the first arrondissement had only 42,000 inhabitants. The fifth, sixth, and ninth had 118,000, 100,000, and 103,000, respectively. See Wendell Cox Consultancy, "Paris Arrondissements: Post 1860 Population and Population Density," Demographia, last modified March 24, 2001, http://www.demographia.com/db-paris-arr1999. htm.

4 For a discussion of the development of multiple film programs in France, see Crisp, *Classic French Cinema*, 15–17. Just as in the United States, these programs were not uncontroversial. Many film distributors and producers argued against them and also argued against film screenings that began after midnight. There were various injunctions passed in France against double bills and early morning screenings in the 1930s, but none was ever implemented.

5 *Pour Vous*, October 12, 1933, 15; October 5, 1933, 15.

6 *Pour Vous*, October 12, 1933, 15; October 19, 1933, 15.

7 "Paris Hideaway Coins Money with Silents," *Variety*, June 7, 1932, 11.

8 *Le Chanteur de jazz* opened in Paris in January 1929 at the Aubert-Palace on the boulevard des Italiens. See *La Semaine à Paris*, January 25, 1929, 85.

9 *Pour Vous*, January 8, 1931, 15; April 9, 1931, 15; November 5, 1931, 15.

10 *Pour Vous*, April 9, 1931, 15.

11 *Pour Vous*, April 9, 1931, 15.

12 For a history of the building, see the website of the Bellevilloise at http://www .labellevilloise.com/.

13 For details of the opening of Chaplin's film in Paris, see Lucette Benissier, "Lettre à M. Charlie Chaplin," *Pour Vous*, March 26, 1931, 2; "L'accueil de Paris à Charlie Chaplin," *Pour Vous*, March 26, 1931, 3; and for information about the opening at Théâtre Marigny, see *Pour Vous*, April 9, 1931, 15.

14 Benissier, "Du monde entier . . . ," *Pour Vous*, March 5, 1931, 11.

15 For a discussion of German screenings of *All Quiet on the Western Front*, and the subsequent banning of the film in Germany, see Thomas Doherty, *Hollywood and Hitler, 1933–1939* (New York: Columbia University Press, 2013), 1–10.

16 For *All Quiet on the Western Front* in Germany, see Guido Enderis, "Nazis Renew Fight on Remarque Film," *New York Times*, December 10, 1931, 10. For *À l'Ouest rien de nouveau* in Paris, see, for example, *La Semaine à Paris*, February 6, 1931, 59.

17 For *La Fin du monde* and *L'Énigmatique Mr. Parkes*, see *La Semaine à Paris*, February 6, 1931, 68; for *No, No, Nanette*, see page 61; for *Le Chant de bandit*, see page 67; for *The Love Parade*, see *La Semaine à Paris*, July 4, 1930, 23.

18 Raymond Villette, "*Jeunes Filles en uniforme*," *Hebdo*, July 2, 1932, 44.

19 Villette, "*Quatre dans le tempête*," *Hebdo*, July 2, 1932, 43.

20 Villette, "*Frankenstein*," *Hebdo*, July 2, 1932, 42.

21 *La Semaine à Paris*, July 1, 1932, 30; November 4, 1932, 26.

22 François Ribadeau Dumas, "*Le Shanghai Express*," *La Semaine à Paris*, April 28, 1932, 11.

23 "Why Paris Goes to the Movies," *Literary Digest*, March 9, 1929, 21–22.

24 "Why Paris Goes to the Movies," 21.

25 "Paris Raps Our Movie Methods," *Literary Digest*, April 11, 1931, 17.

26 For an examination of Matthews's career as well as his experiences reporting on Castro, see Anthony DePalma, *The Man Who Invented Fidel: Castro, Cuba, and Herbert Matthews of the* New York Times (New York: PublicAffairs, 2007).

27 Douglas Gomery, one of the few film historians to discuss air-conditioning, writes that "Balaban & Katz's Central Park Theatre, opened in 1917, was the first mechanically air cooled theatre in the world," and then further examines the Balaban and Katz theatre chain's efforts to bring the technology to other sites. See Gomery, *Shared Pleasures: A History of Movie Presentation in the United States* (Madison: University of Wisconsin Press, 1992), 53–54.

28 Herbert L. Matthews, "The Screen in Paris," *New York Times*, September 18, 1932, X4.

29 Matthews, "The Screen in Paris," X4.

30 Matthews, "Paris Views New Films and Theatres," *New York Times*, January 15, 1933, X4.

31 Matthews, "Paris Views New Films and Theatres," X4.

32 Matthews, "A Glimpse at the Cinema of Paris," *New York Times*, April 2, 1933, X4.

33 Jacques Chabannes, "Les Nouveaux films," *La Semaine à Paris*, December 16, 1932, 25.

34 *La Semaine à Paris*, January 29, 1937, 23.

35 Matthews wrote about the Marignan in "The Cinema in Paris," *New York Times*, June 11, 1933, X2. The Marignan was "less pretentious than the Rex, but its simplicity and comfort make it quite as attractive." The Gaumont-Palace, in the eighteenth arrondissement, was even larger than the Rex, with around six thousand seats.

36 "More Theatres in Paris," *New York Times*, April 23, 1933, E3. This report also noted increases in Parisian theatrical venues, from 509 in 1930, to 641 in 1932. In addition, 1932 "saw 12 street fairs in Paris, and 156 in the suburbs," while "ten gambling halls opened," and the city hosted "two hundred and thirty-seven open air concerts."

37 For a discussion of the French preference for French films, see, for example, Matthews, "Paris Screen Notes," *New York Times*, May 1, 1932, X4.

38 Matthews, "The Cinema in Paris: To Dub or Not to Dub Films—Successful Original American Pictures," *New York Times*, June 4, 1933, X2.

39 *La Semaine à Paris*, May 5, 1933, 37.

40 *La Semaine à Paris*, May 26, 1933, 46.

41 *Pour Vous*, September 8, 1933, 15.

42 My listings from *Pour Vous* begin on June 9, 1933, when *L'Ange bleu* was already playing at the Corso-Opèra. *Pour Vous*, June 9, 1933, 15. On November 24, 1933, the film finally was replaced by *Jeunes Filles en uniforme*, the famous Leontine Sagan film that also enjoyed a long run at the Corso. *Pour Vous*, November 23, 1933, 15.

43 In the second arrondissement, the Cinéphone and the Cinéac showed only newsreels, with the latter presenting only those made by Fox, the American film company. In the ninth, the newsreel cinemas were the Ciné-Actualités and the Ciné-Paris-Midi. The Pathé-Journal showed Pathé newsreels in the tenth, and the Ciné-*Paris-Soir*, associated with the newspaper *Paris-Soir*, showed newsreels in the eleventh.

44 The Italian-French coproduction was *Je vous aimerai toujours* (1933), directed by Mario Camerini, and starring French actors Lisette Lanvin and Alexander D'Arcy. The Spanish-French film was *Pax* (1932), directed by Francisco Elias, with Gina Manès and Camille Bert. The French-Belgian film was *Le Mariage de Mlle Beulemans* (1932). It is also possible that, for instance, the Italian-French coproduction was an Italian film made in multiple languages.

45 Films made by American, German, and British corporations, produced in French and often in France, were relatively common during the early 1930s. For

example, MGM made its French films in Hollywood, while Paramount made French films at the Joinville studio outside Paris. German companies, which, after the US film firms, produced the most French films, made them at the Neubabelsburg studio near Berlin and at the Epinay studio in France. During this period, René Clair, Julien Duvivier, and Jacques Feyder all made films for German concerns. See Crisp, *Classic French Cinema*, 24.

46 For information about exhibition strategies and practices in the United States during the period, see Tino Balio, *Grand Design: Hollywood as a Modern Business Enterprise, 1930–1939* (Berkeley: University of California Press, 1995), and especially chapter 4, "Feeding the Maw of Exhibition," 73–107.

47 The two cinemas in the ninth arrondissement showing *La Maternelle* were the Ciné Vol-Opéra and the Agriculteurs. *Pour Vous*, September 7, 1933, 15; and September 21, 1933, 15.

48 Lucien Wahl wrote the review of *King Kong* for *Pour Vous*, in "Les films nouveaux," September 14, 1933, 6.

49 For play dates for *Théodore et Cie*, see *Pour Vous*, June 8, 1933, 15; and August 31, 1933, 15.

50 "Sur les écrans d'Alger," *L'Echo d'Alger*, January 18, 1934, 4; "Au Régent Cinéma," *Oran-Sports*, February 9, 1934, 4.

51 "Tout clair d'optimisme *Toto* amusera," *Le Petit Parisien*, September 8, 1933, 6.

52 A very partial list of these problems would include the French film industry's inability to exploit fully the foreign market during the early sound era; egregious government taxes on the motion picture industry; and the inability of film firms to stay in business (in 1933, fifty-eight film production companies faced bankruptcy, and by 1935 both Pathé and Gaumont had collapsed). Colin Crisp has written the most extensive history of the magnitude of the problems facing the French film industry at this time. In *The Classic French Cinema*, see page 19 for details about France's conversion to sound as well as the country's foreign markets; for the effect of tax issues on the industry, see pages 17–18; see page 21 for information about firms going into bankruptcy, and page 31 for the collapse of Gaumont and Pathé. Crisp discusses the problem of postmidnight screenings on page 17. Other histories of French national cinema also discuss the industry's chronic problems. In Alan Williams's *Republic of Images: A History of French Filmmaking* (Cambridge, MA: Harvard University Press, 1992), see chapter 3, "The Golden Age of Sound Cinema," 157–212. For a more measured view of the industry's problems during the 1930s, see Yann Darré, *Histoire sociale du cinéma français* (Paris: Éditions La Découverte, 2000), 49–58.

53 In France and the United States, there has been only sporadic historical interest in charting the film cultures of France's colonies. See, for example, Roger Aubry, "Le Cinéma au Cameroun," *African Arts* 2, no. 3 (spring 1969): 66–69; Peter Bloom, *French Colonial Documentary: Mythologies of Humanitarianism* (Minneapolis: University of Minnesota Press, 2008); and Harold Salemson, "A Film at War," *Hollywood Quarterly* 1, no. 4 (July 1946): 416–19 (about Tunisia).

54 All of these examples come from one issue: "Sur les écrans des quatre coins de la France," *Pour Vous*, July 7, 1932, 14.

55 Leo Charney and Vanessa Schwartz, "Introduction," in *Cinema and the Invention of Modern Life*, ed. Leo Charney and Vanessa Schwartz (Berkeley: University of California Press, 1996), 3.

Chapter 2: The Ciné-Clubs

1 André de Fouquières, "La Semaine à Paris: Annoncée et commentée par André de Fouquières," *La Semaine à Paris*, April 12, 1935, 6–7.

2 Abel, *French Cinema*; Dudley Andrew, "Cinematic Politics in Postwar France: Bazin Before Cahiers," *Cinéaste* 12, no. 1 (1982): 12–16.

3 See, for instance, Darré, *Histoire sociale du cinéma français*, 61.

4 Paul Léglise, *Histoire de la politique du cinéma français: Le cinéma et la IIIe république* (R. Pichon et R. Durand-Auzias: Paris, 1970), 234.

5 Geneviève Guillaume-Grimau discusses the founding of the Cinémathèque but not the club that came before it. See Guillaume-Grimaud, *Le Cinéma du Front Populaire* (L'Herminier: Paris, 1986), 32.

6 The materials from the Bibliothèque nationale de France can be found in its digital library, Gallica, at http://gallica.bnf.fr/?lang=EN.

7 For examples of screenings at these locations, see *La Semaine à Paris*, March 29, 1935, 32; and April 12, 1935, 34.

8 *Annuaire général des lettres* (Paris: Annuaire general des lettres, 1933), 466. After the war, as well, while the ciné-club movement remained centered in Paris, there were clubs throughout France. See, for example, Suzanne Frère, "Les Loisirs à Auxerre," *Cahiers internationaux de sociologie* 7 (1949): 101–8.

9 For a discussion of the economic upheaval of the period, see Crisp, *Classic French Cinema*, 1–42.

10 For a discussion of the Congrès des ciné-clubs, see "Le Congrès des ciné-clubs," *Cinéa-Ciné*, December 1, 1929, 25–28.

11 For the founding of *La Tribune Libre* du Cinéma, see Abel, *French Cinema*, 251–57. For the *Tribune* radio program, see "Les Propos d'Antonio," *Le Figaro*, May 24, 1939, 4B. Bessy was known as a screenwriter, novelist, actor, and journalist.

12 For information about the club Des Amis de *Pour Vous*, see, for instance, *Pour Vous*, May 22, 1940, 15; the film that Friday would be a sneak preview of Christian-Jacque's *L'Enfer des anges* (1941).

13 "Cinémas," *Le Temps*, June 4, 1940, 2.

14 "Une soirée en l'honneur de Jean Grémillon à *La Tribune Libre* du Cinéma," *La semaine à Paris*, December 26, 1930, 64–5. Grémillon became a ciné-club favorite after the war, when he appealed especially to secular cinéphiles, while at the same time Catholic enthusiasts championed the work of Robert Bresson. See Roxane Hamery, "Les Ciné-clubs dans la tourmente: La querelle du non-commercial (1948–1955)," *Vingtième siècle, revue d'histoire* 115 (2012): 76.

15 "Les 'Clubs' de cinéma," *Le Temps*, January 18, 1936, 5; *Le Temps*, February 17, 1938, 5; "Cinémas," *Le Temps*, March 9, 1940, 5.

16 *La Semaine à Paris*, October 11, 1935, 35; *La Semaine à Paris*, January 1, 1937, 7; "Un vrai festival René Clair," *Le Temps*, March 18, 1937, 5.

17 For a sense of the excitement in the French film press when a new Clair film appeared, see the constant coverage in *Pour Vous* of the Paris opening of *Le Million*: January 8, 1931, 14; February 12, 1931, 2; March 26, 1931, 8–9; April 9, 1931, 2; April 23, 1931, 12.

18 *La Semaine à Paris*, May 22, 1936, 38–9.

19 *La Semaine à Paris*, May 22, 1936, 39.

20 "Les 'Clubs' de cinéma," 5.

21 *Le Temps*, December 21, 1938, 5, for Méliès and Zecca; January 11, 1939, 5 for *Le Golem* and *La Charotte fantôme*; and January 18, 1939, 5 for *Metropolis*.

22 "Paris Hideaway Coins Money with Silents," *Variety*, June 7, 1932, 11.

23 For the program of British documentaries, see "Petits Nouvelles," *Le Temps*, February 17, 1940, 5; for the German and Russian films, see "Cinémas," *Le Temps*, March 1, 1940, 3; for the program on "films fantastiques," see "Le cinéma," *Le Temps*, April 3, 1940 3; the Marey-to-Renoir series is mentioned in "Cinémas," *Le Temps*, April 16, 1940, 3; and for the conference on the erotic in cinema see "Petites nouvelles," *Le Temps*, May 5, 1938, 6.

24 *La Semaine à Paris*, May 22, 1936, 40.

25 "Le Problème du film en couleur," *L'Humanité*, April 9, 1927, 4.

26 "Les films à voir: *Ivan le Terrible et La Grande Parade*," *L'Humanité*, April 9, 1927, 4.

27 "Ciné-Informations," *L'Humanité*, February 5, 1935, 6.

28 "Petites nouvelles," *Le Temps*, February 17, 1938, 5.

29 *La Semaine à Paris*, May 22, 1936, 40.

30 *La Semaine à Paris*, March 31, 1933, 42, 49.

31 Darré, *Histoire sociale du cinéma français*, 61.

32 Léglise discusses the ciné-club legislation in *Histoire de la politique du cinéma français*, 224–5.

33 For a discussion of Dulac's significance to the ciné-club movement during the 1920s, see Abel, *French Cinema*, 251–7.

34 "Avant-Garde et clubs," *Ciné Pour Tous*, November 15, 1929, 27.

35 Raymond Villette, "Le cinéma au Conseil national des femmes françaises," *Hebdo*, February 13, 1932, 11. For a brief history of the Conseil national des femmes françaises, see Wikipédia en français, s.v. "Conseil national des femmes françaises," accessed September 1, 2014, http://fr.wikipedia.org/wiki/Conseil _national_des_femmes_françaises.

36 "La Femme moderne," *Le Populaire*, April 5, 1931, 1.

37 *La Semaine à Paris*, October 10, 1930, 51.

38 Derain's article in *Cinémonde* is cited in Pierre Leprohon, "La Leçon de *La Foule*," *Cinéa*, May 1, 1929, 10; *Cinéa* cites her opinion about Florey, March 1930, 6 (it is unclear where Derain's essay about Florey first appeared).

39 *Cinéa*, November 1, 1927, 24.

40 *Annuaire général des lettres*, 459–63.

41 "L'artiste Janie Marèze (sic) tuée près de Sainte-Maxime dans un accident d'auto," *Le Petit Parisien*, August 16, 1931, 1.

42 "Cinémas," *Le Matin*, November 24, 1936, 6; "Cinémas," *Journal des débats politiques et litteraires*, December 2, 1936, 4; February 2, 1937, 4; March 25, 1937, 4.

43 Émile Vuillermoz, "Le Cinéma: Les 'clubs' de cinéma," *Le Temps*, January 18, 1936, 5.

44 For the screening of *L'Aurore*, see *La Semaine à Paris*, May 17, 1935, 29; for Clair, see *La Semaine à Paris*, October 11, 1935, 35.

45 *La Semaine à Paris*, March 29, 1935, 32. For a discussion of Netter's celebrity in France at the time, see Joelle Neulander, *Programming National Identity: The Culture of Radio in 1930s France* (Baton Rouge: Louisiana State University Press, 2009), 109–110.

46 *La Semaine à Paris*, April 12, 1935, 34. For Chaumont's career, see Mary Lynn Stewart, *Dressing Modern Frenchwomen: Marketing Haute Couture, 1919–1939* (Baltimore: Johns Hopkins University Press, 2008), 50.

47 *Pour Vous*, May 15, 1940; May 22, 1940; May 29, 1940, 15.

48 For both club locations, see *Ciné-Mondial*, January 21–28, 1944, 2.

49 "3me séance de notre club," *Ciné-Mondial*, January 7, 1944, 3.

50 "Notre club," *Ciné-Mondial*, July 7–14, 1944, 1.

51 "Notre club," *Ciné-Mondial*, July 7–14, 1944, 1.

52 *Ciné-Mondial*, March 31–April 7, 1944, 1.

53 "Notre club," *Ciné-Mondial*, January 21–28, 1944, 2.

54 "Gabriello au club," *Ciné-Mondial*, May 26, 1944, 2. In *Death in the City of Light: The Serial Killer of Nazi-Occupied Paris* (New York: Crown Publishers, 2011), 181, David King writes of how "electricity, gas, and many other services no longer worked" toward the end of the Occupation. As early as June 1943, Sartre's *Les mouches* opened during the afternoon rather than the evening, because of mandated "electricity cuts" (see page 61).

55 Vuillermoz, "Le Cinéma," 5.

Chapter 3: Chevalier and Dietrich

1 *Cinéa*, no. 12, February 2, 1931.

2 *Annuaire général des lettres, 1933–34*, 463–65.

3 For a discussion of Tedesco as an early enthusiast of the film archive and film history, see Christophe Gauthier and Laure Brost, "1927, Year One of the French Film Heritage?" *Film History* 17, nos. 2/3 (2005): 289–306.

4 I am indebted here to a significant tradition of scholarship regarding the phenomenon of French stardom, in movies as well as in other forms. See, for example, Susan Hayward, *Simone Signoret: The Star as Cultural Sign* (London: Continuum, 2004); Kelley Conway, *Chanteuse in the City: The Realist Singer in French Film* (Berkeley: University of California Press, 2004); Ginette Vincendeau, Stars and Stardom in French Cinema (London: Continuum, 2000); Jean-Michel Guiraud, "La Vie intellectuelle et artistique à Marseille au

temps du Maréchal Pétain," *Revue d'histoire de la Deuxième Guerre mondiale* (January 1979): 63–90; Gerry Harris, "Regarding History: Some Narratives Concerning the Café-Concert, Le Music Hall, and the Feminist Academic," *TDR* 40, no. 4 (winter 1996): 70–84.

5 *Mon Film*, July 11, 1930, 9. Chevalier won in a landslide, with more than thirteen thousand votes, while Jean Dehelly, in second, received slightly more than two thousand.

6 *Les Spectacles d'Alger*, December 30, 1931, 2.

7 *Cinéa*, April 1930, 14–24.

8 *Cinéa*, April 1930; in this issue, see Jean Tedesco, "Vers un théâtre mecanique," 2; Paul Ramain, "Réflexions sur un film mal compris: *Un chien andalou* de Luis Bunuel," 6–7; Pierre Mac Orlan, "À propos de *La Petite Marchande d'allumettes*," 37; Henri Baranger, "Opinions de cinéastes: Valery Inkischinoff," 35.

9 Jean-Michel Frodon and Dina Iordanova, eds., *Cinemas of Paris* (Edgecliffe, Scotland: St. Andrews Film Studies, 2016), 246–49.

10 *La Semaine à Paris*, December 12, 1930, 67.

11 For the movement from *Whoopee* to *Cocoanuts* to *Reaching for the Moon*, see issues of *Pour Vous* from 1931: March 5, 1931, 15; May 21, 1931, 15; June 11, 1931, 15; August 6, 1931, 15.

12 *La Semaine à Paris*, February 2, 1932, 10.

13 "Bruits de studios," *Paris-Soir*, December 27, 1931, 5.

14 "Voici les films qui passent à Paris," *Pour Vous*, October 12, 1933, 15.

15 J. M., "Le Cinéma 'les Miracles' inauguré avec *Hallelujah*," *La Semaine à Paris*, December 26, 1930, 61–62.

16 For attitudes toward *À l'Ouest rien de nouveau*, see the film review in *Les Spectacles d'Alger* and also "Chronique d'Argus et de Judex," December 9, 1931, 2, 4. For reports about *Sous les toits de Paris* and its global importance, see *Pour Vous*, January 8, 1931, 8; and February 19, 1931, 10.

17 Charles de Saint-Cyr, "Vingt chose à propos de *L'Ange bleu*, le très grand succès des Ursulines," *La Semaine à Paris*, December 26, 1930, 62–64.

18 "Dans les maisons de production," *Les spectacles*, June 3, 1931, 4.

19 M. P., "*L'Ange bleu*," *Les Spectacles d'Alger*, June 17, 1931, 3.

20 Patrice Petro, "*The Blue Angel* in Multiple-Language Versions: The Inner Thighs of Miss Dietrich," in *Dietrich Icon*, ed. Gerd Gemünden and Mary R. Desjardins (Durham, NC: Duke University Press, 2007), 159n1.

21 "*La Chanson de Paris*," *Les Spectacles d'Alger*, January 28, 1930, 11.

22 "Régent Cinéma," *Les Spectacles d'Alger*, January 21, 1930, 9.

23 "Splendid Select Cinéma," *Les Spectacles d'Alger*, February 4, 1930, 12–13.

24 "*Le Chanteur de jazz*," *Les Spectacles d'Alger*, February 25, 1930, 7.

25 Paul Bachellion, "Les tendances actuelles du cinéma," *Cinéa*, April 1931, 3.

26 Aline Bourgoin, "Qui préférez-vous: Greta Garbo ou Marlène Dietrich," *Pour Vous*, February 5, 1931, 11.

27 Aline Bourgoin, "Résultats d'une petite enquête: Greta Garbo? Ou Marlène Dietrich?," *Pour Vous*, February 19, 1931, 7.

28 For *Grand Hôtel* in Hanoi, see "Prochainement au Chanatecler," *Chantecler Revue*, May 12, 1934, 2, which seems to be the newsletter for a major cinema in the city.

29 *La Semaine à Paris*, March 31, 1933, 49.

30 Philie, "Splendid Cinéma: *La Belle Ténébreuse*," *Les Spectacles d'Alger*, June 24, 1931, 2.

31 Philie, "Splendid Cinéma: *La Belle Ténébreuse*," *Les Spectacles d'Alger*, June 24, 1931, 2.

32 René Lehmann, "*Anna Christie*," *Pour Vous*, March 19, 1931, 9.

33 "C'est un film Paramount," *Les Spectacles*, January 23, 1931, 7.

34 "*Un dimanche à New York*," *Les Spectacles d'Alger*, January 21, 1930, 10.

35 "*Une heure près de toi*," *Les Spectacles d'Alger*, February 22, 1933, 2.

36 "Mistinguett dans 'C'est Paris,'" *Les Spectacles d'Alger*, December 24, 1930, 2; "Mistinguett," *Les Spectacles d'Alger*, December 28, 1932, 2.

37 Bernard Gervaise, "Les gaietés de la semaine," *Le Journal amusant*, August 31, 1930, 2.

38 References to *Parade d'amour* and "M. C." come from *Cinéa*, April 1930, 10, 17.

39 "*La Chanson de Paris*," *Les Spectacles d'Alger*, January 28, 1930, 11–12.

40 "Les succès du jour," *Hebdo*, September 5, 1931, 5.

41 "*L'Ange bleu*," *Les spectacles*, March 20, 1931, 6.

42 "En courant la prétentaine," *Pour Vous*, March 5, 1931, 2.

43 *L'Association Médicale*, December 1931, 656–7.

44 For Chevalier's departure from Hollywood, see Edward Behr, *The Good Frenchman: The True Story of the Life and Times of Maurice Chevalier* (New York: Villard Books, 1993), 210–16.

45 "Débobinons," *Ciné France*, December 3, 1937, 5.

46 "Maurice Chevalier," *Les Spectacles d'Alger*, March 16, 1938, 2.

47 For a discussion of the charges against Chevalier and the French Communist Party's interest in his case, see Behr, *Good Frenchman*, 285–318.

Chapter 4: Violence at the Cinema

1 "Au Moulin-Rouge: Le public manifeste contre la projection d'un film sonore américain," *Le Figaro*, December 9, 1929, 3. I learned of the incident at the screening from Greg M. Colón Semenza and Bob Hasenfratz, *The History of British Literature on Film, 1895–2015* (London: Bloomsbury Academic, 2015), 155.

2 Xavier Delamare, "Moulin Rouge Theatre," Cinema Treasures, accessed December 4, 2018, http://cinematreasures.org/theaters/7133. For information about the Moulin Rouge as part of the Pathé chain, see *Comoedia*, November 9, 1930, 5.

3 "Paris pêle mêle," *La Rampe*, November 1, 1929, 15.

4 "Le gala d'ouverture du Moulin-Rouge-Cinéma," *Les Spectacles*, December 13, 1929, 8.

5 "Au Moulin-Rouge Cinéma," *Cinéa*, December 15, 1929, 6.

6 "Au Moulin-Rouge," *Le Figaro*, 3.

7   "Au Moulin-Rouge," *Le Figaro*, 3; *Les Trois masques* was playing at the
     Max Linder cinema in the ninth arrondissement. See *La Semaine à Paris*,
     December 13, 1929, 78.

8   "Au Moulin-Rouge," *Le Figaro*, 3.

9   Claude Jeantet, "L'Écran de la Semaine: La chute des *Folies-Fox*," *L'Action
     française*, December 13, 1929, 4.

10   Jeantet, "L'Écran de la Semaine," 4.

11   R. L., "À propos des progrès du cinéma," *La Renaissance*, December 14, 1929, 12.

12   Philippe Soupault, "Le cinéma," *Europe*, March 15, 1930, 427–9.

13   For the reopening of Studio 28, see Paul Hammond, *L'Âge d'or* (London: British
     Film Institute, 1997), 64. For the listing of the films at Studio 28 that week, see
     Pour Vous, March 5, 1931, 15. The Starevich film is unnamed in the *Pour Vous*
     listing.

14   Emilie de Brigard discusses *Les Mangeurs d'hommes*—and the hoax—in "The
     History of Ethnographic Film," in *Toward a Science of Man: Essays in the History
     of Anthropology*, ed. Timothy H. Thoresen (Paris: Mouton Publishers, 1975), 42.

15   For a narrative of the actions of the Jeunesses patriotes and Jean Chiappe, see
     Hammond, *L'Âge d'or*, 60–61. See also Georges Sadoul, *Dictionnaire des films*
     (Paris: Éditions du Seuil, 1965), 9.

16   "Police Check Joyous Parisians at Showing of U.S. Newsreels," *Los Angeles Times*,
     October 16, 1944, 1.

17   "Scène et l'écran: Les premiers films étrangers à Paris," *Combat*, October 18,
     1944; collected in *"Eve a commence," film de Henry Koster*, Bibliothèque
     nationale de France, département Arts du spectacle, 8-RSUPP-1535, accessed
     May 10, 2018, http://catalogue.bnf.fr/ark:/12148/cb426750620.

18   See, for instance, Steve Neale, "*Triumph of the Will*: Notes on Documentary and
     Spectacle," *Screen* 20, no. 1 (Spring 1979): 63–86.

19   Crisp, *Classic French Cinema*, 33–35.

20   Darré, *Histoire sociale du cinéma français*, 49–50.

21   In fact, no French cabinet "lasted longer than three years, and several collapsed
     within days." Benjamin F. Martin, *France in 1938* (Baton Rouge: Louisiana State
     University Press, 2005), 9.

22   For a review of this debate, see Steven Ricci, *Cinema and Fascism: Italian Film
     and Society, 1922–1943* (Berkeley: University of California Press, 2008), and in
     particular pages 1–18.

23   See Robert Soucy's two volumes, *French Fascism: The First Wave, 1924–1933*
     (New Haven, CT: Yale University Press, 1986); and *French Fascism: The Second
     Wave, 1934–1939* (New Haven, CT: Yale University Press, 1995). Soucy takes on
     the argument as to whether or not these groups were fascist in the first volume.
     See "Preface," xi–xix.

24   Zeev Sternhell, "Anatomie d'un movement fasciste en France: Le faisceau de
     Georges Valois," *Revue française de science politique* 26, no. 1 (February 1976):
     5–40. See page 6 in particular.

25   Meusy, *Écrans français de l'entre-deux-guerres,* volume II, 196–97.

26 Sean Kennedy provides an excellent history of the development of French fascist groups during the period in *Reconciling France against Democracy: The Croix de Feu and the Parti Social Français, 1927–1945* (Montreal: McGill-Queen's University Press, 2007). See especially pages 18–19.

27 Soucy, in *French Fascism: The First Wave*, provides an outstanding review of the motivating forces in the development of French fascism. See in particular chapter 1, "Origins and Background," 1–26.

28 Philip Nord, in *France's New Deal: From the Thirties to the Postwar Era* (Princeton, NJ: Princeton University Press, 2010), provides a compelling history of the contributions of the French right to the construction of "modern" France in the 1930s and the immediate postwar period. See in particular chapter 1, "The Crisis of the Thirties," 25–87.

29 See chapter 1 of Kennedy, *Reconciling France against Democracy*, 17–50, for the issues motivating French fascists and their frequent common cause with other rightwing groups.

30 Kevin Passmore establishes this historiography of French fascism during the period in "Boy Scouting for Grown-Ups? Paramilitarism in the Croix de Feu and the Parti Social Français," *French Historical Studies* 19, no. 2 (autumn 1995): 527–57. See in particular pages 527–32.

31 Soucy, *French Fascism: The First Wave*, 3–4.

32 Precise numbers of cinemas in the two chains would vary over the 1930s. My numbers here come from the Parisian newspaper *Comoedia*, November 9, 1930, 5.

33 "Violentes manifestations dans un cinéma des boulevards," *Ciné-Comoedia*, November 9, 1930, 1.

34 For new films and reissues that week, see *La Semaine à Paris*, November 7, 1930, 62, 66–67, and 82–83.

35 For a discussion of the two films, see Morienval, "Toutes les horreurs de la guerre dans *Quatre de l'infanterie*," *La Semaine à Paris*, December 19, 1930, 60–61. For a discussion of the opening of the Ermitage cinema, see Meusy, *Écrans français de l'entre-deux-guerres*, volume II, 125.

36 In French periodicals from the period, the version of *À l'Ouest rien de nouveau* in Paris is advertised as being "sonore" rather than "parlant," which typically indicated a silent version with sound effects rather than a speaking version. As just one example among many, see *La Semaine à Paris*, January 16, 1931, 51.

37 For cinema listings regarding *À l'Ouest rien de nouveau* and *Quatre de l'infanterie*, see *Pour Vous*, page 15 of each issue, from December 1930 to February 1931. For listings for the week of February 27, see the issue from February 26, 1931, 15.

38 SNEG, *Étude du comportement*, part 2, section 2.

39 The name of the station itself has a political charge. September 4, 1870, marks the end of Napoleon III's reign and the beginning of the Third Republic. By 1931, many French fascists would have had enough of the republic's various center-right and center-left governing coalitions.

40 In assessing metro routes to the Aubert cinema, I am relying on the 1929 and 1934 metro maps provided by Mark Ovenden in *Paris Underground: The Maps, Stations, and Design of the Métro* (New York: Penguin Books, 2009), 63, 69.

41 "Un incident dans un cinéma des boulevards," *Le Petit Parisien*, January 19, 1931, 2.

42 Soucy, *French Fascism: The First Wave*, 11.

43 At least by 1900, those arrondissements, like the eighteenth, in the northern and eastern sections of the city accounted for many of the new members of fascist organizations, and for many of the newly emigrated Eastern European Jews. See Peter M. Rutkoff, "The Ligue des Patriotes: The Nature of the Radical Right and the Dreyfus Affair," *French Historical Studies* 8, no. 4 (Autumn 1974): 585–603. See in particular page 597. See also Rutkoff, *Revanche and Revision: The Ligue des Patriotes and the Origins of the Radical Right in France, 1882–1900* (Athens: Ohio University Press, 1981), 116.

44 "Au Mozart et à l'Aubert Palace: Steeg, chauté au ciné par des camelots du roi," *L'Humanité*, January 19, 1931, 1.

45 Martin, *France in 1938*, 39. Camelots du roi has come to be translated in several ways, but it is very roughly "Newsboys of the King," a reference to the members selling the newspaper *L'Action française* on the street.

46 For the meeting of November 8, see "Conférences, enseignement," *La Semaine à Paris*, November 7, 1930, 90. For the December meeting, see "Communications diverses," *Le Populaire*, December 27, 1930, 5.

47 See Wikipedia, s.v. "Théâtre de l'Ambigu-Comique," accessed June 14, 2018, https://en.wikipedia.org/wiki/Théâtre_de_l%27Ambigu-Comique.

48 For La Rocque's letter, see "L'Affaire Dreyfus et les Croix de feu," *Comoedia*, March 4, 1931, 2; see also "La représentation de l'Affaire Dreyfus à l'Ambigu n'a pas eu lieu hier soir," *Le Matin*, March 5, 1931, 3; and "Le scandale de l'interdiction de l'affaire Dreyfus: L'opinion publique exige la reprise de la pièce," *Le Populaire*, March 8, 1931, 5.

49 "Le gouvernement et sa police aux ordres du fascisme," *Le Populaire*, March 6, 1931, 1–2.

50 Martin, *France in 1938*, 41.

51 "Échec au fascisme à Drancy," *L'Humanité*, May 25, 1934, 2.

52 "Bagarres à Moulins," *L'Humanité*, May 30, 1934, 2.

53 "Toute la population de Cachan dressée contre les fascists," *L'Humanité*, May 25, 1934, 2.

54 "Ce soir, à Saint-Denis, front unique d'action contre le fascism," *L'Humanité*, May 30, 1934, 1.

55 "Manifestation fasciste avortée à Vitry," *L'Humanité*, March 3, 1935, 2.

56 "... Et à Argenteuil," *L'Humanité*, May 25, 1934, 2.

57 Magali Della Sudda, "Right-Wing Feminism and Conservative Women's Militancy in Interwar France," in *The French Right Between the Wars: Political and Intellectual Movements from Conservatism to Fascism*, ed. Samuel Kalman and Sean Kennedy (New York: Berghann Books, 2014), 97–111.

58 "The Paris Riots," *Spectator*, March 19, 1937, 2, accessed July 31, 2017, http://archive.spectator.co.uk/article/19th-march-1937/2/the-paris-riots-the-riot-which-broke-out-at-clichy.

59 Tyler Stovall, "French Communism and Suburban Development: The Rise of the Paris Red Belt," *Journal of Contemporary History* 24, no. 3 (July 1989): 437–60. See especially page 438.

60 "1937: L'émeute de Clichy divise le front populaire," *Alternative Libertaire*, accessed June 29, 2016, http://www.alternativelibertaire.org/?1937-L-emeute-de-Clichy-divise-le.

61 For Clichy population figures in the 1930s and currently, see Wikipédia en français, s.v. "Clichy," accessed June 11, 2019, https://fr.wikipedia.org/wiki/Clichy.

62 My information comes from the July 8, 2015 issue of *Pariscope*, 85.

63 For a description of the geography of the battle, see "Les témoins établissent avec éclat les responsabilités fascistes et policières," *L'Humanité*, March 18, 1937, 2.

64 *La Semaine à Paris*, January 26, 1934, 34; March 9, 1934, 37; July 26, 1935, 18.

65 See advertisement for *Le Jardin d'Allah* in *Le Matin*, March 17, 1937, 6.

66 For Farrére's fascism, see Kennedy, *Reconciling France against Democracy*, 63. For a discussion of the literary and intellectual followers of the fascists, see Alice Kaplan, *The Collaborator: The Trial and Execution of Robert Brasillach* (Chicago: University of Chicago Press, 2001).

67 Mary-Elizabeth O'Brien discusses the theatre and cinema as sites of Nazi surveillance in *Nazi Cinema as Enchantment: The Politics of Entertainment in the Third Reich* (Rochester, NY: Camden House, 2004). See in particular pages 143–4.

68 "Says Nazis Seize Priests," *New York Times*, September 2, 1941, 6.

69 "Says Nazis Seize Priests," 6.

70 There is at least some anecdotal evidence of Nazi authorities patrolling the interiors of Parisian cinemas during the Occupation. In *Death in the City of Light*, David King tells the story of a woman who was almost arrested for walking out of a Nazi newsreel and going to the powder room. See page 140.

71 "Deux agitateurs communistes sont arrêtés à Melun," *Le Matin*, September 1, 1941, 4.

72 "Le film *Face au bolchevisme* projeté dans les salles parisiennes et de banlieue," *Le Matin*, September 8, 1941, 2.

Chapter 5: Occupied Paris

1 *Le Matin*, January 1, 1941, 4.

2 For a listing of cinemas before the surrender, see *Pour vous*, June 5, 1940, 2 (the journal's final issue). The exact number is difficult to determine. The latest listing readily available, in *La Semaine à Paris* for January 29–February 4, 1937, 21, names 233 cinemas, but this does not include the myriad specialty cinemas or cinema clubs. Regarding the closure of all cinemas at the time of the surrender, see Evelyn Ehrlich, *Cinema of Paradox: French Filmmaking under the German Occupation* (New York: Columbia University Press, 1985), 10.

3   Simone de Beauvoir, *Wartime Diary* (Champaign: University of Illinois Press, 2009). As early as September 1, even before France's official entry into the war, de Beauvoir writes of all of the Parisians leaving the city, and the "unending line of cars passing on the quay, crammed with suitcases and sometimes with kids" (see page 38). David King writes of Parisians leaving the city early in 1940, and then claims that "The scale of departures from the French capital had accelerated in May 1940," with the exodus increasing in June, after the surrender. See King, *Death in the City of Light*, 9. See also Hanna Diamond, *Fleeing Hitler: France 1940* (Oxford: Oxford University Press, 2008).

4   See film listings in *Pour Vous*, June 5, 1940, 2.

5   Jean-Pierre Jeancolas provides an excellent, brief history of cinema during the first few months of the Occupation in *Histoire du cinéma français* (Paris: Armand Colin, 2015), 45–48.

6   In Ehrlich, *Cinema of Paradox*, see pages 1–43 for discussion of the film scene in Paris as the war started and the German policy toward cinema once the Occupation began, including the formation of Continental Films. See pages 147–48 for an analysis of German "benevolence" toward the French film industry. Jean-Pierre Jeancolas, in *15 ans d'années trente: Le cinéma des français 1929–1944* (Paris: Éditions Stock, 1983), discusses the closing and reopening of cinemas, Continental Films, and the ban on American films; see pages 300–312. For the ban on British films (as well as those films with Jewish actors or production talent), see Jean-Pierre Bertin-Maghit, *Le Cinéma français sous l'Occupation* (Paris: Presses universitaires de France, 1994), 8, 39. For information about the surprisingly high film attendance during the early months of the war, see François Garçon, *De Blum à Pétain: Cinéma et société française (1936–1944)* (Paris: Éditions du Cerf, 1984), 27–28.

7   Paul Virilio, *War and Cinema: The Logistics of Perception* (London: Verso Books, 1989), 8–9.

8   "Les Programmes," *Le Matin*, July 6, 1940, 2.

9   For listings of these reopened cinemas, see *Comoedia*, June 28, 1941, 8.

10 *Comoedia*, September 13, 1941, 8.

11 For these listings, see *Comoedia*, June 28, 1941, 8.

12 *Comoedia*, June 28, 1941, 8.

13 *Comoedia*, June 28, 1941, 8.

14 Eric Rentschler discusses the making of *Münchausen* in *The Ministry of Illusion: Nazi Cinema and Its Afterlife* (Cambridge, MA: Harvard University Press, 1996), 194.

15 Issues of *Ciné-Mondial* listed the weekly closures. See, for instance, the issue of April 28, 1944, 13.

16 Robert Gildea cites two example of cinema surveillance, although not in Paris. One took place in Saint-Nazaire and the other in Le Mans, when men were arrested during newsreels, in the first instance for causing "a disturbance," in the second "for applauding the bombing of a German hospital by the RAF." See Gildea, *Marianne in Chains: In Search of the German Occupation 1940–1945* (New York: Macmillan, 2002), 152.

17 Ronald C. Rosbottom, *When Paris Went Dark: The City of Light Under German Occupation, 1940–1944* (New York: Little, Brown and Company, 2014), xxxi.

18 Susan Quinn, *A Mind of Her Own: The Life of Karen Horney* (Reading, MA: Addison-Wesley, 1988).

19 Quinn, *Mind of Her Own*, 238–39.

20 For a review and analysis of Harvey's film career, see Antje Ascheid, "Nazi Stardom and the 'Modern Girl': The Case of Lilian Harvey," *New German Critique* 74 (Spring–Summer 1998): 57–89.

21 For information about the prewar popularity of MacDonald, see the discussion of her 1939 film *Broadway Serenade* in "Cinémas," *Le Matin*, February 5, 1940, 4.

22 "On travaille activement à Neubabelsberg," *L'Afrique du Nord*, January 19, 1935, 14.

23 H. T. S., "The Screen," *New York Times*, May 25, 1935, 12; June 25, 1938, 7; September 11, 1939, 24; May 27, 1939, 19.

24 See the advertisement for *Les Mains libres* in *Le Petit Parisien*, December 20, 1940, 3.

25 François Vinneuil, "Le Cinéma," *Le Petit Parisien*, December 22, 1940, 2.

26 "Cinémas," *Le Matin*, December 20, 1940, 4.

27 "Dossier: Les Champs-Elysées et les salles de cinéma," Salles-Cinéma, accessed May 16, 2018, https://salles-cinema.com/actualites/les-cinemas-des-champs-elysees. For a brief history of the Cinéma des Champs-Élysées, see Meusy, *Écrans français,* volume II, 133.

28 *Pour Vous*, April 2, 1931, 15.

29 *Pour Vous*, January 10, 1940, 15.

30 See, for instance, Francine Muel-Dreyfus, *Vichy and the Eternal Feminine: A Contribution to a Political Sociology of Gender*, trans. Kathleen A. Johnson (Durham, NC: Duke University Press, 2001). For the "new woman" in National Socialist Cinema, see Ascheid, "Nazi Stardom."

31 *Le Petit Parisien*, December 23, 1940, 2.

32 "Le Grand Gala de Radio-Paris," *Ciné-Mondial*, April 24, 1942, 12.

33 See the film listings in *Le Petit Parisien*, December 22, 1940, 2.

34 Ehrlich, *Cinema of Paradox*, 154, 220n31.

35 See the advertisement for *Les Mains libres*, *Le Matin*, January 18, 1941, 3.

36 For a description of the Congress of European Writers, see Olivier Corpet and Claire Paulhan, *Collaboration and Resistance: French Literary Life under the Occupation*, trans. Jeffrey Mehlman et al. (Brooklyn, NY: Five Ties Publishing, 2010), 150.

37 Guy Bertret, "Hello! Miss Marika," *Ciné-Mondial*, April 17, 1942, 1–2. The citations come from captions on page 1.

38 For Chevalier's performance at the camp, see Behr, *Good Frenchman*, 280–84.

39 The trip has received scant scholarly attention. The best source for information is René Chateau, *Le Cinéma français sous l'Occupation: 1940–1944* (Courbevoie: Éditions René Chateau, 1996), 212–19. See also "Il y a un mois, l'Allemagne enthousiaste accueillait nos artistes de cinéma," *Le Matin*, April 25–26, 1942, 1.

For Heuzé's dispatches, see the following articles from *Ciné-Mondial*: "En route pour Berlin!," March 27, 1942, 1; "Mieux qu'un rêve ... la réalité de l'avenir," April 10, 1942, 10; "Premier contact avec Berlin," April 17, 1942, 5–6; "Voyage des vedettes françaises en Allemagne," April 24, 1942, 3–4; "Premier rendez-vous à Berlin," May 1, 1942, 8–9; "Avec les artistes dans leur maison," May 8, 1942, 3–4; and "Á Berlin dans l'air de Paris," May 15, 1942, 5–6. For his part in the trip, as well as for working for Continental Films and welcoming the German star Heinrich George at the Comédie-Française, Préjean spent six weeks in prison after the war (Chateau, *Le Cinéma français*, 463).

40 For Annabella's Berlin trip, see Nino Frank, "Avant son depart pour Berlin, Annabella nous confie ses premiers rêves," *Pour Vous*, April 2, 1931, 7; and "Studios en plein air," *Pour Vous*, April 9, 1931, 14. *Pour Vous* wrote about Illéry's trip to Dusseldorf in "Studios en plein air," February 19, 1931, 14.

41 Many of Darrieux's obituaries mentioned the reasons for her activities during the war. See, for instance, "French Film Legend Who Worked for the Nazis 'to Free Her Playboy Diplomat Husband from an Internment Camp' (Before He Ran off with Rich American Doris Duke) Dies Aged 100," *Daily Mail*, October 19, 2017, accessed May 10, 2018, http://www.dailymail.co.uk/news/article-4996462 /French-actress-Danielle-Darrieux-died-aged-100. html.

42 Pierre Heuzé, "Mieux qu'un rêve ... la réalité de l'avenir," *Ciné-Mondial*, April 10, 1942, 10.

43 Heuzé, "Premier contact avec Berlin," *Ciné-Mondial*, April 17, 1942, 5.

44 Heuzé, "Voyage des vedettes françaises en Allemagne," *Ciné-Mondial*, April 24, 1942, 3–4. As for the historical importance of *La Nuit est à nous*, it was not the first French sound film. Alan Williams identifies *Le Collier de la reine* (1929) as the first French sound picture, "although this was in reality a silent film with a recorded music score, some sound effects, and a small number of interpolated, synchronous sound close-ups." He goes on to write that "the first real French talkie [was] *Les Trois Masques*" from 1929 and directed by André Hugun. *La Nuit est à nous* was probably the first French sound film to be made in multiple languages; the German version of the film was indeed directed by Froelich. See Williams, *Republic of Images*, 161–62.

45 Heuzé, "Premier rendez-vous à Berlin," *Ciné-Mondial*, May 1, 1942, 8.

46 Heuzé, "Avec les artistes dans leur maison," *Ciné-Mondial*, May 8, 1942, 3–4.

47 Heuzé, "Avec les artistes," 4.

48 David Mayers, "Nazi Germany and the Future of Europe: George Kennan's Views, 1939–1945," *International History Review* 8, no. 4 (November 1986): 550–72. For the "cosmopolitan character" of the European aristocracy, see page 565.

49 See, for example, Leonidas E. Hill, "The Wilhelmstrasse in the Nazi Era," *Political Science Quarterly* 82, no. 4 (December 1967): 546–70. See pages 565–66 for the discussion of the rightwing "aristocratic cosmopolitanism" of the 1930s.

50 Pierre Leprohon, "Un visage sans fard, un jeu sans artifice, un coeur en pleine lumiére ... Brigitte Horney," *Ciné-Mondial*, March 13, 1942, 6.

51 "*Illusion*," *Le Matin*, November 18, 1942, 2.

52 For information about the production and historical importance of the film, see *"Les aventures fantastiques du Baron Münchausen,"* *Ciné-Mondial*, March 1944, 11–12. The link to a period when the cinema was only "hesitantly" (*balbutiait*) beginning seems inaccurate; Meliès made *Les Hallucinations du baron de Münchausen* late in his career, in 1911.

53 "4 ans de guerre, 4 ans de cinema," *Ciné-Mondial*, January 7, 1944, 11–12.

54 Ehrlich, *Cinema of Paradox*, 42.

55 *Le Matin*, June 3–4, 1944, 2.

56 "Pour la premiére fois a l'écran Attile Horbiger et Brigitte Horney," *Ciné-Mondial*, July 7, 1944, 11–12.

57 Crisp, *Classic French Cinema*, 43–52. The exact number of French films can be difficult to determine. Evelyn Ehrlich lists 219 such films, including thirty films from Continental, the German-run studio, in *Cinema of Paradox*, 193–201.

58 Bertin-Maghit, *Le Cinéma français*; Jeancolas, *15 ans d'années trente*.

59 Susan Hayward provides the best summation and examination of the period in English in *French National Cinema* (London: Routledge, 1993). She places the war years within a larger period in chapter 3, "From Clarity to Obscurity: French Cinema's Age of Modernism 1930–1958," while also remarking on significant shifts and differences not only between 1939 and 1945 but throughout this era. For similar examples in French, see Jeancolas's *15 ans d'années trente*. In addition, Garçon notes the fluidities as well as the differences in the shift from the Popular Front of the 1930s to the fascism of Vichy in *De Blum à Pétain*.

60 *Ciné-Mondial*, May 26–June 2, 1944.

61 Françoise Barr, "Si le cinéma n'avait pas existé," *Ciné-Mondial*, March 17–24, 1944, 3.

62 *Le Matin*, May 6–7, 1944, 2.

63 For Arletty's wartime relationship with an officer in the Luftwaffe, see Bertin-Maghit, *Le Cinéma français*, 69.

Chapter 6: Liberation Cinema, Postwar Cinema

1 *Le Petit Parisien*, July 22, 1944, 2.

2 Louis Daquin, "Ce que nous voulons," *Bulletin officiel du CLCF*, October 23, 1944, 1.

3 "La Reouverture des salles," *Bulletin officiel du CLCF*, October 23, 1944, 4.

4 For the look of Paris just before and after the Liberation, see Julian Jackson, *France: The Dark Years 1940–1944* (New York: Oxford University Press, 2001), especially chapter 23, "Liberations," 544–70. Jean-Paul Sartre also wrote about the appearance of Paris during the war, and how part of the horror of the Occupation was the manner in which everyday life could seem so unchanged. See Sartre, "Paris under the Occupation," *Sartre Studies International* 4, no. 2 (1998): 1–15, originally published as "Paris sous l'Occupation," *Situations III* (Paris: Gallimard, 1949).

5 "La Reouverture des salles," *Bulletin officiel du CLCF*, October 23, 1944, 4.

6 *Le Petit Parisien*, August 14, 1944, 2.

7   *Le Petit Parisien*, August 14, 1944, 2.

8   *Ce soir*, October 1, 1944, 2.

9   *L'Humanité*, October 15, 1944, 2.

10 "Les Spectacles," *L'Humanité*, October 15, 1944, 2.

11 For evidence of Durbin's popularity during this period, see Jackie Stacey, *Star-Gazing: Hollywood Cinema and Female Spectatorship* (London: Routledge, 1994).

12 *Ciné France*, October 22, 1937, 1; "Favoris et favorites du public dans l'intimité," *Le Petit Parisien*, November 29, 1937, 1; Claude Sylvane, "J'ai rencontré Michèle Morgan," *Ciné France*, February 25, 1938, 4; "Vedettes de Hollywood," *La Nouvelliste d'Indochine*, January 16, 1938, 7. For evidence of Durbin on French radio, see "La radio," *L'Humanité*, July 27, 1937, 7. Radio-Cité that night played "Le concours Deanna Durbin" at 10:05 in the evening.

13 "Les Spectacles—The Shows," *L'Echo d'Alger*, August 4, 1944, 2; August 27, 1944, 2.

14 "Les Spectacles—The Shows," *L'Echo d'Alger*, October 18, 1944, 2.

15 "Scène et l'écran: Les premiers films étrangers à Paris," *Combat*, October 18, 1944, collected in *"Eve a commencé," film de Henry Koster*, Bibliothèque nationale de France, département Arts du spectacle, 8-RSUPP-1535, accessed May 10, 2018, http://catalogue.bnf.fr/ark:/12148/cb426750620; "Les Spectacles," *L'Echo d'Alger*, November 26, 1944, 2.

16 "Scène et l'écran."

17 *"Eve a commencé," film de Henry Koster.*

18 Roger Leenhardt, "Sunlights et salles: *Eve a commencé*," *Les lettres française*, October 28, 1944; Jeander, "Ciné critique: *Eve a commencé*," *Libération*, October 21, 1944; Paul Barbellion, "*Eve a commencé*," *Carrefour*, October 21, 1944; André Bazin, "L'écran parisien: *Eve a commencé*," *Le parisien libéré*, October 22–23, 1944. All can be found in *"Eve a commencé," film de Henry Koster*." For a history of Bazin's work with *Le parisien libéré*, see Geneviève Sellier, "André Bazin, Film Critic for *Le Parisien libéré*, 1944–1958: An Enlightened Defender of French Cinema," *Paragraph* 36, no. 1 (2013): 118–32.

19 Bazin, "L'Écran parisien."

20 Bazin, "L'Écran parisien."

21 *L'Humanité*, November 7, 1944, 2.

22 *Ce soir*, December 28, 1944, 2.

23 "La grande quinzaine du cinéma français," *L'Humanité*, December 9, 1944, 2.

24 "La grande quinzaine du cinéma français," 2. Also, see Jeancolas, *Histoire du cinéma français*, 52, for a brief discussion of *Goupi mains rouges*.

25 "Gros plans," *L'Humanité*, December 9, 1944, 2.

26 "À Paris cette semaine," *Cinévie* supplement, November 7, 1945.

27 "À Paris cette semaine," *Cinévie* supplement, November 7, 1945.

28 "À Paris cette semaine," *Cinévie* supplement, December 24, 1946.

29 "À Paris cette semaine," *Cinévie* supplement, October 17, 1945.

30 For film listings in this paragraph, see "À Paris cette semaine," *Cinévie* supplement, October 10–November 14, 1945.

31 François Truffaut, *Les Films de ma vie* (Paris: Flammarion, 1975), 208.

32 Colin Burnett, *The Invention of Robert Bresson: The Auteur and His Market* (Bloomington: Indiana University Press, 2017), 68.

33 "À Paris cette semaine," *Cinévie* supplement, October 10, 17, 24, and 31, 1945.

34 "À Paris cette semaine," *Cinévie* supplement, October 17, 1945.

35 Eric Hurel, "Merci, Monsieur René Clair," *Cinévie*, October 17, 1945, 2.

36 J. Roy, "Je compte bientöt de revenir en France dit René Clair," *Cinévie*, March 26, 1946, 2.

37 "René Clair, le meilleur de ses interprètes, a pour vedette un metteur en scène," *Cinévie*, December 31, 1946, 4.

38 "À Paris cette semaine," *Cinévie* supplement, October 10, 1945.

39 "À Paris cette semaine," *Cinévie* supplement, February 27, 1946.

40 "À Paris cette semaine," *Cinévie* supplement, November 14, 1945; February 27, 1946; April 2, 1946.

41 "À Paris cette semaine," *Cinévie* supplement, October 17, 1945; November 7, 1945.

42 "À Paris cette semaine," *Cinévie* supplement, October 31, 1945.

43 "À Paris cette semaine," *Cinévie* supplement, February 27, 1946; December 31, 1946.

44 "À Paris cette semaine," *Cinévie* supplement, January 9, 1946.

45 See, for example, the advertisement for *Quai des brumes*, playing at the Ermitage cinema, in *Le Matin*, October 23, 1938, 6; also the film listings in *L'Humanité*, January 10, 1939, 7, for a sense of the film's continuous showings in Paris.

46 Memorandum of Conversation, October 5, 1941, 811.4061 Motion Pictures/438, NND 730032.

47 "Paris a été le cadeau de Noël de Simone Simon," *Cinévie*, January 2, 1946, 5–6; Simone Simon, "L'Amérique en cinq episodes," *Cinévie*, January 16, 1946, 11; January 23, 1946, 12; January 30, 1946, 11.

48 On prepare pour vous . . . Le 50me crime de Sessue Hayakawa," *Cinévie*, April 16, 1946, 7–8.

49 Michèle Morgan, "Cinq ans d'Amérique," *Cinévie*, January 2, 1946, 11.

50 "Une nouvelle Morgan est née . . . dans un salon de coiffure," *Cinévie*, January 23, 1946, 7.

51 *Cinévie*, April 16, 1946.

52 Feuillère appeared on the cover of the January 23, 1946 issue. See also "Mon histoire: Des histoires, par Edwige Feuillère," *Cinévie*, March 26, 1946, 11; and April 16, 1946, 11. For Darrieux's marriage, see "Danielle Darrieux se marie pour la 3me fois!," *Cinévie*, January 16, 1946, 7–8.

53 "*Cinévie* a vu pour vous l'unique représentation du film: *Le Magician d'Oz*," *Cinévie*, March 13, 1946, 1.

54 "À Paris cette semaine," *Cinévie* supplement, October 10, 1945; October 17, 1945; November 7, 1945.

55 "À Paris cette semaine," *Cinévie* supplement, October 31, 1945.

56 "À Paris cette semaine," *Cinévie* supplement, October 17, 1945; November 14, 1945; February 27, 1946.

57 *L'Écran français*, supplement 81, January 14, 1947.

58 See Crisp, *Classic French Cinema*, 6, for a graph of French film production from 1924 to 1960, and for the varying estimates of films produced.

59 For the play dates of *Symphonie inachevée* at the Studio de l'Étoile cinema, see issues of *La Semaine à Paris*, from July 24 to August 28, 1936.

60 "La vie des ciné-clubs," *Ciné-Club*, March 1948, 7.

61 "Dans les ciné-clubs," *Ciné-Club*, November 1947, 6.

62 "La vie des ciné-clubs," *Ciné-Club*, March 1948, 7; "Calendrier des conférences du mois de mars," *Ciné-Club*, April 1948, 7.

63 "La vie des ciné-clubs," *Ciné-Club*, December 1947, 6.

64 "La vie des ciné-clubs," *Ciné-Club*, October 1948, 6.

65 "Ciné-Club et ses lecteurs," *Ciné-Club*, May 1948, 8; "La vie des ciné-clubs," *Ciné-Club*, January–February 1948, 7; October 1948, 6.

66 "Programme des ciné-clubs," *Ciné-Club*, March 1949, 6.

67 "La vie des ciné-clubs," *Ciné-Club*, December 1948, 6.

68 "Programme des ciné-clubs," *Ciné-Club*, January 1949, 6.

69 "Programme des ciné-clubs," *Ciné-Club*, January 1949, 6.

70 "Programme des ciné-clubs," *Ciné-Club*, January 1949, 6; February 1949, 6.

71 "La vie des ciné-clubs," *Ciné-Club*, January–February 1948, 7.

72 "La vie des ciné-clubs," *Ciné-Club*, June 1948, 6.

73 There is a great deal of literature about the Blum-Byrnes accords. For a study of the results of the agreement as well as its impact on French thinking about postwar film history and national cinema, see Jacques Portes, "Les origins de la légende noire des accords Blum-Byrnes sur le cinéma," *Revue d'histoire modern et contemporaine* 33, no. 2 (1986): 314–29. See also Crisp, *Classic French Cinema*, 73–75. Crisp writes that by the end of 1947 and the beginning of 1948, 54 percent of all films in France would come from Hollywood, up from 41 percent in 1946 (see page 75).

74 Portes, "Les origins de la légende noire," 314.

75 H. Raymond, "*Maria Candelaria*," *Terre et ciel*, June 1947, 21.

76 Raymond, "Pour un ciné-club Air France," *Terre et ciel*, June 1947, 21.

77 Raymond, "René Clair, le plus français de nos réalisateurs," *Terre et ciel*, June 1947, 21.

78 For a discussion of the charges against Chevalier, see Behr, *Good Frenchman*, 285–316.

Conclusion: A Final Stroll

1 For immigration figures, see Patrick Weil, *How to Be French: Nationality in the Making since 1789*, trans. Catherine Porter (Durham, NC: Duke University Press, 2008), 153; Leslie Page Moch, *The Pariahs of Yesterday: Breton Migrants in Paris* (Durham, NC: Duke University Press, 2012), 162.

2 SNEG, *Étude du comportement*, part 2, section 2.

3 SNEG, *Étude du comportement*. See section 2, question 8 for statistics regarding waiting in line; question 32 for dubbing; question 21 for ticket price; and question 26 for attending after work.

4   SNEG, *Étude du comportement*, section 2, question 5.

5   Claude Degand, *Étude de marché du cinéma français* (Paris: Centre national de la cinématographie, 1954). The phrase comes from the title of chapter 2, on page 8.

6   Crisp, *Classic French Cinema*, 64.

7   Renaitour, *Où va le cinéma français?* The citations here can be found on page 5. For press reports, see "Notes de lecture," *L'Humanité*, April 9, 1937, 8; "Où va le cinéma français?" *Le Petit Parisien*, June 22, 1937, 6; "Où va le cinéma français?" *Les Annales colonials*, June 23, 1937, 6; "Où va le septième art français?" *L'Homme libre*, August 13, 1937, 3; "C'est le moment!" *Marianne*, October 6, 1937, 19.

8   Renaitour, *Où va le cinéma français?* For numbers of cinemas, see page 99; for film releases, page 116; shooting schedules and returns, pages 50 and 52; Parisian cinemas refusing to play French films, page 43; the provinces and their taste in stars, page 49.

9   Degand, *Étude de marché*, 7.

10 Degand, *Étude de marché*, 3.

11 Degand, *Étude de marché*. See page 11 for the percentages of men and women, and page 9 for the assessment of Paris attendance.

12 Degand, *Étude de marché*. The report discusses the impact of television on page 48.

13 Degand, *Étude de marché*. For activities during intermissions and for an assessment of women's pleasures at the cinema, see page 39.

14 Degand, *Étude de marché*, 4.

15 Degand, *Étude de marché*. For the age and class of audiences, see page 5; for numbers from Paris, see page 11; for how audiences made their choices, see page 29.

16 Degand, *Étude de marché*, 17.

17 Degand, *Étude de marché*. See page 12 for national considerations, and page 16 for discussion of Limoges and Nantes.

18 Degand, *Étude de marché*, 28.

19 Degand, *Étude de marché*, 8.

20 Degand, *Étude de marché*, 9.

21 Degand, *Étude de marché*, 45.

22 *Pariscope*, no. 1108, August 16, 1989. See pages 51–112 for the cinema listings.

23 Xavier Delamare, "Louxor," Cinema Treasures, accessed October 24, 2016, http://cinematreasures.org/theaters/7521.

24 "Cinéma Gaumont les Fauvettes," Les Cinémas Pathé Gaumont, accessed October 24, 2016, http://www.cinemalesfauvettes.com/.

BIBLIOGRAPHY

Abel, Richard. *Americanizing the Movies and "Movie-Mad" Audiences, 1910–1914.* Berkeley: University of California Press, 2006.

Abel, Richard. *The Ciné Goes to Town: French Cinema 1896–1914.* Berkeley: University of California Press, 1994.

Abel, Richard. *French Cinema: The First Wave, 1915–1929.* Princeton, NJ: Princeton University Press, 1984.

Abel, Richard. *The Red Rooster Scare: Making Cinema American.* Berkeley: University of California Press, 1999.

Altenloh, Emilie. "A Sociology of the Cinema: The Audience (1914)." Translated by Kathleen Cross. *Screen* 42, no. 3 (2001): 249–93.

Andrew, Dudley. "Cinematic Politics in Postwar France: Bazin Before Cahiers." *Cinéaste* 12, no. 1 (1982): 12–16.

Ascheid, Antje. "Nazi Stardom and the 'Modern Girl': The Case of Lilian Harvey." *New German Critique* 74 (Spring–Summer 1998): 57–89.

Aubry, Roger. "Le Cinéma au Cameroun." *African Arts* 2, no. 3 (Spring 1969): 66–69.

Bachellion, Paul. "Les tendances actuelles du cinéma." *Cinéa*, April 1931, 3.

Balio, Tino. *Grand Design: Hollywood as a Modern Business Enterprise, 1930–1939.* Berkeley: University of California Press, 1995.

Baranger, Henri. "Opinions de cinéastes: Valery Inkischinoff." *Cinéa*, April 1930, 35.

Barr, Françoise. "Si le cinéma n'avait pas existé." *Ciné-Mondial*, March 17–24, 1944, 3.

Behr, Edward. *The Good Frenchman: The True Story of the Life and Times of Maurice Chevalier.* New York: Villard Books, 1993.

Benissier, Lucette. "Du monde entier . . ." *Pour Vous*, March 5, 1931, 11.

Benissier, Lucette. "Lettre à M. Charlie Chaplin." *Pour Vous*, March 26, 1931, 2.

Benjamin, Walter. *The Arcades Project.* Translated by Kevin McLaughlin. Cambridge, MA: Harvard University Press, 2002.

Berneau, Pierre, and Jeanne Berneau. *Le spectacle cinématographique à Limoges de 1896 à 1945: Cinquante ans de culture Populaire.* Preface by Jean A. Gili. Paris: Association française de recherche sur l'histoire du cinema, 1992.

Bertin-Maghit, Jean-Pierre. *Le Cinéma français sous l'Occupation.* Paris: Presses universitaires de France, 1994.

Bertret, Guy. "Hello! Miss Marika." *Ciné-Mondial*, April 17, 1942, 1–2.

Bloom, Peter. *French Colonial Documentary: Mythologies of Humanitarianism.* Minneapolis: University of Minnesota Press, 2008.

Bosséno, Christian-Marc. "La Place du spectateur." *Vingtième siècle: Revue d'histoire* 46 (April–June 1995): 143–54.

Bourgoin, Aline. "Qui préférez-vous: Greta Garbo ou Marlène Dietrich." *Pour Vous*, February 5, 1931, 11.

Bourgoin, Aline. "Résultats d'une petite enquête: Greta Garbo? Ou Marlène Dietrich?" *Pour Vous*, February 19, 1931, 7.

Burnett, Colin. *The Invention of Robert Bresson: The Auteur and His Market.* Bloomington: Indiana University Press, 2017.

Chabannes, Jacques. "Les nouveaux films." *La Semaine à Paris*, December 16, 1932, 25; January 29, 1937, 23.

Chaplain, Renaud. "Les exploitants des salles de cinéma lyonnaise: Des origins à la second guerre mondiale." *Vingtième siècle: Revue d'histoire* 79 (July–September 2003): 19–35.

Charney, Leo, and Vanessa Schwartz, eds. *Cinema and the Invention of Modern Life.* Berkeley: University of California Press, 1996.

Chateau, René. *Le Cinéma français sous l'Occupation: 1940–1944.* Courbevoie: Éditions René Chateau, 1996.

Conway, Kelley. *Chanteuse in the City: The Realist Singer in French Film.* Berkeley: University of California Press, 2004.

Corpet, Olivier, and Claire Paulhan. *Collaboration and Resistance: French Literary Life under the Occupation.* Translated by Jeffrey Mehlman et al. Brooklyn, NY: Five Ties Publishing, 2010.

Crisp, Colin. *The Classic French Cinema, 1930–1960.* Bloomington: Indiana University Press, 1997.

Daquin, Louis. "Ce que nous voulons." *Bulletin officiel du CLCF*, October 23, 1944, 1.

Darré, Yann. *Histoire sociale du cinéma français.* Paris: Éditions La Découverte, 2000.

de Beauvoir, Simone. *Wartime Diary.* Champaign: University of Illinois Press, 2009.

de Brigard, Emilie. "The History of Ethnographic Film." In *Toward a Science of Man: Essays in the History of Anthropology*, edited by Timothy H. Thoresen, 33–63. Paris: Mouton Publishers, 1975.

de Certeau, Michel. *The Practice of Everyday Life.* Translated by Steven Rendall. Berkeley: University of California Press, 1984.

de Certeau, Michel. "Walking in the City." In *The Cultural Studies Reader*, edited by Simon During, 151–60. London: Routledge, 1993.

de Fouquières, André. "La Semaine à Paris: Annoncée et commentée par André de Fouquières." *La Semaine à Paris*, April 12–18, 1935, 6–7.

Degand, Claude. *Étude de marché du cinéma français.* Paris: Centre national de la cinématographie, 1954.

Della Sudda, Magali. "Right-Wing Feminism and Conservative Women's Militancy in Interwar France." In *The French Right Between the Wars: Political and Intellectual Movements from Conservatism to Fascism*, edited by Samuel Kalman and Sean Kennedy, 97–111. New York: Berghann Books, 2014.

DePalma, Anthony. *The Man Who Invented Fidel: Castro, Cuba, and Herbert Matthews of the* New York Times. New York: PublicAffairs, 2007.

de Saint-Cyr, Charles. "Vingt chose à propos de *L'Ange bleu*, le très grand success des Ursulines." *La Semaine à Paris*, December 26, 1930, 62–64.

Diamond, Hanna. *Fleeing Hitler: France 1940*. Oxford: Oxford University Press, 2008.

Doherty, Thomas. *Hollywood and Hitler, 1933–1939*. New York: Columbia University Press, 2013.

Ehrlich, Evelyn. *Cinema of Paradox: French Filmmaking under the German Occupation*. New York: Columbia University Press, 1985.

Epstein Nord, Deborah. "The City as Theater: From Georgian to Early Victorian London." *Victorian Studies* 31, no. 2 (1988): 159–88.

Fee, Annie. *Male Cinephiles and Female Movie-Fans: A Counter-History of French Cinephilia, 1918–1925*. PhD diss., University of Washington, 2014.

Frère, Suzanne. "Les Loisirs à Auxerre." *Cahiers Internationaux de Sociologie* 7 (1949): 101–8.

Frodon, Jean-Michel, and Dina Iordanova, eds. *Cinemas of Paris*. Edgecliffe, Scotland: St. Andrews Film Studies, 2016.

Fuller-Seeley, Kathy, ed. *Hollywood in the Neighborhood: Historical Case Studies of Local Moviegoing*. Berkeley: University of California Press, 2008.

Fuller-Seeley, Kathy. "Introduction: Spectatorship in Popular Film and Television." *Journal of Popular Film and Television* 29, no. 3 (2001): 98–99.

Garçon, François. *De Blum à Pétain: Cinéma et société française (1936–1944)*. Paris: Éditions du Cerf, 1984.

Garçon, François. *La Distribution cinématographique en France 1907–1957*. Paris: CNRS Éditions, 2006.

Gauthier, Christophe. *La Passion du cinéma: Cinéphiles, ciné-clubs et salles specialisées à Paris de 1920 à 1929*. Paris: Association française de recherche sur l'histoire du cinéma, 1999.

Gauthier, Christophe, and Laure Brost. "1927, Year One of the French Film Heritage?" *Film History* 17, no. 2/3 (2005): 289–306.

Gervaise, Bernard. "Les gaietés de la semaine." *Le Journal amusant*, August 31, 1930, 2.

Gildea, Robert. *Marianne in Chains: In Search of the German Occupation 1940–1945*. New York: Macmillan, 2002.

Gomery, Douglas. *Shared Pleasures: A History of Movie Presentation in the United States*. Madison: University of Wisconsin Press, 1992.

Grieveson, Lee. *Policing Chicago: Movies and Censorship in Early-Twentieth-Century America*. Berkeley: University of California Press, 2004.

Guillaume-Grimaud, Geneviève. *Le cinéma du Front Populaire*. Paris: L'Herminier, 1986.

Guiraud, Jean-Michel. "La vie intellectuelle et artistique à Marseille au temps du Maréchal Pétain." *Revue d'histoire de la Deuxième Guerre mondiale* (January 1979): 63–90.

Hamery, Roxane. "Les ciné-clubs dans la tourmente: La querelle do non-commercial (1948–1955)." *Vingtieme siècle, revue d'histoire* 115 (2012): 75–88.

Hammond, Paul. *L'Âge d'or*. London: British Film Institute, 1997.

Harris, Gerry. "Regarding History: Some Narratives Concerning the Café-Concert, le Music Hall, and the Feminist Academic." *TDR* 40, no. 4 (Winter 1996): 70–84.

Hayward, Susan. *French National Cinema*. London: Routledge, 1993.

Hayward, Susan. *Simone Signoret: The Star as Cultural Sign*. London: Continuum, 2004.

Hervé, Frédéric. "Encombrante censure: La place de la Commission de contrôle des films dans l'organigramme de la politique du cinéma (1959–1969)." In *Le cinéma: Une affaire d'État 1945–1970*, edited by Dimitri Vezyroglou, 123–32. Paris: Comité d'histoire du ministère de la culture et de la communication, 2014.

Heuzé, Pierre. "A Berlin dans l'air de Paris." *Ciné-Mondial*, May 15, 1942, 5–6.

Heuzé, Pierre. "Avec les artistes dans leur maison." *Ciné-Mondial*, May 8, 1942, 3–4.

Heuzé, Pierre. "En route pour Berlin!" *Ciné-Mondial*, March 27, 1942, 1.

Heuzé, Pierre. "Mieux qu'un rêve . . . la réalité de l'avenir." *Ciné-Mondial*, April 10, 1942, 10.

Heuzé, Pierre. "Premier contact avec Berlin." *Ciné-Mondial*, April 17, 1942, 5–6.

Heuzé, Pierre. "Premier rendez-vous à Berlin." *Ciné-Mondial*, May 1, 1942, 8.

Heuzé, Pierre. "Voyage des vedettes françaises en Allemagne." *Ciné-Mondial*, April 24, 1942, 3–4.

Higson, Andrew. "The Concept of National Cinema." *Screen* 30, no. 4 (1989): 36–47.

Higson, Andrew. *Waving the Flag: Constructing a National Cinema in Britain*. Oxford: Oxford University Press, 1995.

Hill, Leonidas E. "The Wilhelmstrasse in the Nazi Era." *Political Science Quarterly* 82, no. 4 (December 1967): 546–70.

H. T. S. "The Screen." *New York Times*, May 25, 1935, 12; June 25, 1938, 7; May 27, 1939, 19; September 11, 1939, 24.

Hugault, Henri. "Au Moulin-Rouge: Le public manifeste contre la projection d'un film sonore américain." *Le Figaro*, December 9, 1929, 3.

Hurel, Eric. "Merci, Monsieur René Clair." *Cinévie*, October 17, 1945, 2.

Jackson, Julian. *France: The Dark Years 1940–1944*. New York: Oxford University Press, 2001.

Jäger, Lorenz. *Adorno: A Political Biography*. New Haven, CT: Yale University Press, 2004.

Jeancolas, Jean-Pierre. *Histoire du cinéma français*. Paris: Armand Colin, 2015.

Jeancolas, Jean-Pierre. *15 ans d'années trente: Le cinéma des français 1929–1944*. Paris: Éditions Stock, 1983.

Jeantet, Claude. "L'écran de la semaine: La chute des *Folies-fox*." *L'Action française*, December 13, 1929, 4.

J. M. "Le Cinéma 'les Miracles' inauguré avec *Hallelujah*." *La Semaine à Paris*, December 26, 1930, 61–62.

Kaplan, Alice. *The Collaborator: The Trial and Execution of Robert Brasillach*. Chicago: University of Chicago Press, 2001.

Kennedy, Sean. *Reconciling France against Democracy: The Croix de Feu and the Parti Social Français, 1927–1945*. Montreal: McGill-Queen's University Press, 2007.

King, David. *Death in the City of Light: The Serial Killer of Nazi-Occupied Paris.* New York: Crown Publishers, 2011.

Kuhn, Annette. *Dreaming of Fred and Ginger: Cinema and Cultural Memory.* New York: New York University Press, 2002.

Le Bret, André. "Cinéma." *Le Petit Parisien*, March 21, 1938, 8.

Léglise, Paul. *Histoire de la politique du cinéma français: Le cinéma et la IIIe république.* Paris: R. Pichon et R. Durand-Auzias, 1970.

Lehmann, René. "*Anna Christie.*" *Pour vous*, March 19, 1931, 9.

Leprohon, Pierre. "La leçon de *La Foule.*" *Cinéa*, May 1, 1929, 10.

Leprohon, Pierre. "Un visage sans fard, un jeu sans artifice, un coeur en pleine lumiére . . . Brigitte Horney." *Ciné-Mondial*, March 13, 1942, 6.

Martin, Benjamin F. *France in 1938.* Baton Rouge: Louisiana State University Press, 2005.

Matthews, Herbert L. "The Cinema in Paris." *New York Times*, June 11, 1933, X2.

Matthews, Herbert L. "The Cinema in Paris: To Dub or Not to Dub Films—Successful Original American Pictures." *New York Times*, June 4, 1933, X2.

Matthews, Herbert L. "A Glimpse at the Cinema of Paris." *New York Times*, April 2, 1933, X4.

Matthews, Herbert L. "Paris Views New Films and Theatres." *New York Times*, January 15, 1933, X4.

Matthews, Herbert L. "The Screen in Paris." *New York Times*, September 18, 1932, X4.

Mayers, David. "Nazi Germany and the Future of Europe: George Kennan's Views, 1939–1945." *International History Review* 8, no. 4 (November 1986): 550–72.

Meusy, Jean-Jacques. *Écrans français de l'entre-deux-guerres, volumes I et II: Les années sonores et parlantes.* Paris: Association française de recherche sur l'histoire du cinéma, 2017.

Meusy, Jean-Jacques. *Paris-Palaces, ou, Le temps des cinémas (1894–1918).* Paris: CNRS Éditions, 1995.

Midkiff DeBauche, Leslie. "Reminiscences of the Past, Conditions of the Present: At the Movies in Milwaukee in 1918." In *American Movie Audiences: From the Turn of the Century to the Early Sound Era*, edited by Melvyn Stokes and Richard Maltby, 129–39. London: BFI, 1999.

Moch, Leslie Page. *The Pariahs of Yesterday: Breton Migrants in Paris.* Durham, NC: Duke University Press, 2012.

Morgan, Michèle. "Cinq ans d'Amérique." *Cinévie*, January 2, 1946, 11.

Morienval. "Toutes les horreurs de la guerre dans *Quatre de l'infanterie.*" *La Semaine à Paris*, December 19, 1930, 60–61.

M. P. "*L'Ange bleu.*" *Les Spectacles d'Alger*, June 17, 1931, 3.

Muel-Dreyfus, Francine. *Vichy and the Eternal Feminine: A Contribution to a Political Sociology of Gender.* Translated by Kathleen A. Johnson. Durham, NC: Duke University Press, 2001.

Neale, Steve. "*Triumph of the Will*: Notes on Documentary and Spectacle." *Screen* 20, no. 1 (Spring 1979): 63–86.

Neulander, Joelle. *Programming National Identity: The Culture of Radio in 1930s France*. Baton Rouge: Louisiana State University Press, 2009.

Nord, Philip. *France's New Deal: From the Thirties to the Postwar Era*. Princeton, NJ: Princeton University Press, 2010.

O'Brien, Charles. *Cinema's Conversion to Sound: Technology and Film Style in France and the U.S.* Bloomington: Indiana University Press, 2005.

O'Brien, Mary-Elizabeth. *Nazi Cinema as Enchantment: The Politics of Entertainment in the Third Reich*. Rochester, NY: Camden House, 2004.

Orlan, Pierre Mac. "À propos de *La Petite Marchande d'allumettes.*" *Cinéa*, April 1930, 37.

Ovenden, Mark. *Paris Underground: The Maps, Stations, and Design of the Métro*. New York: Penguin Books, 2009.

Passmore, Kevin. "Boy Scouting for Grown-Ups?: Paramilitarism in the Croix de Feu and the Parti Social Français." *French Historical Studies* 19, no. 2 (Autumn 1995): 527–57.

Petro, Patrice. "*The Blue Angel* in Multiple-Language Versions: The Inner Thighs of Miss Dietrich." In *Dietrich Icon*, edited by Gerd Gemünden and Mary R. Desjardins, 141–61. Durham, NC: Duke University Press, 2007.

Philie. "Splendid cinéma: *La Belle Ténébreuse.*" *Les Spectacles d'Alger*, June 24, 1931, 2.

Portes, Jacques. "Les origines de la légende noire des accords Blum-Byrnes sur le cinema." *Revue d'histoire modern et contemporaine (1954–)* 33, no. 2 (April–June 1986): 314–29.

Quinn, Susan. *A Mind of Her Own: The Life of Karen Horney*. Reading, MA: Addison-Wesley, 1988.

Rab, Sylvie. "Le cinéma dans l'entre-deux-guerres; une politique culturelle municipal impossible? L'exemple de Suresnes." *Le Mouvement social* 184 (July–September 1998): 75–98.

Ramain, Paul. "Réflexions sur on film mal compris: *Un chien andalou* de Luis Buñuel." *Cinéa*, April 1930, 6–7.

Raymond, H. "*Maria Candelaria.*" *Terre et ciel*, June 1947, 21.

Raymond, H. "Pour un ciné-club Air France." *Terre et ciel*, June 1947, 21.

Raymond, H. "René Clair, le plus français de nos réalisateurs." *Terre et ciel*, June 1947, 21.

Reff, Theodore. "Manet and the Paris of Haussmann and Baudelaire." In *Visions of the Modern City: Essays in History, Art, and Literature*, edited by William Sharpe and Leonard Wallock, 135–67. Baltimore: Johns Hopkins University Press, 1987.

Renaitour, Jean-Michel, ed. *Où va le cinéma français?* Paris: Editions Baudinière, 1937.

Rentschler, Eric. *The Ministry of Illusion: Nazi Cinema and Its Afterlife*. Cambridge, MA: Harvard University Press, 1996.

Ricci, Steven. *Cinema and Fascism: Italian Film and Society, 1922–1943*. Berkeley: University of California Press, 2008.

R. L. "À propos des progrès du cinéma." *La Renaissance*, December 14, 1929, 12.

Rosbottom, Ronald C. *When Paris Went Dark: The City of Light under German Occupation, 1940–1944*. New York: Little, Brown and Company, 2014.

Roy, J. "Je compte bientöt de revenir en France dit René Clair." *Cinévie*, March 26, 1946, 2.

Rutkoff, Peter M. "The Ligue des Patriotes: The Nature of the Radical Right and the Dreyfus Affair." *French Historical Studies* 8, no. 4 (Autumn 1974): 585–603.

Rutkoff, Peter M. *Revanche and Revision: The Ligue des Patriotes and the Origins of the Radical Right in France, 1882–1900.* Athens: Ohio University Press, 1981.

Sadoul, Georges. *Dictionnaire des films.* Paris: Éditions du Seuil, 1965.

Salemson, Harold. "A Film at War." *Hollywood Quarterly* 1, no. 4 (July 1946): 416–19.

Sartre, Jean-Paul. "Paris under the Occupation." *Sartre Studies International* 4, no. 2 (1998): 1–15.

Sedgwick, John, and Clara Pafort-Overdun. "Understanding Audience Behavior through Statistical Evidence: London and Amsterdam in the Mid-1930s." In *Audiences: Defining and Researching Screen Entertainment Reception*, edited by Ian Christie, 96–110. Amsterdam: Amsterdam University Press, 2012.

Sellier, Geneviève. "André Bazin, Film Critic for *Le Parisien libéré*, 1944–1958: An Enlightened Defender of French Cinema." *Paragraph* 36, no. 1 (2013): 118–32.

Semenza, Greg M. Colón, and Bob Hasenfratz. *The History of British Literature on Film, 1895–2015.* London: Bloomsbury Academic, 2015.

Simon, Simone. "L'Amérique en cinq épisodes." *Cinévie*, January 16, 1946, 11; January 23, 1946, 12; January 30, 1946, 11.

Singer, Ben. "Manhattan Nickelodeons: New Data on Audiences and Exhibitors." *Cinema Journal* 34, no. 2 (2001): 5–35.

Smoodin, Eric. "American Madness." In *America First: Naming the Nation in US Film*, edited by Mandy Merck, 65–82. London: Routledge, 2007.

Smoodin, Eric. "The History of Film History." In *Looking Past the Screen: Case Studies in American Film History and Method*, edited by Jon Lewis and Eric Smoodin, 1–33. Durham, NC: Duke University Press, 2007.

Société nouvelle des établissements Gaumont (SNEG). *Étude du comportement des spectateurs du Gaumont.* Paris: Societé nouvelle des établissements Gaumont, 1948.

Soucy, Robert. *French Fascism: The First Wave, 1924–1933.* New Haven, CT: Yale University Press, 1986.

Soucy, Robert. *French Fascism: The Second Wave, 1934–1939.* New Haven, CT: Yale University Press, 1995.

Soupault, Philippe. "Le cinéma." *Europe*, March 15, 1930, 427–9.

Stacey, Jackie. *Star-Gazing: Hollywood Cinema and Female Spectatorship.* London: Routledge, 1994.

Sternhell, Zeev. "Anatomie d'un movement fasciste en France: Le faisceau de Georges Valois." *Revue française de science politique* 26, no. 1 (February 1976): 5–40.

Stewart, Mary Lynn. *Dressing Modern Frenchwomen: Marketing Haute Couture, 1919–1939.* Baltimore: Johns Hopkins University Press, 2008.

Stokes, Melvyn, and Richard Maltby, eds. *American Movie Audiences: From the Turn of the Century to the Early Sound Era.* London: BFI, 1999.

Stovall, Tyler. "French Communism and Suburban Development: The Rise of the Paris Red Belt." *Journal of Contemporary History* 24, no. 3 (July 1989): 437–60.

Tedesco, Jean. "Vers un théâtre mecanique." *Cinéa*, April 1930, 2.

Thissen, Judith. "Jewish Immigrant Audiences in New York City, 1905–14." In *American Movie Audiences: From the Turn of the Century to the Early Sound Era*, edited by Melvyn Stokes and Richard Maltby, 15–28. London: BFI, 1999.

Truffaut, François. *Les films de ma vie*. Paris: Flammarion, 1975.

Vasey, Ruth. *The World According to Hollywood, 1918–1939*. Madison: University of Wisconsin Press, 1997.

Villette, Raymond. "Le cinéma au Conseil national des femmes françaises." *Hebdo*, February 13, 1932, 11.

Vincendeau, Ginette. *Stars and Stardom in French Cinema*. London: Continuum, 2000.

Virilio, Paul. *War and Cinema: The Logistics of Perception*. London: Verso Books, 1989.

Vuillermoz, Émile. "Les 'clubs' de cinema." *Le Temps*, January 18, 1939, 5.

Wahl, Lucien. "Les films nouveaux." *Pour Vous*, September 14, 1933, 6.

Waller, Gregory. "Hillbilly Music and Will Rogers: Small-Town Picture Shows in the 1930s." In *American Movie Audiences: From the Turn of the Century to the Early Sound Era*, edited by Melvyn Stokes and Richard Maltby, 164–79. London: BFI, 1999.

Waller, Gregory. *Main Street Amusements: Movies and Commercial Entertainment in a Southern City, 1896–1930*. Washington, DC: Smithsonian Institution Press, 1995.

Weil, Patrick. *How to Be French: Nationality in the Making since 1789*. Translated by Catherine Porter. Durham, NC: Duke University Press, 2008.

Williams, Alan. *Republic of Images: A History of French Filmmaking*. Cambridge, MA: Harvard University Press, 1992.

Commission d'action militaire, 123

Conduisez-moi, Madame (*Lead Me, Madam*; 1932), 35

Congress of European Writers, 111

Conseil national de la Résistance, 123

Conseil national des femmes françaises, 53

Continental Films, 101–2, 104, 107, 110, 112, 117, 119, 122, 129, 140

conversion to sound, 23–26, 30, 67–71, 75; multiple-language productions, 9, 11, 23, 25, 34, 67; reactions to, 77–80; stardom, effects on, 60–61, 63–65, 119

Cooper, Gary, 73

La Coquille et le clergyman (*The Seashell and the Clergyman*; 1928), 53

Le Corbeau (*The Raven*; 1943), 141

Corso-Opéra cinema, 23, 32, 50, 67, 154

Coup de tête (1944), 125

Le Couple invisible (*Topper*; 1937), 17

Courcelles cinema, 17–18

La Courtisane (*Susan Lennox: Her Fall and Rise*; 1931), 70

Le Crapouillot (satirical magazine), 29

Crawford, Joan, 33, 63–64

Le Crime de Monsieur Lange (*The Crime of Monsieur Lange*; 1936), 141

Crisp, Colin, 11, 82–83, 117

The Crowd Roars (1932), 33

Le Cuirassé Potemkine (*Battleship Potemkin*; 1925), 45

Cukor, George, 56

Les Dames du Bois du Boulogne (*The Ladies of the Bois de Boulogne*; 1945), 127, 132

Danton cinema, 154

Darré, Yann, 52, 83

Darrieux, Danielle, 18, 147; Germany, visit to, 112–13; during World War II, 104; following World War II, 136

Dary, René, 101

Davis, Bette, 48

Dead End Kids, 134

Deanna et ses boys (*One Hundred Men and a Girl*; 1937), 126

Dearly, Max, 31, 77

de Certeau, Michel, 6

de Fouquières, André, 41–42, 50, 59

Degand, Paul, 149

Dehelly, Jean, 63–65

Déjeuner pour deux (*Breakfast for Two*; 1937), 18

de la Falaise, Henri, 87

Delair, Suzy, 112–13

Delambra cinema, 131

Delannoy, Jean, 58, 125, 129

de la Rocque, François, 91, 95, 98

Delluc, Louis, 49

Delta cinema, 134, 143

De Mayerling à Sarajevo (*Sarajevo*; 1940), 138

DeMille, Cecil B., 50

de Nagy, Kate, 108

Denfert cinema, 131

De Poligny, Serge, 34

Derain, Lucie, 54, 56–57, 59

Der Gouverneur (*The Governor*; 1939), 108

de Saint-Cyr, Charles, 67, 73

Désordre (*Disorder*; 1930), 54

Destry Rides Again (1939), 74

Deuxième bureau contre kommandantur (*Second Commander against Kommandantur*; 1939), 101, 125

Les Deux 'Monsieur' de Madame (*The Two "Monsieur" of Madame*; 1933), 35

Les Deux timides (*Two Timid Souls*; 1928), 48

The Devil Is a Woman (1935), 74

Le Diable au corps (*The Devil in the Flesh*; 1947), 142

Le Diable en bouteille (*Liebe, Tod, und Teufel*; 1935), 107–8

Dickens, Charles, 7

Dictateur (*The Great Dictator*; 1941), 133

Dietrich, Fritz, 113

Dietrich, Marlene, 5, 17, 23, 28, 33, 76, 96, 107; and Greta Garbo, 65–66, 70–71; as international star, 18, 23, 60–61, 63, 73, 74–75, 119; voice of, 67–68, 71, 74

Feyder, Jacques, 48–49, 52, 57
Fields, W. C., 17
Le Figaro (newspaper), 7–8, 17, 77–79, 127
La Fille du Puisatier (*The Well-Digger's Daughter*; 1940), 140
Film Complet (magazine), 109
Les Films Diamant, 64
Les Films Minerva, 129
La Fin du monde (*End of the World*; 1931), 26
First Love (1939), 127
Fleurs meurtriers (1930), 81
Florelle, 9
Florence est folle (1944), 129
Florey, Robert, 54
Florida cinema, 140
Folies Bergère (1935), 74
Folies-Dramatiques cinema, 91, 104, 110
Fonda, Henry, 101
Fontainebleau, 144
Forbidden (1932), 21
Ford, John, 18, 33
La Forêt pétrifiée (*The Petrified Forest*; 1936), 48
Forfaiture (*The Cheat*; 1915), 136
La Foule (*The Crowd*; 1928), 54, 65
Fox folies (*Fox Movietone Follies of 1929*), 10, 76–80, 85, 97
Français cinema, 111
France libre (1944), 125
Franju, Georges, 42
Frankenstein (1931), 21, 27, 33
Fréhel, 111
French Indochina: Hanoi, 70; Saigon, 126
Fresnay, Pierre, 118
Froelich, Carl, 112–13
Front National (newspaper), 127
Fuller-Seeley, Kathryn, 5, 39

Gabin, Jean, 18, 32, 34, 77, 99, 141; during World War II, 110, 136; following World War II, 135–36, 140, 149
Gaël, Josseline, 118
Gaité-Clichy cinema, 129

Les Gaietés de l'infanterie (*With Love and Hisses*; 1927), 86
Gambetta-Aubert-Palace cinema, 103, 154
Gambetta-Étoile cinema, 96
Gance, Abel, 26, 44, 49
Garbo, Greta, 5, 17, 33, 77, 109; and Marlene Dietrich, 66, 70–71; silent films, 23–25
Garçon, François, 11–12
Gaumont, 6, 44, 155–56; Gaumont British, 4; Gaumont-Franco-Film-Aubert exhibition chain, 13, 85; Société nouvelle des établissements Gaumont, 12, 87, 147
Gaumont, Léon, 14
Gaumont Champs-Élysées cinema, 154
Gaumont cinema, 103
Gaumont-Palace cinema, 12–13, 18, 28, 30, 33, 87, 123, 125, 130; audience statistics, 147–49; history of, 14–15
Gauthier, Christophe, 3
Gaynor, Janet, 7–8
Gigi (1958), 74
Gloria cinema, 140
Godard, Jean-Luc, 144
Le Golem (*The Golem*; 1920), 49
Le Goujat (*The Scoundrel*; 1935), 56
Goupi mains rouges (*It Happened at the Inn*; 1943), 129
La Grande Mare (*The Big Pond*; 1930), 71
La Grande Parade (*The Big Parade*; 1925), 51
Grande Quinzaine du cinéma français, 129
La Grande révolte (*Condottieri*; 1937), 103
Grand Hotel (1932), 70
Le Grand Jeu (1934), 52, 57
Grant, Cary, 17–18
Gravey, Fernand, 71
Grémillon, Jean, 48
Grenoble, 53
Greven, Alfred, 112
Gribouille (1937), 135
Grieveson, Lee, 5
La griffe du hasard (1937), 103
Griffith, D. W., 49

Mostaganem, Algeria, 38
Moulin, Charles, 58
Moulin Rouge cinema, 36, 128; violence at, 76–80, 85
Moulins, 92
Mozart-Pathé cinema, 17–18, 86–91, 96, 98
Murder My Sweet (1944), 141
Murders in the Rue Morgue (1932), 33
Murnau, F. W., 49–50, 56
Musée de l'Homme, 48, 143
Musique de rêve (1940), 103
Myrrha cinema, 140

Nantes, 11, 151; Majestic cinema, 9; Palace cinema, 18
national cinema, 6, 18, 37–39
Netter, Yvonne, 56
New York Times (newspaper), 29, 32–33, 37, 97, 108
Nice (city), 11, 44, 78, 118
Nîmes, 38–39
Noël-Noël, 131
No, No, Nanette (1930), 26
Normandie cinema, 102, 104, 123, 125, 129, 134–35, 140, 145
Nos maîtres les domestiques (*Our Masters, the Servants*; 1930), 85
Nouveau-Théâtre cinema, 131
Le nouvelliste d'Indochine (newspaper), 126
Novelty-Palace cinema, 154
Nu comme un ver (*Naked as a Worm*; 1933), 33–34, 77
La Nuit est à nous (*The Night Is Ours*; 1930), 113

Occupation of Paris, 14–15, 18–19, 91, 99, 104, 138, 140–41; banned films, 101, 126–27, 135–36, 139; ciné-clubs, 43, 57–59; closing cinemas, 123; in contemporary cinema, 120–21; electricity shortage, 58, 106; film policy, 101–2, 117–18; German surrender, 125; reopening

cinemas, 102–3, 108–9, 116; resistance to, 122–23; soldatenkino, 106; surveillance at cinemas, 106; uses of celebrity, 112–17; violence at cinemas, 97
Olympia cinema, 21, 33, 85, 135, 140
L'Ombre du doute (*Shadow of a Doubt*; 1943), 131
Ondra, Anny, 108
L'Opéra de quat'sous (*The Threepenny Opera*; 1931), 66
L'Operateur (*The Cameraman*; 1928), 85
Ophüls, Max, 21, 138
Orage (1938), 103
Oran, Algeria, 36
Ordet (*The Word*; 1943), 141
Osso film studio, 44
Où va le cinéma français? (*Where Is French Cinema Going?*; Groupe du cinématographe publication), 12, 149–50

Pabst, G. W., 9, 50, 66, 86, 121, 143
The Pagan Lady (1931), 57
Pagnol, Marcel, 11, 73, 104, 140
Pagode cinema, 10, 25
Painlevé, Jean, 52, 122, 142, 144
Paisà (1946), 143
Palais de Chaillot, 152, 156
Palais-Rochechouart cinema, 13, 123
Palmy Days (1931), 33
Panique (1946), 140
Panthéon cinema, 26, 66, 134, 140
Papa longues jambes (*Daddy Long Legs*; 1931), 7
Parade d'amour (*The Love Parade*; 1929), 26, 64, 71–72
Paradis-Palace-Aubert cinema, 13
Paramount cinema, 21, 30, 85, 101, 125, 145, 154, 156
Paramount Pictures Corporation, 30; French films, production of, 8, 11, 34, 64, 71, 73, 85; link to Pathé, 13
Paris-Ciné cinema, 135
Le Paris cinema, 17
Pariscope (magazine), 1

Trenet, Charles, 118
La Tribune Libre (newspaper), 45
Triomphe cinema, 131
Les Trois masques (*The Three Masks*; 1929), 78
Truffaut, François, 15, 132, 142, 144
Tueur à gages (*This Gun for Hire*; 1942), 139

UFA (German film studio), 23, 104, 113; French productions, 34–35, 107–8
Universal, 25, 67, 132
Univers-Palace cinema, 131
Ursulines cinema, 54, 110, 138; showing *L'Ange bleu*, 66, 86

Vampyr (1932), 31
Van Parys, Georges, 141
Variety (magazine), 23
Vasey, Ruth, 38
Les Vautours de la jungle (*Hawk of the Wilderness*; 1938), 131
Vedettes (tabloid), 58
Veidt, Conrad, 10, 134
Verklungene Melodie (*Faded Melody*; 1938), 108
Vernon, Suzy, 73
Viala, Line, 101
Vidor, King, 54, 65, 67
La Vie brûlante de Marlène Dietrich (Lasserre), 73
La Vie de Plaisir (1944), 104
La Vie privée de Henry VIII (*The Private Life of Henry VIII*; 1933), 34
Vieux-Colombier cinema, 61
Vigo, Jean, 44, 48, 52, 59
Ville frontière (*Bordertown*; 1935), 48
Vincent-Bréchignac, Jean, 26
Virilio, Paul, 101
Vivienne cinema, 129
La Voie sans disque (1933), 21

Voilà Paris, 72
Le Voleur de Bagdad (*The Thief of Bagdad*; 1924), 23
Volpone (1941), 103
Voltaire-Aubert-Palace cinema, 13, 103
von Sternberg, Josef, 21, 28, 33, 50, 66, 73–74
von Stroheim, Erich, 49
Vous ne l'emporterez pas avec vous (*You Can't Take It with You*; 1938), 138
Le Voyage dans la Lune (*A Trip to the Moon*; 1902), 138

Waller, Gregory, 5, 39
Warner Bros., 17, 34
Wegener, Paul, 49
Weingartner, Felix, 91
Werner, Ilse, 99, 104
West, Mae, 33
Whale, James, 49
The White Shadows (1924), 28
Whoopee (1930), 66
Wieck, Dorothea, 63, 108
Wiene, Robert, 49
Wilder, Billy, 74
Williams, Esther, 15, 148
Winterset (1936), 56
Wolf, Pierre, 150
Wray, Fay, 10
Wyler, William, 54, 148

X-27 (*Dishonored*; 1931), 28, 33

Yoshiwara (1937), 138

Zay, Jean, 52
Zecca, Ferdinand, 49
Ziel in den Wolken (*Target in the Clouds*; 1939), 108
Zenith cinema, 103
Zouzou (1934), 131